QUARKXPRESS 5
DESIGN PROFESSIONAL

By Elizabeth Eisner Reding

THOMSON

COURSE TECHNOLOGY

QuarkXPress™ 5—Design Professional

by Elizabeth Eisner Reding

Managing Editor:
Nicole Jones Pinard

Senior Product Manager:
Rebecca Berardy

Associate Product Manager:
Christina Kling Garrett

Editorial Assistant:
Elizabeth Harris

Production Editors:
Karen Jacot, Jennifer Goguen

Developmental Editor:
Mary-Terese Cozzola

Technical Reviewer:
Mary Juliano, ssj

Composition House:
GEX Publishing Services

QA Manuscript Reviewers:
Harris Bierhoff, Jeffrey Schwartz, Ashlee Welz

Text Designer:
Ann Small

Illustrator:
Philip Brooker

Cover Design:
Philip Brooker

Design Professional Series Vision

The Design Professional Series is your guide to today's hottest multimedia applications. These comprehensive books teach the skills behind the application, showing you how to apply smart design principles to multimedia products, such as dynamic graphics, animation, Web sites, and video.

A team of design professionals including multimedia instructors, students, authors, and editors worked together to create this series. We recognized the unique learning environment of the digital media or multimedia classroom and have created a series that:

- Gives you comprehensive step-by-step instructions
- Offers in-depth explanation of the "why" behind a skill
- Includes creative projects for additional practice
- Explains concepts clearly using full-color visuals

It was our goal to create a book that speaks directly to the multimedia and design community—one of the most rapidly growing computer fields today.

This series was designed to appeal to the creative spirit. We would like to thank Philip Brooker for developing the inspirational artwork found on each unit opener and book cover. We would also like to give special thanks to Ann Small of A Small Design Studio for developing a sophisticated and instructive book design.
—The Design Professional Series

Author's Vision

One of the aspects that makes the Design Professional series special is that its target audience is the savvy student who wants important information, needs little hand-holding, has an interest in design and a healthy dose of creativity. This person is fun to write for because he/she wants to learn.

Another important aspect of this series is the participants who make it happen. This book was created by a dynamic team, many of whom have worked together on other projects. If you've ever worked in such an environment, then you know how much fun this can be. If you haven't, then you're in for a treat. It's such a rewarding experience to work with professionals who know what they're supposed to do, and when and how they're supposed to do it. Like a well-oiled machine, events happen in an orderly fashion with few surprises.

Special thanks to the following team members:

- Rebecca Berardy: who was a constant champion in making this book happen and was always there for a good laugh or cry.
- MT Cozzola: who shaped the manuscript into its current form and made my ramblings coherent.
- Mary Juliano, ssj (Associate Professor of Mathematics and Computer Science, Caldwell College, Caldwell, NJ): who provided timely and professional advice (and was a true joy).
- Larry Sullivan and Paul Flexner: who reviewed each unit and made important suggestions that kept the content on track.
- Harris Bierhoff, Jeffrey Schwartz, and Ashlee Welz: who got rid of errors and inconsistencies through their tireless efforts.
- Karen Jacot, and all those at Course Technology who participated in this project.
- Nicole Pinard: who helped make this vision a reality.

I would like to add a special thanks to my husband, Michael, for his emotional and professional support, and to my mother, Mary Eisner, for her support and enthusiasm. Their contributions make this book possible.
—Elizabeth Eisner Reding

UNIT B
CREATING A DOCUMENT

1. Set preferences and defaults.

2. Add text to a document.

3. Modify and reposition a text box.

4. Copy and move text.

35

What You'll Do

A What You'll Do figure begins every lesson. This figure gives you an at-a-glance look at the skills covered in the unit and shows you the completed project file of the lesson. Before you start the lesson, you will know—both on a technical and artistic level—what you will be creating.

Comprehensive Conceptual Lessons

Before jumping into instructions, in-depth conceptual information tells you "why" skills are applied. This book provides the "how" and "why" through the use of professional examples. Also included in the text are helpful tips and sidebars to help you work more efficiently and creatively.

Introduction to QuarkXPress 5

Welcome to *QuarkXPress 5—Design Professional*. This book offers creative projects, concise instructions, and complete coverage of basic to intermediate QuarkXPress skills, helping you to create dynamic document layout! Use this book both in the classroom and as your own reference guide.

This text is organized into eleven units. In these units, you will learn many skills including how to create a document, work with text, manage a multi-page document, work with objects, add artwork, use drawing, text, and color tools, understand the printing process, and create content for the Web!

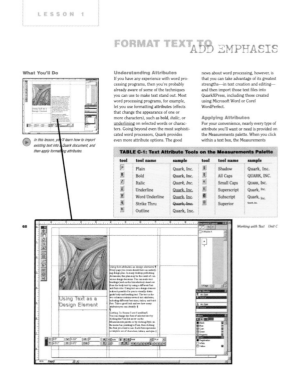

LESSON 1

FORMAT TEXT TO ADD EMPHASIS

iv

Step-by-Step instructions

This book combines in-depth conceptual information with concise steps to help you learn QuarkXPress. Each set of steps guides you through a lesson where you will apply QuarkXPress tasks to a dynamic and professional project file. Step references to large colorful images and quick step summaries round out the lessons.

At the back of the book, you will find a Steps Summary. The Steps Summary is a listing by Unit of all the tasks performed in the lessons.

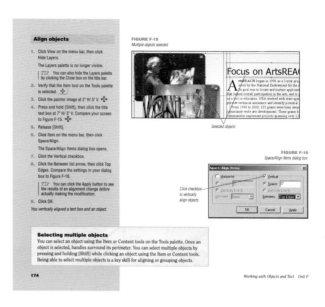

Projects

This book contains a variety of end-of-unit material for additional practice and reinforcement. The *Skills Reference* is a table of keyboard shortcut keys and quick references, showing you the most efficient way to complete a task. The *Skills Review* contains hands-on practice exercises that mirror the progressive nature of the lesson material. The unit concludes with four projects: two Project Builders, one Design Project, and one Group Project. The Project Builder cases, require you to apply the skills you've learned in the unit to create one document. Design Projects examine design principles and send students to the Web to research desktop publishing issues. Group Projects encourage group activity as students utilize the resources of a team to create a project.

What instructor resources are available with this book?

The Instructor's Resources are Course Technology's way of putting the resources and information needed to teach and learn effectively into your hands. All the resources are available for both Macintosh and Windows operating systems, and many of the resources can be downloaded from *www.course.com*.

Assessing Your Students
Solution Files

Solution Files are Project Files completed with comprehensive sample answers. Use these files to evaluate your students' work. Or, distribute electronically or in hard copy so students can verify their work.

ExamView

ExamView is a powerful testing software package that allows instructors to create and administer printed, computer (LAN-based), and Internet exams. ExamView includes hundreds of questions that correspond to the topics covered in this text, enabling students to generate detailed study guides that include page references for further review. The computer-based and Internet testing components allow students to take exams at their computers, and also save the instructor time by grading each exam automatically.

Presenting Your Class
Figure Files

Figure Files contain all the figures from the book in bitmap format. Use the figure files to create transparency masters or in a PowerPoint presentation.

Planning Your Class
Instructor's Manual

Available as an electronic file, the Instructor's Manual is quality-assurance tested and includes unit overviews, detailed lecture topics for each unit with teaching tips, and comprehensive sample solutions to all lessons and end-of-unit material. The Instructor's Manual is available on the Instructor's Resource CD-ROM, or you can download it from *www.course.com*.

Sample Syllabus

Prepare and customize your course easily using this sample course outline (available on the Instructor's Resources CD-ROM).

Student Tools
Project Files and Project Files List

To complete most of the units in this book, your students will need Project Files. Put them on a file server for students to copy. The Project Files are available on the Instructor's Resource CD-ROM, the Review Pack, and can also be downloaded from *www.course.com*. Instruct students to use the Project Files List at the end of the book. This list gives instructions on copying and organizing files.

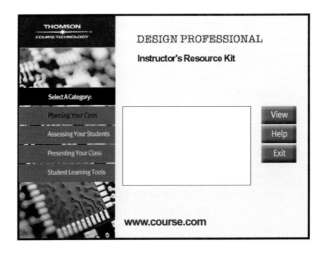

Unit	Location	Photograph
A	Skills Review	Beach, Carol Cram
B	Project Builder 1	Eiffel Tower, Carol Cram
	Group Project	Beach Girl, Carol Cram
C	Lessons	Lava Skies, Carol Cram
	Skills Review	Hydrangea, Carol Cram
	Project Builder 1	Zion 3, Carol Cram
	Project Builder 2	Bike, Carol Cram
D	Lessons	Tula, Carol Cram
	Project Builder 1	Guards Changing, Carol Cram
	Project Builder 2	Rose, Carol Cram
E	Skills Review	Brittany Sunset North, Carol Cram
	Project Builder 1	Child Asleep, Carol Cram
	Project Builder 2	Election Signs, Carol Cram
F	Lessons	Artist Painting, Native Son, Hanging Show, Carol Cram
	Skills Review	Rose, Daffodils, Tree Reflection, Carol Cram
	Project Builder 1	Futurescope
	Project Builder 2	Glacier Bay Mid View, Glacier Closeup, Glacier Bay Entrance Ship, Glacier Bay Boat Vertical, Carol Cram
G	Lessons	Mansion 1, Girl Sand, Mandala, Carol Cram
	Skills Review	Cold Front
	Project Builder 1	Helicopters Landing
	Project Builder 2	TKD, Carol Cram
	Design Project	Okanagan Sunset, Carol Cram
	Group Project	Colorful Car, Carol Cram
H	Lessons	Hawaii Girl Car, Carol Cram
	Skills Review	Louvre Pyramid, Carol Cram
	Project Builder 1	London Guard, Carol Cram
	Project Builder 2	PontduGard, Carol Cram
K	Lessons	Seasonal Backgrounds, Siede Preis/Getty Images™
	Lessons	Alaska Ocean Ripples, Arial Mountains, Quark FlorenceArno, Tower, Holland Canal Scene Miniature, Amsterdam Canal Wide, Paris Skyline, Paris Seine, Carol Cram
	Skills Review	Seasonal Backgrounds, Siede Preis/Getty Images™
	Project Builder 1	Shapes and Patterns, Rowan Moore/Getty Images™ Travel and Vacation Icons, Getty Images™
	Group Project	Shapes and Patterns, Rowan Moore/Getty Images™

UNIT F WORKING WITH OBJECTS AND TEXT

UNIT G WORKING WITH PICTURES

UNIT K   CREATING CONTENT FOR WEB USE

Intended audience

This text is designed for the beginner or intermediate student who wants to learn how to use QuarkXPress 5. The book is designed to provide basic and in-depth material that not only educates but encourages the student to explore the nuances of this exciting program.

Lesson 4 in Unit K is for Windows users only due to the inconsistencies found within the Quark program on Macintosh operating systems.

Measurements

In general, when measurements are shown in this book, they are presented in inches. If necesary, use the following instructions to change the way Quark displays units of measure to inches

1. Click Edit on the menu bar, point to Preferences, click Preferences, then click Measurements.

2. Click the Horizontal and/or Vertical list arrows, then click Inches.

3. Click OK.

If rulers are not displayed, you can show them by clicking View on the menu bar, then clicking Show Rulers, or by pressing [Ctrl][R] (Win) or [command][R] (Mac). You can hide visible rulers by clicking View on the menu bar, then clicking Hide Rulers, or by pressing [Ctrl][R] (Win) or [command][R] (Mac).

Note: In Unit K, where we work with Web documents, measurements are presented in pixels rather than inches. However, there is no need to change your preferences. When you create or open a Web page in Quark, the ruler automatically adjusts to show pixels, the standard unit of measure on a Web page.

Icons, buttons, and pointers

Symbols for icons, buttons, and pointers are shown *each time they are used in each unit*. Note to Macintosh users: some buttons look slightly different on this platform. For example, the Delete tool looks like an "X" in Windows but looks like a trash can in Macintosh.

Fonts

Documents opened or created in the lessons employ common fonts such as Arial, Times New Roman, and Impact. However, a goal of this book is encouraging students to develop and extend their page layout skills, including their familiarity with fonts. Therefore, a wider variety of fonts are used in the end of unit projects. In cases where fonts are used in files, each font is identified. If any of the fonts in use are not available on your computer, please make a substitution.

Quark XTensions

XTensions are mini-programs (having the extension .xnt) that can be added to or deleted from QuarkXPress *without* causing harm to the rest of the program. The Quark XTensions used in this book are Jabberwocky, Index, Step and Repeat, Guide Manager, and Type Effects. You can check to see which XTensions are installed on your computer by clicking Utilities on the menu bar, then by clicking XTensions Manager. The XTensions Manager dialog box, shown in Figure 1, opens. This dialog box lists all the XTensions currently in your installation of Quark. You can disable a selected XTension by clicking the Enable list arrow, then by clicking No. If you are unsure what a particular XTension does, you can click the About button. A description of the selected XTension displays at the bottom of the About dialog box. The About Jabberwocky dialog box is shown in Figure 2.

Get XTensions

If you are missing any QuarkXPress XTensions, the best place to get them is the Quark website *www.quark.com*. Here you'll find pages for Downloads and XTensions for QuarkXPress 5. When you find an XTension that you want for the computer platform you are using (for example, Macintosh or Windows), click its link. (*Hint*: If a dialog box opens asking you for a password, it means that site is busy and that you should try again later.) Click the link to download the file, decompress it if necessary, then drag the XTension file to the XTension folder in the Quark folder on your hard drive. (*Note*: If you are working in an institutional or networked environment, it's best to consult systems personnel *before* making any modifications.)

FIGURE 1
XTensions Manager dialog box

FIGURE 2
About Jabberwocky dialog box

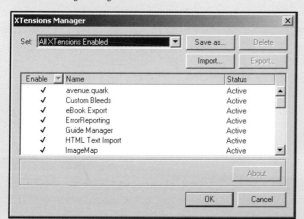

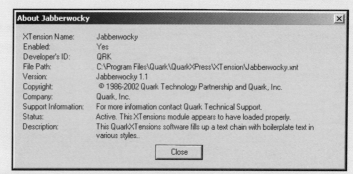

Use Table 1 to determine which XTensions can be downloaded to enable specific features. (*Note*: Quark is continually updating its Web site. XTension names and version numbers may change.)

Menu commands in tables

In tables, menu commands are abbreviated using the following format: Edit ➤ Preferences ➤ Preferences ➤ Measurements. This command translates as follows: Click Edit on the menu bar, point to Preferences, click Preferences, then click Measurements.

Power User Shortcuts table

The Power User Shortcuts table contains the most expedient method of completing tasks covered in the unit *for the first time*. It is meant for the more experienced user, or for the user who wants to become more experienced. Buttons are shown rather than named.

Grading tips

Many students have Web-ready accounts to which they can post their completed assignments. The instructor can access the student accounts using a browser and view the documents online. Using this method, it is not necessary for the student to include his/her name on the document, as all of their assignments are in an individual password protected account.

Creating a portfolio

One method for students to submit and keep a copy of all of their work is to create a portfolio of their projects that is linked to a simple Web page that can be saved on a CD.

If it is necessary for students to print completed projects, work can be printed and mounted at a local copy shop; a student's name can be printed on the back of the document.

Web addresses

Students will be referred to the Student Online Companion (SOC) for End-of-Unit projects involving the Internet. If any URL referenced in an End-of-Unit project becomes inactive, please encourage students to use their favorite search engine to find a substitute site.

File locations

Several lessons in Unit K require files that are supplied with QuarkXPress. It is strongly encouraged that students copy these files to the folder that contains their project files. In Windows, these files are located in \Program Files\Quark\QuarkXPress\Tutorials\avenue.quark Tutorial. In Macintosh, they are located in \QuarkXPress\Tutorials\avenue.quark Tutorial. It may be advisable to have the installation CD handy just in case these files are not installed.

TABLE 1: XTensions guide

XTension to download	to enable feature
Line Check	Type Tricks
Jabberwocky	Jabberwocky
Step and Repeat	Step and Repeat
Guide Manager	Guide Manager

GETTING STARTED WITH QUARKXPRESS

1. Start QuarkXPress 5.0.

2. Learn how to open and save a document.

3. Examine the QuarkXPress window.

4. Use Help to learn about QuarkXPress.

5. View and print a document.

6. Close a document and exit QuarkXPress.

UNIT A
GETTING STARTED WITH QUARKXPRESS

Introduction

Creating a dynamic, attractive series of pages can be a complex task, requiring a keen sense of design, an adventurous spirit, and a robust software program that is up to the task. Professionals who lay out pages—including designers, production staff, and output providers—have made QuarkXPress the industry leader and the standard by which other page layout programs are judged. Due to its superior design controls, QuarkXPress is *the* software program to know for anyone who wants to create, manage, and deliver content for print and Web-based forums.

Learning About QuarkXPress

QuarkXPress (also called "Quark", for short) is available on both Windows and Macintosh platforms, and operates similarly on both, except for keyboard commands that have equivalent functions. The [Ctrl] and [Alt] keys are used for keyboard commands in Windows, and the [command] and [option] keys are used on Macintosh computers. There are different ways of starting Quark, depending on the computer platform you are using. When you start Quark, the computer displays a **splash screen**—a window that provides information about the software—and then the Quark window opens. Quark contains elements in a work area. You use the toolbar, palettes, dialog boxes, and pull-down menus to create and manipulate pages.

4

Tools You'll Use

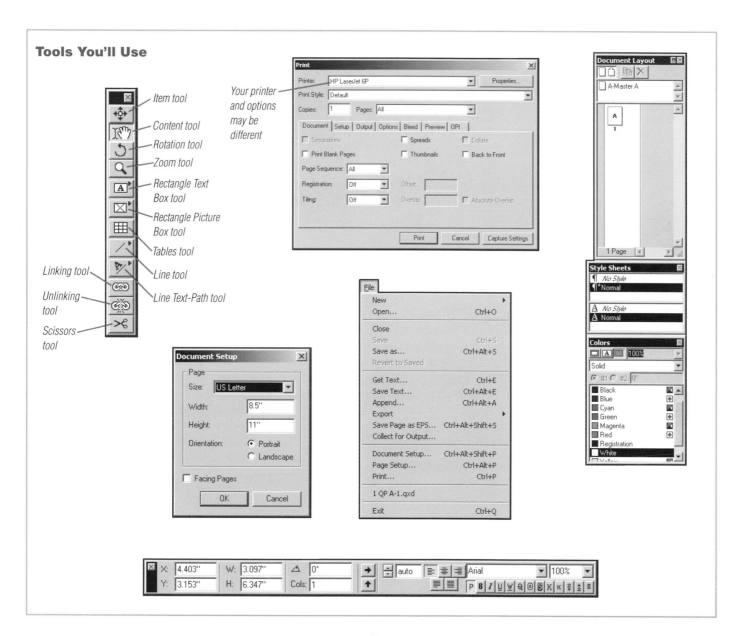

Item tool

Content tool

Rotation tool

Zoom tool

Rectangle Text Box tool

Rectangle Picture Box tool

Tables tool

Line tool

Linking tool

Line Text-Path tool

Unlinking tool

Scissors tool

Your printer and options may be different

Print

Printer:	HP LaserJet 6P	▼	Properties...
Print Style:	Default		▼
Copies:	1	Pages:	All	▼

Document | Setup | Output | Options | Bleed | Preview | OPI |

☐ Separations   ☐ Spreads   ☐ Collate
☐ Print Blank Pages   ☐ Thumbnails   ☐ Back to Front
Page Sequence: All
Registration: Off   Offset:
Tiling: Off   Overlap: ☐ Absolute Overlap

Print   Cancel   Capture Settings

Document Layout

A-Master A

A
1

1 Page

Style Sheets

¶ *No Style*
¶⁺ Normal

A *No Style*
A Normal

Colors

100%
Solid
⊙ #1 ○ #2 0°

■ Black
■ Blue
■ Cyan
■ Green
■ Magenta
■ Red
■ Registration
☐ White

Document Setup

Page
Size: US Letter ▼
Width: 8.5"
Height: 11"
Orientation: ⊙ Portrait   ○ Landscape
☐ Facing Pages

OK   Cancel

File

New	▶
Open...	Ctrl+O
Close	
Save	Ctrl+S
Save as...	Ctrl+Alt+S
Revert to Saved	
Get Text...	Ctrl+E
Save Text...	Ctrl+Alt+E
Append...	Ctrl+Alt+A
Export	▶
Save Page as EPS...	Ctrl+Alt+Shift+S
Collect for Output...	
Document Setup...	Ctrl+Alt+Shift+P
Page Setup...	Ctrl+Alt+P
Print...	Ctrl+P
1 QP A-1.qxd	
Exit	Ctrl+Q

X: 4.403"   W: 3.097"   △ 0°   auto   Arial   100%
Y: 3.153"   H: 6.347"   Cols: 1   P B Z U W Ø S K K

START QUARKXPRESS 5.0

What You'll Do

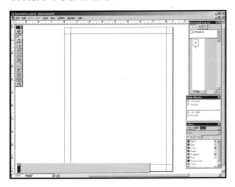

In this lesson, you'll start QuarkXPress 5.0.

Defining Page Layout Software

Quark is a desktop publishing program that is used to lay out pages for publication. **Page layout software** lets you combine text and graphics (such as worksheets, charts, and artwork) created in other programs to produce typeset-quality documents for output on a computer printer or by a commercial printer, or for publication to the World Wide Web. Table A-1 lists examples of uses of desktop publishing documents, and some common features.

QUICKTIP

Work created in Quark is called a **document**, and each document can contain anywhere from 1 to 2000 pages.

Managing Content

Desktop publishing has been—and always will be—a key tool in **content management**, the process of organizing and formatting all types of information so it can be easily accessed by end users. Content management has become further complicated by the explosion of businesses that have expanded their print-based content to include an electronic, Web-based sector. Now, content that was used solely for print must also be published electronically for use on the Web. **Repurposing**, or adapting one type of content such as a paper-based document into another format such as a Web page, can be expensive and time consuming.

Using Media-independent Publishing

Quark technology lets you repurpose content, while minimizing any effort needed to adapt existing documents for the Web. This means that you can create your documents without deciding which media will be used. You create one document, and let Quark make the adjustment for the media. This concept is called **media-independent publishing**.

Working with Multiple Pages

Quark makes it easy to work with multi-page publications. Pages can be easily added, deleted, and moved within a document. Text that flows from one page to another can be linked, and you can insert continued on and continued from notices that help readers find related text.

Adding Consistency to Your Work

Quark has many tools to help you create consistency within a document. **Master pages,** for example, let you create a template for a type of page that contains repetitive elements. Perhaps every right or left lesson page has a gold band on its outer edge. Instead of creating this effect each time you want a lesson page, you can create a master page that contains this information. Inserting a lesson page then becomes as easy as clicking a master page icon.

Emphasizing Special Text

Even great writing can seem boring if all the text looks the same. Using varied text styles to express different meanings and convey messages can add interest. You can use headlines to grab a reader's focus and lead him to stories of specific significance. You can use a sidebar to make a short statement more noticeable, or a pull quote to make an important story stand out and grab a reader's attention. Altering the appearance of text by bolding, italicizing, or underlining it can emphasize its significance.

QUICKTIP

On a Windows computer, you press [Enter] at the end of a sentence; on a Macintosh computer, you press [return].

Publishing Web Documents

In addition to its standard tools, Quark provides special tools for use in Web documents. While working in the Quark Web mode, the Web Tools palette provides you with form controls and image map tools that make your Web documents more effective.

TABLE A-1: Common Uses and Features of Desktop Publishing Documents

publication type	example
Informational	Brochures, signs, calendars, forms
Periodical	Newsletters, catalogs, books, indexes, tables, hyperlinks
Promotional	Advertisements, flyers, press releases
World Wide Web	Web pages, HTML, XML, hyperlinks, form controls, image maps, rollovers, meta tags, tables
Stationery	Letterhead, labels, business cards, envelopes, postcards, invitations
Specialty	Banners, resumes, award certificates, gift certificates

Start QuarkXPress (Windows)

1. Click the Start button on the taskbar.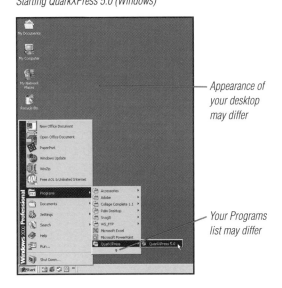

2. Point to Programs, point to the QuarkXPress folder, then click the QuarkXPress 5.0 program icon, as shown in Figure A-1.

3. Click File on the menu bar, point to New, then click Document.

4. Click OK to create a document using the default settings.

   > TIP Unless the default settings have been modified by a previous user, this is a one-page 8 ½" × 11" document.

5. Click View on the menu bar, then click Fit in Window. Compare your screen to Figure A-2.

You started QuarkXPress for Windows.

FIGURE A-1
Starting QuarkXPress 5.0 (Windows)

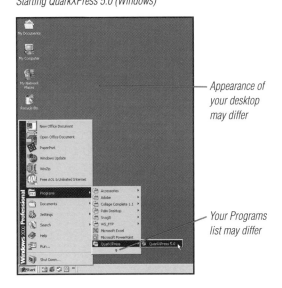

Appearance of your desktop may differ

Your Programs list may differ

FIGURE A-2
New QuarkXPress document

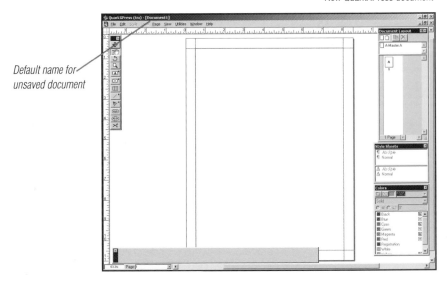

Default name for unsaved document

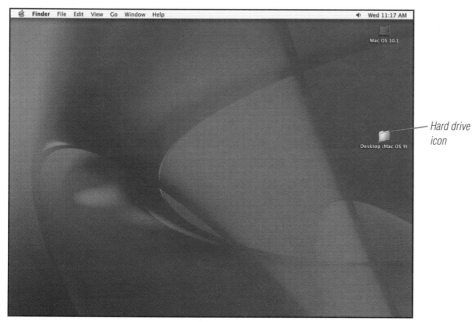

Hard drive
icon

Start QuarkXPress (Macintosh)

1. Double-click the hard drive icon shown in Figure A-3, then double-click the QuarkXPress 5.0 folder.

2. Double-click the QuarkXPress 5.0 program icon. 🌀 QuarkXPress 5.0

3. Click File on the menu bar, point to New, then click Document.

4. Click OK.

5. Click View on the menu bar, then click Fit in Window.

You started QuarkXPress for Macintosh.

Understanding XTensions (Win)

You may have noticed that some of the menu commands shown in this book are missing from your computer. If this is the case, don't panic. Many Quark features are XTensions, small applications that increase functionality, but are not essential to the operation of the program. Some of the commands you may be missing are the Guide Manager, Jabberwocky, Step and Repeat, and the recent files list (at the bottom of the File menu). If you are missing any of these features, please notify your technical support person. You can find these features at the Quark web site, www.quark.com, on the Downloads page.

LEARN HOW TO OPEN AND SAVE A DOCUMENT

What You'll Do

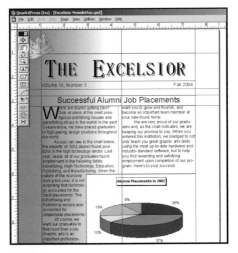

In this lesson, you'll locate and open a file, then save the file with a new name.

Opening and Saving Files

Quark provides several options for opening a file. Often, the project you're working on may determine the techniques you use for opening and saving files. For example, you may want to preserve the original version of a file while you modify a copy. You can open a file, then immediately save it with a different filename, as well as open and save a Quark file in a document, template, library, or book format. Table A-2 describes different Quark file formats. Quark offers different file formats for different page layout needs. The Web Documents format, for example, has properties better suited to the Web than the Documents format.

Using Save as Versus Save

Sometimes it's more efficient to create a new document by modifying an existing one, especially if it contains elements that you would like to use in the new document. When you open a file, its name appears in the document's title bar. When you click File on the menu bar, then click Save as, the Save as dialog box opens, as shown in Figure A-4. The Save as command creates a copy of the file with a new name. The new filename appears in the document's title bar. Use the Save as command to name an unnamed document, or to save an existing document with a new name. For example, throughout this book, you will be instructed to open your project files and then use the Save as command to save them with new names. Saving your project files with new names keeps them intact in case you have to start the lesson over again, or you wish to repeat an exercise. When you use the Save command, you save the changes you made to the open document. Use the Save command often as you work to make sure your changes are saved to disk. You can save an existing document by clicking File on the menu bar, then clicking Save.

QUICKTIP
No dialog box opens when you click the Save command on the File menu.

TABLE A-2: Quark File Formats

file format	description	extension
Document	A typical single- or multi-page file that can be printed	.qxd
Template	A file that can only be saved using a new name and cannot be overwritten	.qxt
Library	Organizes and stores repetitively used information	.qxl
Book	A multi-document publication	.qxb
Web Document	Defines the first page and default Master Page of a Web document	.qwd
Web Template	A Web document that can only be saved using a new name and cannot be overwritten	.qwt
XML Document	A Web document that contains eXtensible Markup Language (XML) code	.xml
XML Template	A Web document containing eXtensible Markup Language (XML) code that can only be saved using a new name and cannot be overwritten	.xmt

FIGURE A-4
Save as dialog box

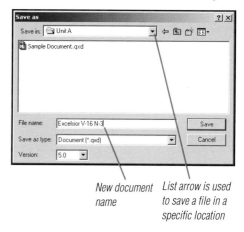

New document name

List arrow is used to save a file in a specific location

Open a file

1. Click File on the menu bar, then click Open.

2. Click the Look in list arrow (Win) or the Current file location list arrow (Mac) shown in Figure A-5, then click the drive where your project files are stored.

3. Click QP A-1.qxd, then click Open.

   TIP   The font used at the top of the page is MS Mincho. If your computer does not have this font, a warning box tells you that fonts used in the document are not available. If you see this warning box, click List Fonts, click MS Mincho in the Missing Fonts list, click Replace, click the Replacement Font list arrow, click Arial Narrow, click OK, then click OK again.

You used the Open command on the File menu to locate and open a file.

FIGURE A-5
Open dialog box for Windows and Macintosh

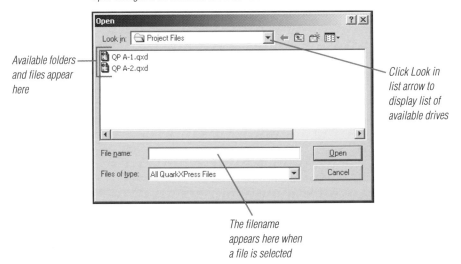

Available folders and files appear here

Click Look in list arrow to display list of available drives

The filename appears here when a file is selected

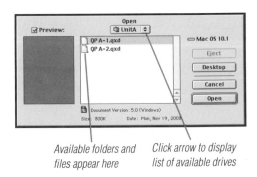

Available folders and files appear here

Click arrow to display list of available drives

Replacing missing fonts

You will see a warning box if you open a document that uses fonts that are not installed on your computer. When this happens, you can click the Continue button and Quark will make substitutions for you based on the fonts that *are* installed on your computer. You can choose to make your own substitutions by clicking the List Fonts button. When you do this, the Missing Fonts for *document name* will open, and all missing fonts used in the document will be listed. Click an item in the list, click Replace, click the Replacement Font list arrow in the Find Replacement Font dialog box, then click OK. Continue making substitutions until you exhaust the list or are satisfied with the number of replacements you made, then click OK. The document will open with your replacement fonts.

FIGURE A-6

Save as dialog box

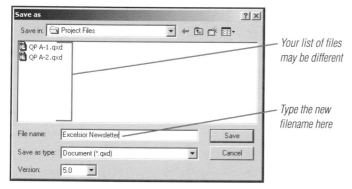

Your list of files may be different

Type the new filename here

FIGURE A-7

Excelsior Newsletter document

New filename

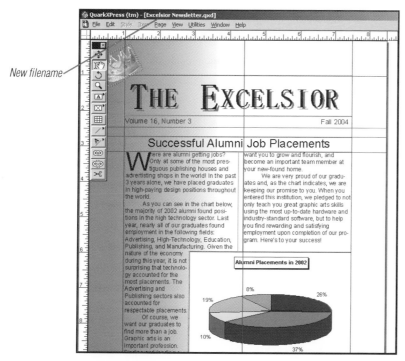

1. Click File on the menu bar, then click Save as.

2. If the drive containing your project files is not visible, click the Save in list arrow (Win) or the Current file location list arrow (Mac), then click the drive and folder where your project files are stored.

3. Select the current filename in the File name text box, if necessary, then type **Excelsior Newsletter**, as shown in Figure A-6.

4. Click Save. Compare your screen to Figure A-7.

You used the Save as command on the File menu to save the file with a new name.

EXAMINE THE QUARKXPRESS WINDOW

What You'll Do

View	
Fit in Window	Ctrl+0
50%	
✔ 75%	
Actual Size	Ctrl+1
200%	
Thumbnails	Shift+F6
Hide Guides	F7
Show Baseline Grid	Ctrl+F7
✔ Snap to Guides	Shift+F7
Hide Rulers	Ctrl+R
Show Invisibles	Ctrl+I
Hide Visual Indicators	
Show Tools	F8
Hide Measurements	F9
Show Document Layout	F4
Hide Style Sheets	F11
Hide Colors	F12
Show Trap Information	Ctrl+F12
Show Lists	Ctrl+F11
Show Layers	
Show Profile Information	
Show Hyperlinks	
Show Index	
Show Sequences	
Show Placeholders	

 In this lesson, you'll learn about the components in the Quark window, and you'll use the Show and Hide commands on the View menu to show and hide rulers and palettes in the document window.

Identifying Windows

The **program title bar** displays the program name (QuarkXPress) and the filename of the open document (in this case, Excelsior Newsletter). The title bar also contains a Close button and Minimize, Maximize, and Restore buttons for the program.

QUICKTIP

You may see two title bars if the document is not maximized—one for the program window and one for the document window.

The **document window** is the window beneath the program title bar and menu bar that includes the document image, rulers, and other objects (from the rulers at the top of your screen to the status bar (Win) at the bottom). Desktop items are visible in this area (Mac).

Understanding Menu Commands

The **menu bar** contains menus from which you can choose Quark commands. You can choose a menu command by clicking it, or by pressing [Alt] (Win) or [option] (Mac)

plus the underlined letter in the menu name. Some commands display shortcut keys on the right side of the menu. **Shortcut keys** provide an alternate way to activate menu commands. Some commands may appear dimmed, which means they are not currently available. An ellipsis after a command indicates you must make additional choices before completing the command. Still other commands may contain a right-pointing arrowhead. This means there are additional, related commands on another menu.

QUICKTIP

If it is not maximized, the document window will appear *beneath* the menu bar, and the document name will appear in the document window title bar.

Learning About the Document Window

A **palette** is a small moveable window you use to verify and modify settings. The document window contains several palettes whose appearances change depending on what you're doing, or what is clicked. These **palettes** contain buttons that let you make changes in a document, or display information. For example, if you click any text in the document, the Measurements palette displays information. The Measurements palette contains different data if text is selected than if a chart or picture is selected. Other palettes in the document window are described in Table A-3. Palettes can be turned on and off using commands on the View menu.

Rulers can help you precisely measure and position an object in the work area. The **status bar** is located at the bottom of the program window (Win) or document window (Mac). It displays current page and magnification information. The **Pasteboard** is the area surrounding the document. It can be used to create or modify elements, or as a holding area for future use.

QUICKTIP

Most palettes—such as the Measurements palette and the Tools palette—can be moved by clicking and dragging their title bars to a new location. You might want to move a palette if it is obscuring your view.

FIGURE A-8
Screen elements

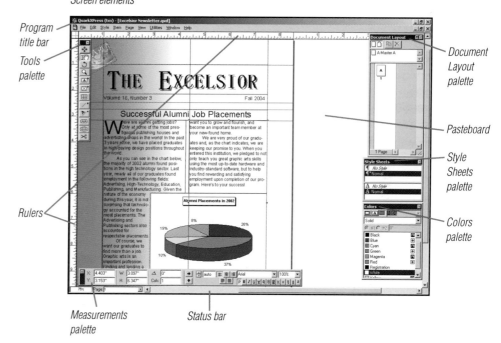

Program title bar
Tools palette
Rulers
Measurements palette
Status bar
Document Layout palette
Pasteboard
Style Sheets palette
Colors palette

TABLE A-3: Document Window Palettes

palette name	description
Tools	Lets you perform tasks such as creating boxes, lines, tables, and text, and enlarging and reducing the document view
Measurements	Lets you view and edit data pertaining to the current selection
Document Layout	Lets you add, delete, and modify pages within a document
Style Sheets	Lets you create, delete, and modify paragraph and character qualities that have been saved
Colors	Lets you add color to the current selection

Select a tool

1. Click the Rectangle Text Box tool on the Tools palette, then press and hold the mouse button until the list of hidden tools appears, as shown in Figure A-9. ⒜▸

2. Click the Concave-corner Text Box tool. ⊠

3. Click the Line Text-Path tool. ☇▸

4. Click Edit on the menu bar, point to Preferences, then click Preferences.

5. Click Tools. Compare the Tool Defaults shown in your Preferences dialog box to Figure A-10.

   | TIP Your Tools palette settings may differ if another user modified the settings.

6. Click Default Tool Palette, then click OK.

   Rectangle Text Box tool appears in the Tools palette. If the program was modified, it will now display the default settings.

You selected the Rectangle Text Box tool in the Tools palette, used shortcut keys to select another tool in the Tools palette, then you reset the Tools palette to its default settings.

FIGURE A-9
Hidden tools

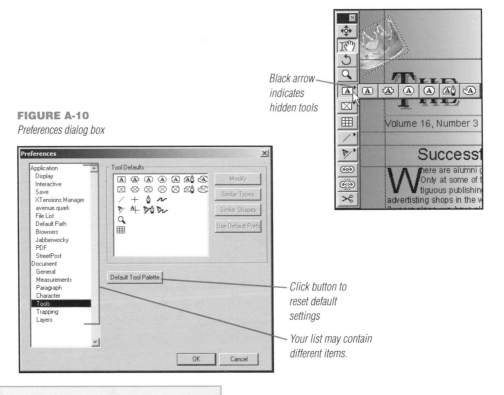

FIGURE A-10
Preferences dialog box

Black arrow indicates hidden tools

Click button to reset default settings

Your list may contain different items.

Using shortcut keys

Most tools on the Tools palette have a shortcut key (or a combination of keys) that lets you select tools *without* having to use the mouse. Many menu commands have shortcut keys as well. For example, the shortcut key that lets you select the tool beneath the current tool is [Ctrl][Alt][Tab] (Win) or [command][option][tab] (Mac). Once you are more familiar with shortcut keys, you can work faster and become less dependent on the mouse. Some tools, such as the Rectangle Text Box tool and the Line tool, have additional tools hidden beneath them. These tools have a small black triangle in the upper-right corner. You can display the hidden tools by pressing and holding the mouse over the triangle.

FIGURE A-11

View menu

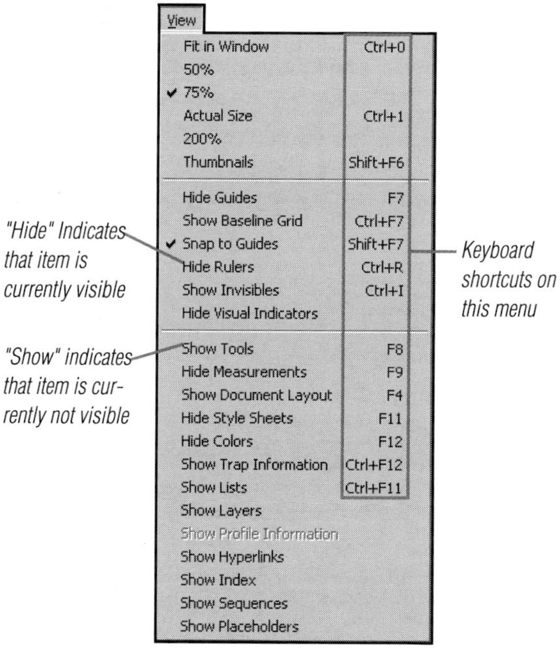

```
View
  Fit in Window          Ctrl+0
  50%
✓ 75%
  Actual Size            Ctrl+1
  200%
  Thumbnails             Shift+F6

  Hide Guides            F7
  Show Baseline Grid     Ctrl+F7
✓ Snap to Guides         Shift+F7
  Hide Rulers            Ctrl+R
  Show Invisibles        Ctrl+I
  Hide Visual Indicators

  Show Tools             F8
  Hide Measurements      F9
  Show Document Layout   F4
  Hide Style Sheets      F11
  Hide Colors            F12
  Show Trap Information   Ctrl+F12
  Show Lists             Ctrl+F11
  Show Layers
  Show Profile Information
  Show Hyperlinks
  Show Index
  Show Sequences
  Show Placeholders
```

"Hide" Indicates that item is currently visible

Keyboard shortcuts on this menu

"Show" indicates that item is currently not visible

Hide and show palettes

1. Click View on the menu bar, then click Hide Tools.

2. Click View on the menu bar, then click Hide Document Layout.

3. Click View on the menu bar. Compare your menu to Figure A-11.

   Any hidden item, such as the Document Layout palette, now says Show Document Layout, so that you can re-display the element.

4. Click Show Tools. This command re-displays all hidden tools.

5. Click View on the menu bar then click Show Document Layout.

6. Click View on the menu bar, then click Hide Rulers.

7. Click View on the menu bar, then click Show Rulers.

   > TIP   You can also use shortcut keys to hide and show palettes, and other screen elements. These shortcuts are listed in Table A-4.

You used the View menu to show and hide palettes.

TABLE A-4: Show/Hide Keyboard Shortcuts

to hide or show	shortcut
Guides	[F7]
Rulers	[Ctrl][R] (Win) or [Command][R] (Mac)
Tools palette	[F8]
Measurements palette	[F9]
Document Layout palette	[F4] (Win) or [F10] (Mac)
Style Sheets palette	[F11]
Colors palette	[F12]

USE HELP TO LEARN ABOUT QUARKXPRESS

What You'll Do

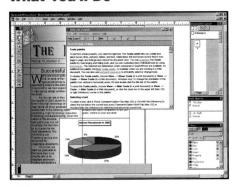

 In this lesson, you'll open the Help utility, then view and find information.

Understanding the Power of Help

QuarkXPress features an extensive Help system that you can use to access definitions, explanations, and useful tips. Help information appears in its own window, and can be viewed on the screen as you read or practice steps in Quark. Help topics can also be printed.

Using Help Topics

The initial Help window has three tabs that you use to retrieve information about QuarkXPress commands and features: Contents, Index, and Find, as shown in Figure A-12. The Contents tab allows you to browse topics by category; the Index tab provides each letter in the alphabet, which you can click to view keywords and topics alphabetically. The Find tab allows you to enter keywords as your search criteria. When you choose a topic using any of the three methods, information about that topic appears in its own window, which can be moved, resized, or kept onscreen so that you can read it while Quark is open.

FIGURE A-12
Tabs in the Help window

Click a tab for the Help
method you want to use

Contents tab in the Help Topics dialog box

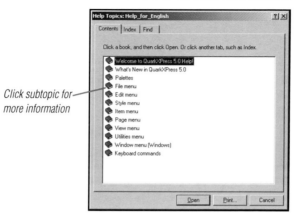

Find information in Help Contents

1. Click Help on the menu bar, then click Help Topics (Win) or Help Contents (Mac), if necessary.

   The Help Topics dialog box opens, as shown in Figure A-13.

   | TIP   You can also open the Help window by pressing [F1].

2. Double-click File menu in the list of topics.

3. Click Get Picture command, then click Display. Compare your screen to Figure A-14.

4. Click Print, then click Print in the Print dialog box.

You used the Contents tab in Help to view and print a topic.

FIGURE A-14

Get Picture command information in Help

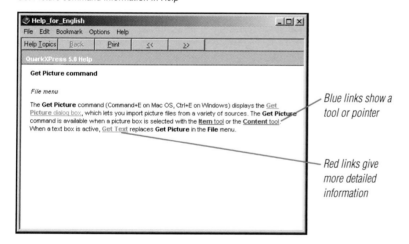

Click subtopic for more information

Blue links show a tool or pointer

Red links give more detailed information

Using Help hyperlinks

Most Help topics contain hyperlinks within the window, which you can click to see information about related topics. You can always return to the original list of topics by clicking the Help Topics button beneath the menu bar in the Help window.

Find information in the Index

1. Click the Help Topics button in the Help window, then click the Index tab.

2. Type **T**, then click Tools palette, as shown in Figure A-15.

3. Click Display.

> TIP   In most cases, double-clicking an option has the same results as single-clicking and then clicking a command.

You used the Index tab in Help to view a topic.

Keep Help information on top

1. Click Options on the menu bar in the Help window, then point to Keep Help on Top. Compare your screen to Figure A-16.

2. Click On Top.

3. Click the title bar in the Quark window, then compare your screen to Figure A-17. Notice that the Help window remains on top even though another window is active.

> TIP   You can click the Minimize button if the window obscures your view and you don't want to close Help.

4. Click File on the Help window menu bar, then click Exit (Win) or Quit (Mac) when you are finished reading the topic.

You made the Help window visible on top of the Quark window.

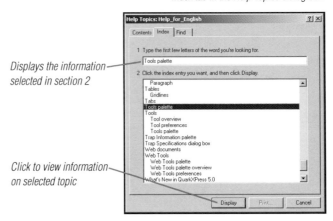

Displays the information selected in section 2

Click to view information on selected topic

FIGURE A-16
Options menu

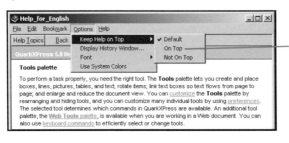

Click to display Help window on top of program

FIGURE A-17
Help window on top of Quark window

Help window can be resized and repositioned so you can see both the screen and Help

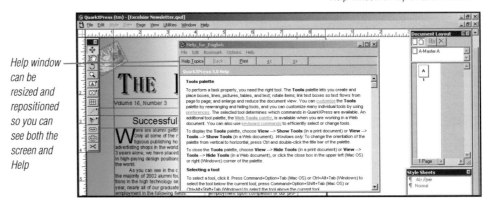

Find tab in the Help Topics dialog box

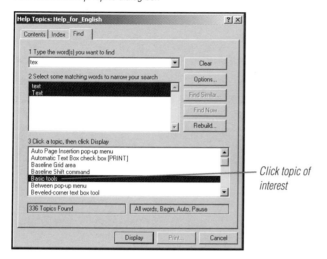

Click topic of
interest

Get information using Find

1. Click Help on the menu bar, click Help Topics, then click the Find tab.

2. If necessary, click Next to minimize the database size, then click Finish.

3. Type **tex**.

4. Use the scroll bar in section 3 to find and click Basic tools. Compare your screen to Figure A-18.

5. Click Display.

   The keyword *text* may be highlighted in the Basic tools Help window, as shown in Figure A-19.

6. Click File on the menu bar of the Help window, then click Exit.

You found information in Help by typing text using the Find tab.

FIGURE A-19
Basic tools topic in Help window

Keywords may be
highlighted

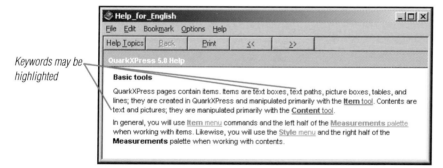

VIEW AND PRINT A DOCUMENT

What You'll Do

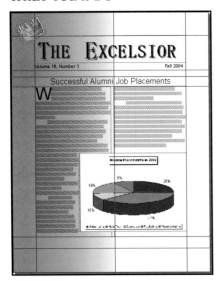

In this lesson, you'll use the Zoom tool on the Tools palette to increase and reduce your view of the document. You'll also temporarily modify the page orientation setting, return to the original setting, and print the document.

Getting a Closer Look

When you edit a document in QuarkXPress, it is sometimes necessary to have an "up-close" view of a specific area. Quark has several methods you can use to enlarge or reduce your current view. You can use the Zoom tool to zoom in or zoom out on areas of your document. Zooming in or out enlarges or reduces your viewpoint, *not* the actual image. Once you select the Zoom tool on the Tools palette, you can click the pointer on the area you want to enlarge. You can reduce an area by pressing [Alt] (Win) or [option] (Mac) while clicking the pointer over an area.

Zooming Around

The current zoom percentage appears in the document's status bar, as shown in Figure A-20. When you click a document with the Zoom tool, the document window—frame surrounding the image—will be resized as the image is magnified or reduced. You can also use the View menu to change the zoom percentage. In some cases, the range in which you can zoom is

Using a scanner and a digital camera

If you have a scanner, you can use print images—such as those taken from photographs, magazines, or line drawings—in Quark. Scanners are relatively inexpensive and simple to use. They come in many types, including flatbed or single-sheet feed. Once an image is scanned and saved as an electronic file, you can use it in a Quark document. See your instructor to learn how to use the available scanner. You can also use a digital camera to create your own images. Although it operates much like a film camera, a digital camera contains some form of electronic media, such as a floppy disk or SmartMedia card, onto which it captures images. Once you upload the images from your camera to your computer, you can use them in Quark.

a limitation of your hardware settings; in other cases, it is a property of your operating system. For example, on the Mac, the range in which you can zoom is 10% to 800%. In Windows (with a default value of 96 dpi) the zoom range is 10% to 692%.

Printing Your Document

In many cases, you may opt to have a professional print shop reproduce your Quark creations. Generally, this is your best option if you need high-quality results. You can, however, print a Quark document using a standard black-and-white or color printer. Of course, the quality of your printer and paper will affect the appearance of your output. The Print dialog box, shown in Figure A-21, displays options for printing, such as paper orientation. **Orientation** is the direction an image appears on the page. In **portrait orientation**, a document is printed with the short edge of the paper at the top and bottom. In **landscape orientation**, a document is printed with the long edge of the paper at the top and bottom.

QUICKTIP

Options available in the Print dialog box may vary with each printer.

FIGURE A-20

Zoom tool and percentage

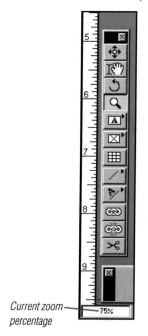

Current zoom
percentage

FIGURE A-21

Print dialog box

Your printer and print
options may vary

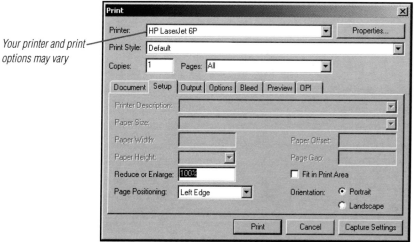

Use the Zoom tool

1. Click the Zoom tool on the Tools palette. Q

2. Scroll to the chart, if necessary; position the pointer over the center of the chart, then click. Compare the enlarged area to Figure A-22. ⊕

   TIP When enlarging or reducing the image of a document, position the pointer over the area you want to view.

3. Press and hold [Alt] (Win) or [option] (Mac), click the center of the chart twice, then release [Alt] (Win) or [option] (Mac). Compare your screen to Figure A-23. ⊖

   TIP Text too small to be read is **greeked**, meaning that it appears as gray bars instead of actual characters. Greeking speeds up redrawing and has no effect on what is printed.

4. Click View on the menu bar, then click Fit in Window.

You used the Zoom tool to visually enlarge and reduce an area of the document.

FIGURE A-23
Document area reduced

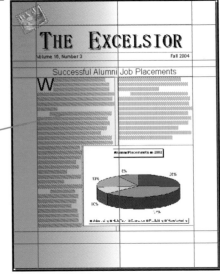

Tiny text is
'greeked'

FIGURE A-24

Setup tab in the Print dialog box

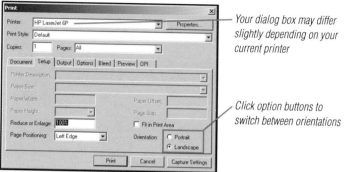

Your dialog box may differ
slightly depending on your
current printer

Click option buttons to
switch between orientations

FIGURE A-25

Preview tab in the Print dialog box

Red area indicates
document

Your imageable area may
differ slightly depending on
your current settings

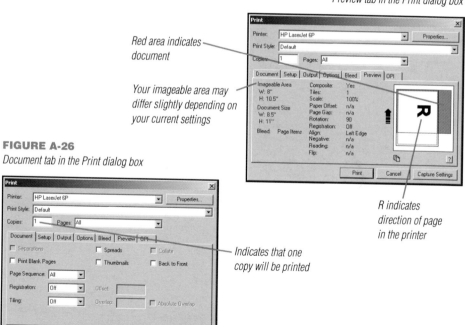

R indicates
direction of page
in the printer

FIGURE A-26

Document tab in the Print dialog box

Indicates that one
copy will be printed

Examine print settings

1. Click File on the menu bar, then click
   Page Setup.

   TIP   If you have not selected a printer
   using the Chooser, a warning box may
   appear. (Mac)

2. Click the Landscape option button, as shown
   in Figure A-24.

3. Click the Preview tab in the Print dialog box.
   Compare your dialog box to Figure A-25.

4. Click the Setup tab in the Print dialog box,
   then click the Portrait option button.

5. Click the Document tab.

6. Adjust your settings so they look like those
   shown in Figure A-26.

7. Click Print, then click OK to close the warning
   box if necessary

*You changed the print orientation and printed a
document.*

CLOSE A DOCUMENT AND EXIT QUARKXPRESS

What You'll Do

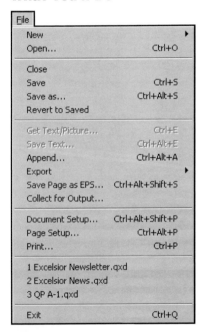

 In this lesson, you'll use the Close and Exit (Win) or Quit (Mac) commands on the File menu to close a document and exit Quark.

Concluding Your Work Session

By the end of your work session, you may have opened several documents, and now must decide which ones you want to save.

QUICKTIP

You should periodically save your documents while you're working. Although there is no hard-and-fast rule about how often you should save, every 10-15 minutes is a good interval.

Closing Versus Exiting

When you finish working on a document, you need to save and close it. You can close one document at a time, or close all open documents at the same time by exiting the program. If you have not modified a document, Quark will close it automatically. Closing a file leaves Quark open, which allows you to open or create another file. To close all open documents, you can click the Close button in the Program title bar. Quark will prompt you to save any changes before it closes any modified files. Exiting Quark closes the file, closes Quark, and returns you to the desktop, where you can choose to open another program, or shut down the computer.

FIGURE A-27

Closing a document using the File menu

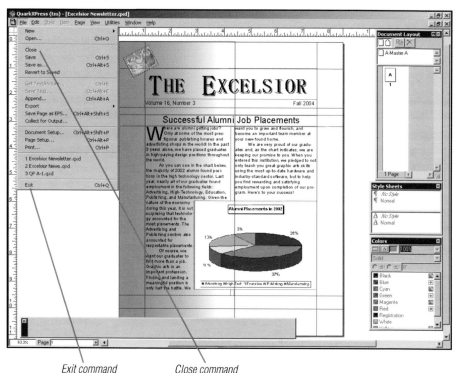

Exit command   Close command

Close the document and exit Quark

1. Click File on the menu bar, then compare your screen to Figure A-27.

2. Click Close.

3. If asked to save your work, click Yes (Win) or Save (Mac).

4. Click File on the menu bar, then click Exit (Win) or Quit (Mac).

> TIP   To exit Quark and close an open file, click the Close button in the Program window. Quark will prompt you to save any unsaved changes before closing.

You closed the active document, saved your changes, then exited QuarkXPress.

Power User Shortcuts

Key: Menu items are indicated by ➤ between the menu name and its command.

to do this:	use this method:
Close a file	File ➤ Close ⌘[W] (Mac), [Ctrl][F4] (Win)
Create a new document	File ➤ New ➤ Document
Exit QuarkXPress	[Ctrl][Q] (Win), [return][Q] (Mac)
Fit document in window	View ➤ Fit in Window
Open a file	[Ctrl][O] (Win), [return][O] (Mac)
Open Help	[F1]
Page setup	[Ctrl][Alt][P] (Win), [return][option] [P] (Mac)
Print a document	[Ctrl][P] (Win), [return][P] (Mac)
Reset Tools palette	Edit ➤ Preferences ➤ Preferences
Save a file	[Ctrl][S] (Win), [return][S] (Mac)
Save a file as	[Ctrl][Alt][S], [return][option] [S] (Mac)
Select tool above current tool	[Ctrl][Alt][Shift][Tab] (Win) [return][option] [Shift] [Tab] (Mac)
Select tool beneath current tool	[Ctrl][Alt][Tab] (Win) [return][option][tab] (Mac)

to do this:	use this method:
Show/Hide Colors palette	[F12]
Show/Hide Document Layout palette	[F4] (Win) [F10] (Mac)
Show/Hide Guides	[F7]
Show/Hide Measurements palette	[F9]
Show/Hide Rulers	[Ctrl][R] (Win), [return][R] (Mac)
Show/Hide Style Sheets palette	[F11]
Show/Hide Tools palette	[F8]
View Help on top of Quark	Options ➤ Keep Help on Top
Zoom in using Zoom tool	🔍
Zoom out using Zoom Tool	[Alt] 🔍 (Win) [Option] 🔍 (Mac)

Start QuarkXPress 5.0.

1. Start Quark.
2. Create a new document using default settings.
3. Locate the title bar and the current zoom percentage.
4. Locate the menu that is used to open a new document.
5. Locate and view the five visible palettes.

Learn how to open and save a document.

1. Open QP A-2.qxd. (*Hint*: The Elephant font is used in this document. If your computer does not have this font, make a substitution.)
2. Save it as **Faraway Travel**.

Examine the QuarkXPress window.

1. Locate the Program title bar, Document title bar (if displayed), and the Maximize and Minimize buttons, without referring back in the unit.
2. Locate the Tools palette, the rulers, and the status bar.
3. Locate the Measurements palette, Document Layout palette, Style Sheets palette, and Colors palette.

Use Help to learn about QuarkXPress.

1. Open the QuarkXPress Help window.
2. Using the Index tab, find information about saving your work. (*Hint*: Type **sav** in the text box at the top of the dialog box.)

3. Print the information you find.
4. Close the Help window.

View and print a document.

1. Click the Zoom tool.
2. Zoom in on the sandy beach.
3. Zoom out to the original perspective.
4. Use the View menu to fit the Faraway Travel document to the page. Compare your image to Figure A-28.

FIGURE A-28
Completed Skills Review

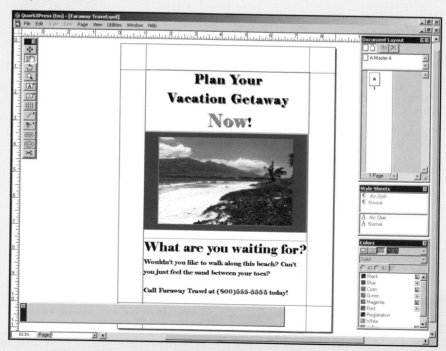

5. Print one copy of the document.
6. Save your work.

Close a document and exit QuarkXPress.

1. Close the Faraway Travel document.
2. Close the unnamed document file.
3. Exit (Win) or Quit (Mac) QuarkXPress.

As a new QuarkXPress user, you are comforted knowing that the Help system provides definitions, explanations, procedures, and other helpful information. It also includes examples and demonstrations that show how Quark features work. Topics include elements such as the work area and palettes, as well as detailed information about Quark commands and options.

1. Open the Quark Help dialog box.
2. Click the Index tab, if necessary.
3. Locate information about the Preferences dialog box.
4. Click the entry for the Measurements pane.
5. Click the link for Horizontal and Vertical pop-up menus. Compare your screen to Figure A-29.
6. Once you have read this topic, print the information.
7. Use the Help dialog box button bar to return to Help Topics.
8. Close the Help dialog box.

FIGURE A-29
Completed Project Builder 1

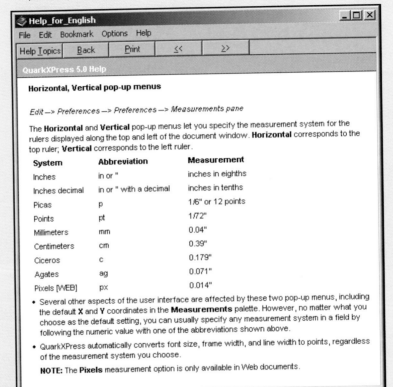

Within the figure:

Help_for_English

File   Edit   Bookmark   Options   Help

Help Topics | Back | Print | << | >>

QuarkXPress 5.0 Help

Horizontal, Vertical pop-up menus

Edit —> Preferences —> Preferences —> Measurements pane

The **Horizontal** and **Vertical** pop-up menus let you specify the measurement system for the rulers displayed along the top and left of the document window. **Horizontal** corresponds to the top ruler; **Vertical** corresponds to the left ruler.

System	Abbreviation	Measurement
Inches	in or "	inches in eighths
Inches decimal	in or " with a decimal	inches in tenths
Picas	p	1/6" or 12 points
Points	pt	1/72"
Millimeters	mm	0.04"
Centimeters	cm	0.39"
Ciceros	c	0.179"
Agates	ag	0.071"
Pixels [WEB]	px	0.014"

- Several other aspects of the user interface are affected by these two pop-up menus, including the default **X** and **Y** coordinates in the **Measurements** palette. However, no matter what you choose as the default setting, you can usually specify any measurement system in a field by following the numeric value with one of the abbreviations shown above.
- QuarkXPress automatically converts font size, frame width, and line width to points, regardless of the measurement system you choose.

NOTE: The **Pixels** measurement option is only available in Web documents.

You are applying for an internship at a local newspaper. If you get the position, you will use QuarkXPress to lay out pages. Because the competition for available internships is stiff, you want to have an advantage over your competitors prior to your interview. You decide to review hiding, showing, and moving palettes.

1. Open a blank Quark document using default settings.

2. Fit the blank document in the window.

3. Hide, then show, each palette in the window.

4. Cycle through the Tools palette using the shortcuts described in the Power User Shortcuts table.

5. Open the Help window, use the Find tab to locate information about handles, then about the Mover pointer topic.

6. Make the Help window visible on top of the Quark window, if necessary. Compare your screen to Figure A-30.

7. Save the document as **Sample Document**.

FIGURE A-30
Completed Project Builder 2

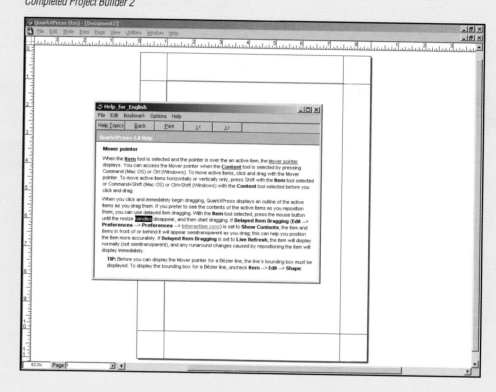

As a novice QuarkXPress user, you would like more information about page layout design principles. You decide to use your favorite browser and search engine to find sites with information about page layout design principles.

1. Connect to the Internet and go to *www.course.com*. Navigate to the page for this book, click the link for the Student Online Companion, then click the link(s) for this project. The site for this unit, shown in Figure A-31, is just one of many informative sites that can help you learn about page layout design principles.

2. If it is permitted, bookmark this URL for future reference.

3. Review the information on the site.

4. Be prepared to discuss what you learned, and how these principles can be incorporated into your upcoming projects.

5. When you finish your research, close your browser.

FIGURE A-31
Completed Design Project

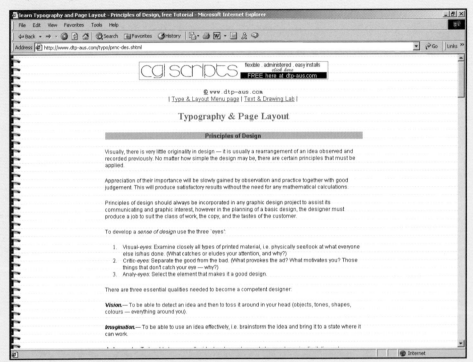

Depending on the size of your group, you can assign elements of the project to individual members, or work collectively to create the finished product.

As a professional desktop publisher, it is important to develop a critical eye when reviewing the work of ourselves and others. Sometimes, it is easier to determine what is *wrong* with a document than what is *right*. After your initial exposure to page layout software, you and your teammates want to critique available newsletters. In addition to your gut reactions, you can use the Internet as a source of information on document critiquing to substantiate your findings.

1. Connect to the Internet and go to *www.course.com*. Navigate to the page for this book, click the link for the Student Online Companion, then click the link(s) for this project. The site for this unit is just one of many informative sites that can help you learn about critiquing a layout.
2. Read up on what makes for a bad newsletter.
3. Each member of your team should locate at least one newsletter received in the mail, or at a library.
4. Analyze each newsletter, keeping track of each negative feature you find.

5. Be prepared to discuss the negative features you located, and why they detract from the document. If you choose, you can write a brief summary of your findings.

FIGURE A-32
Completed Group Project

CREATING A DOCUMENT

1. Set preferences and defaults.

2. Add text to a document.

3. Modify and reposition a text box.

4. Copy and move text.

UNIT B
CREATING A DOCUMENT

Introduction

Once you have learned how to start QuarkXPress and create a new document, it's time to learn some additional basics that'll get you up and running quickly. In addition to adding text to a page, you can also control the environment in which you work by adjusting preferences. **Preferences** are the settings within the Quark program that affect either the document in which you're working, or the application as a whole.

Starting From Scratch

Beginning with a blank document can be overwhelming: all that white space, all that emptiness. Have you ever wondered how text magically gets into a document?

Someone—in this case, you—must create the objects to contain the text, and then either enter or import the text. Someone must position the text objects in just the right location on the page. Again, that someone is you. Each task you perform in Quark has its own methodology, and its own tools you can use to make the experience a snap.

> **QUICKTIP**
>
> Looking at a blank page in QuarkXPress can be intimidating. Feeling overwhelmed by all that white space and all the tools? If so, don't be alarmed. This is part of the normal learning curve; as you use Quark and become more comfortable with it, the way it works will become clear to you. Practice, practice, practice!

Tools You'll Use

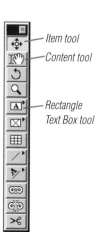

Item tool

Content tool

Rectangle Text Box tool

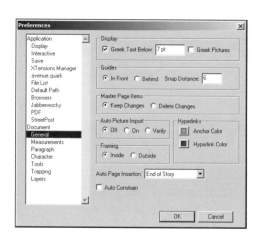

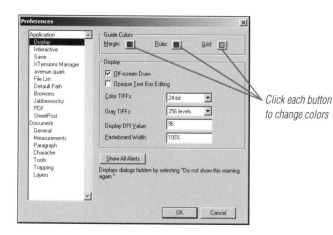

Click each button to change colors

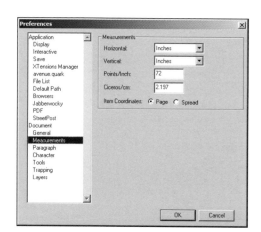

SET PREFERENCES AND DEFAULTS

What You'll Do

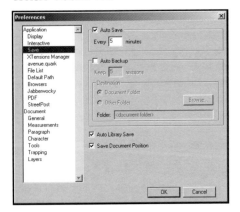

 In this lesson, you'll learn about different kinds of preferences and how to change them.

Understanding Preferences

As you work with Quark, like any program, you'll find there are settings you can adjust to make your working environment more pleasant, comfortable, and convenient. These settings are called **preferences**, and they affect either the program itself, or the particular document in which you are working. Table B-1 lists some of the preferences that can be changed, and whether their modification affects the document or the program.

Selecting Program Versus Document Preferences

Figure B-1 shows the Preferences dialog box. The right side of the dialog box shows the settings for the preference selected on the left side of the dialog box. As you can see, there are two categories: Application and Document. Application-level preferences affect work on all documents. Document preferences affect only the active document. For example, you can set up Quark so that any open file is automatically saved every five minutes (or any interval of minutes you select). This is an example of an *Application* preference. Setting this preference, incidentally, is a good idea, since frequent saving of your work is a vital habit to develop.

The Measurements preference is an example of a *Document* preference. You can choose to display onscreen measurements in picas, points, inches, or other units—whichever suits the requirements of the document you're currently working on. Because this is a Document-level preference, changing this setting affects only the current document.

Changing Preferences When All Documents Are Closed

If you change settings in the Preferences dialog box when no document is open, the document preferences you set will affect the next document you create. That's why the Preferences dialog box looks slightly different when no document is open; it shows a Default Document category and a Default Web Document category, to accommodate whichever type of document you might create next.

TABLE B-1: Quark Preferences

preference	affects the	preference	affects the
Auto Library Save	Program	Margin, Ruler, or Grid Guides	Program
Auto Page Insertion	Document	Measurements	Document
Auto Picture Import	Document	Pasteboard Width	Program
Auto Save/Auto Backup	Program	Save Document Position	Program
Drag and Drop Text	Program	Scroll Speed	Program
Guides In Front/Behind	Document	Smart Quotes	Program
Color/Gray TIFFs	Program	Text Display	Document
Live Refresh	Program	Tool Defaults	Document

FIGURE B-1
Preferences dialog box

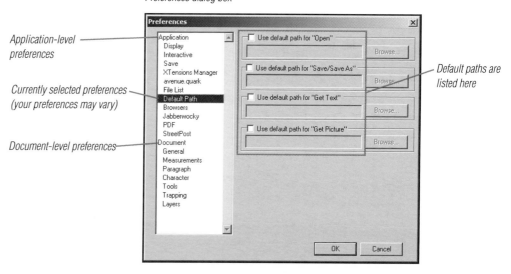

Application-level preferences

Currently selected preferences (your preferences may vary)

Document-level preferences

Default paths are listed here

Determining File Locations

Like most computer users, you probably store your files in specific areas. Maybe your project files are stored in a specific location on a server, and you are allocated space there as well. Perhaps you automatically store your project and solution files on a Zip disk. Regardless of the locations, you can configure Quark so that it always looks in just the right locations for just the right files. In Quark, these 'right locations' are called **default paths**, and you customize these locations for each time you open a document, save a document, save a document under another name, get text, or get a picture.

Modifying File Locations

The Preferences dialog box is opened by clicking Edit on the menu bar, pointing to Preferences, then clicking Preferences. The default path options are displayed by clicking Default Path in the Application category. Each Default Path option contains a checkbox that turns the option on or off, a Browse button that helps you locate the path you want to use, and a text box that displays the location you selected. If, for example, you want the default path for opening files to be in the Project Files folder on the D: drive, you would click the Use default path for "Open" checkbox, click the Browse button to its right, click the

Project Files folder on the D: drive, click OK, then click OK to close the Preferences dialog box. Figure B-2 shows each of the default paths and their modifications.

QUICKTIP

You can *re*modify any default path by clicking the Browse button and redirecting the path. You can turn off any default path by clicking its checkbox so it does not contain a checkmark.

FIGURE B-2
Modified default paths

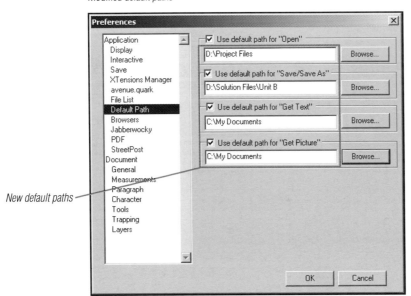

New default paths

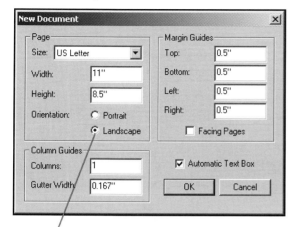

*Click option button to change
orientation to Landscape*

*Value determines
how frequently the
document is saved*

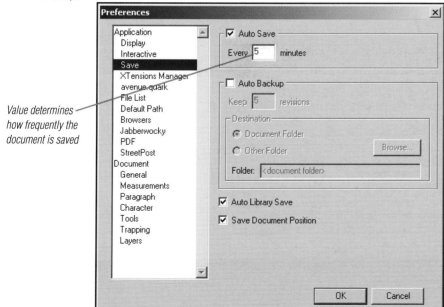

Set Auto Save options

1. Start Quark, click File on the menu bar, point to New, then click Document.

2. Click the Landscape option button, as shown in Figure B-3.

3. Click OK to close the New Document dialog box.

4. Click View on the menu bar, then click Fit in Window.

5. Click Edit on the menu bar, point to Preferences, then click Preferences.

6. Click Save in the Application list, then click the Auto Save checkbox if it does not contain a checkmark. See Figure B-4.

> TIP Using Auto Save is great insurance towards warding off disaster because it saves your work even if you forget. You may want to use this feature only until you become more accustomed to saving frequently on your own, as Auto Save can also save something that was not meant to be permanent.

You started QuarkXPress, opened a new document with a landscape orientation, then you modified the Auto Save preference.

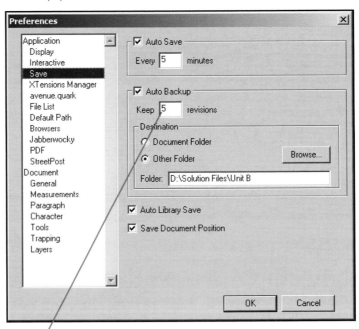

*Value determines the number of
revisions that are maintained*

Using the Auto Backup feature

The Auto Backup feature in the Preferences dialog box is useful if you need to keep in-progress versions of a saved file—say, for example, you have a mission-critical project for which you want to document multiple saved versions of a file. When you click the Auto Backup checkbox, Quark automatically makes a copy of your document when you manually save your work (up to a maximum of 100 revisions). Each revision is automatically saved in the Save/Save as folder you specified in the default path options (unless you indicate otherwise), with a consecutive number following its name. See Figure B-5, which shows that five revisions will be maintained. When the number of revisions *exceeds* the number of revisions specified, the oldest version is deleted to make way for the newest.

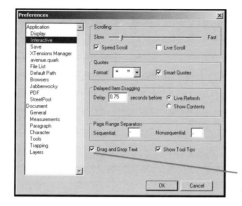

*Click checkbox to enable the
Drag and Drop feature*

Set Drag and Drop option

1. Click Interactive in the Application category.
2. Click the Drag and Drop Text checkbox to add a checkmark, as shown in Figure B-6.
3. Click OK to close the Preferences dialog box.
4. Click File on the menu bar, click Save as, then save the file as **About Quark**.

You turned on the Drag and Drop Text option in the Preferences dialog box.

Saving a document as a template

When using the Save as command, there are two document types from which to choose. In most cases, you'll accept the default choice: a typical Quark file with the extension .qxd. Some files, however, are used as springboards for other documents. They usually contain enough basic information (such as rulers and text boxes) to get you started on a particular project, and offer the advantage of assuring continuity in design and layout. Such a file is called a **template**, and it differs from a document in the following ways:

- It has the file extension .qxt.
- The template icon differs from the document icon.
- When opened, the screen displays the contents of the template, but the title bar indicates that the document is unnamed.

So when would you use a template? Repetitive documents, such as a newsletter, that have common layout features are ideal opportunities. Imagine the following scenario: You are in charge of your company newsletter. In each issue, the masthead remains the same, as does the placement of the table of contents, columns of text, and graphics on the first page. The second page always contains a short bio of the employee of the month, as well as a picture of the employee. Creating a template for the newsletter allows you to create the basic layout of the document, and lets you "fill in the blanks" with monthly content. This saves you lots of time, and you'll like how it makes you look very professional.

ADD TEXT TO A DOCUMENT

What You'll Do

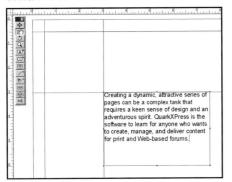

Creating a dynamic, attractive series of pages can be a complex task that requires a keen sense of design and an adventurous spirit. QuarkXPress is the software to learn for anyone who wants to create, manage, and deliver content for print and Web-based forums.

In this lesson, you'll create a text box and add text to it, and create horizontal and vertical ruler guides.

Understanding the Tasks

You may be wondering why you have to learn yet *another* software program. You probably already have a pretty nifty word processing program that says you can use it to lay out pages. The truth is that your word processing program probably *will* let you create really nice pages, but it likely does not give you the control and the options of a full-blown desktop publishing program like Quark. Your word processor is probably sufficient if all you are creating is a sign for a garage sale, or a flyer for a neighborhood talent show. But if you want to create professional-quality pages that can be sent to a commercial printer, you need a program that is up to the task. Consider, for example, the process that goes into creating a book like this one. Figure B-7 shows what a page from an actual book in the Design Professional series would look like if it were laid out using a word processing program. Did you notice that all the elements are aligned at the left margin (even the text in columns 2 and 3)? The word processor lets you create simple layouts that have little variety.

QUICKTIP

You should always use the right tool for the job. A word processing program is best used for composing text. A desktop publishing program is best used to lay out pages. For example, the text for this book is written using Microsoft Word, but prior to being printed, it is laid out using Quark.

Working Together

There are two basic ways of adding text to a document. One is to type text directly into a text box. Another way is to import text from a word processing program document. A word processing program is great for composing and editing text. A desktop publishing program makes that text look good.

Assessing the Limitations

In a word processing document, your primary limitations are the **margins**, those page borders on the top, bottom, left, and right. Items within each page generally cannot exceed these borders. In Quark, each item—whether it is text, a table, or a picture—can be placed *anywhere* on the page. This occurs because each element on a page—whether it is text or an image—is placed in its own object. An **object** is any item that, when selected, is surrounded by handles. (You can select an object by clicking it.) **Handles** are small boxes that appear around the object's perimeter. Each element is constrained by the dimensions of its object rather than the margins on a page. Figure B-8 shows the Design Professional

series content as in Figure B-7, but it is laid out using Quark, the program actually used in the production of this series. While the program window may seem 'messier' in appearance, all those lines actually help you decide what goes where.

QUICK**TIP**

The concept of an object is analogous to a container in that it can be moved and modified *independent* of other elements.

Using the Tools

All those items in Figure B-8 that make it look crowded are what make Quark—and ultimately, you—the power behind the pages. For example, the limits of the page

are defined by the blue margins. The selected object is just right of the pointing finger—which is also an object, but is not selected at the moment. The object that contains the text is called a **text box**, drawn using a tool on the Tools palette. The object that contains the image is called a **picture box**, also drawn using a tool on the Tools palette. The green **ruler guides** are pulled down from the horizontal and vertical rulers to make it easier for you to align objects.

QUICK**TIP**

You can remove a ruler guide using either the Item or Content tool from the Tools palette. Position the pointer over a guide, then click and drag it to the ruler from which it was created.

FIGURE B-7

Design Professional series content laid out in a word processing program

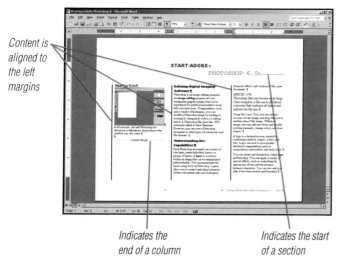

Content is aligned to the left margins

Indicates the end of a column

Indicates the start of a section

FIGURE B-8

Design Professional series content laid out in a desktop publishing program

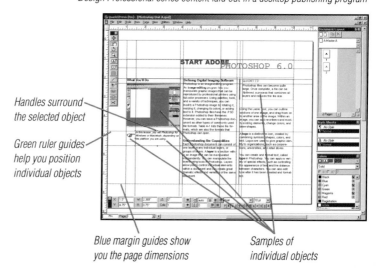

Handles surround the selected object

Green ruler guides help you position individual objects

Blue margin guides show you the page dimensions

Samples of individual objects

Create a text box and add text

1. Click the Rectangle Text Box tool on the Tools palette.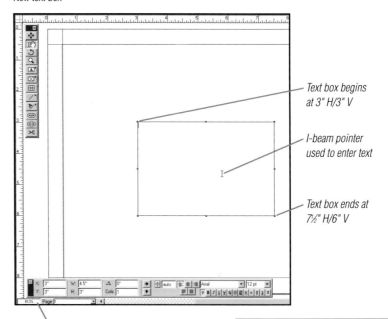

2. Position the pointer at 3" H/3" V. (*Hint*: You can drag a palette out of the way if it obscures your view.) ┼

   > TIP The first measurement refers to the horizontal ruler (H), and the second measurement refers to the vertical ruler (V).

3. Click and drag the pointer to 7 ½" H/6" V. Compare your screen to Figure B-9.

4. Type the text shown in Figure B-10. (*Hint*: You can change the view of your document if you are unable to read the text.)

   > TIP The flashing cursor is called the **insertion point**. Typed characters always occur to the right of the insertion point.

5. Press [Ctrl][A] (Win) or [command][A] (Mac) to select all the text in the text box.

6. Click the Font size list arrow on the Measurements palette.

   > TIP You can change the appearance of the type—the font—by clicking the Font list arrow (to the right of the Font size list arrow) on the Measurements palette.

7. Click 18. Compare your text box to Figure B-11.

You created a text box with the Rectangle Text Box tool, entered text in the text box, then enlarged the text using the Measurements palette.

Text box begins at 3" H/3" V

I-beam pointer used to enter text

Text box ends at 7½" H/6" V

Your zoom factor may be different

FIGURE B-10
Newly entered text

Creating a dynamic, attractive series of pages can be a complex task that requires a keen sense of design and an adventurous spirit. QuarkXPress is the software to learn for anyone who wants to create, manage, and deliver content for print and Web-based forums.

Insertion point

FIGURE B-11
Enlarged text

Creating a dynamic, attractive series of pages can be a complex task that requires a keen sense of design and an adventurous spirit. QuarkXPress is the software to learn for anyone who wants to create, manage, and deliver content for print and Web-based forums.

FIGURE B-12

Pointer on horizontal ruler

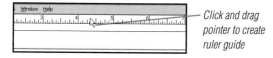

Click and drag
pointer to create
ruler guide

FIGURE B-13

Drawing the horizontal ruler guide

Pointer indicates
horizontal ruler guide

Ruler guide will
appear in green when
drawing is complete

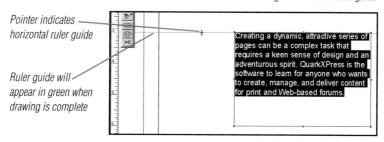

Creating a dynamic, attractive series of
pages can be a complex task that
requires a keen sense of design and an
adventurous spirit. QuarkXPress is the
software to learn for anyone who wants
to create, manage, and deliver content
for print and Web-based forums.

FIGURE B-14

Horizontal and vertical ruler guides

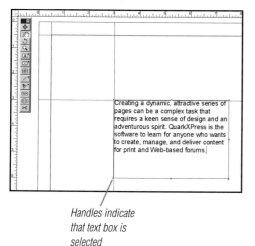

Handles indicate
that text box is
selected

Draw ruler guides

1. Position the pointer anywhere in the horizontal ruler, as shown in Figure B-12.

2. Click and drag the pointer to 3" V, as shown in Figure B-13.

3. Release the mouse button.

   TIP The ruler guide will appear in green when the mouse button is released.

4. Position the pointer anywhere in the vertical ruler.

5. Click and drag the pointer to 3" H, then release the mouse button.

   TIP If you create a ruler guide in error, you can delete it by positioning the pointer over a guide, then dragging it back to its ruler.

6. Click anywhere in the text box to deselect the text.

7. Click File on the menu bar, then click Save. Compare your screen to Figure B-14.

You created vertical and horizontal ruler guides.

Using rulers

Quark provides two rulers to precisely define areas on a page. The rulers run along the top and left sides of the page. Each point on an image has a horizontal and vertical location. These two numbers, called X and Y coordinates, appear in the Measurements palette. The X coordinate refers to the location on the horizontal ruler and the Y coordinate refers to the location on the vertical ruler. In some cases, missing a ruler measurement even slightly can dramatically change the look of your page. If you have difficulty seeing the ruler markings, you can increase the size of the page; the greater the zoom factor, the more detailed the markings.

MODIFY AND REPOSITION A TEXT BOX

What You'll Do

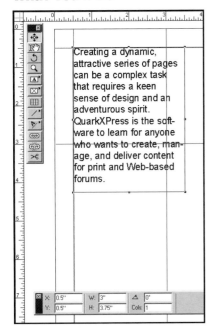

 In this lesson, you'll change the size and location of a text box, and experience the snap-to effect of the guides.

Understanding the Realities of Desktop Publishing

Wouldn't it be nice if you could create the perfect document or page in one sitting? The reality is that this rarely happens. In most cases, pages take quite a bit of tweaking to make a document look just right. Tweaking—a not-so-technical term for making elements on a page come together—can be accomplished in many ways. The most basic type of modification you can make to a text box is to change its size and shape. You can do this by dragging a handle, once it has been selected.

QUICKTIP

Planning is the key to working efficiently. Before you begin, you should have a written—or mental—plan of how you want a page to look, and you should have a rough idea of what items you want to use. Think about all the elements you'll need and how they'll fit together in a pleasing manner. Imagine that you're creating a jigsaw puzzle.

Resizing and Reshaping By Dragging

Figure B-15 contains sample text in a text box that looks like it was plopped on the page without much thought. This particular page has three columns, but our text box doesn't seem to conform to any known shape or size. The first step to resizing a text box is to select it. Once it is selected, you can modify its size and shape by dragging its handles. When you hold the pointer over a text box handle, the pointer changes its appearance to that of a pointing hand. When you click and drag the pointing hand, the pointer changes its appearance again. This click and drag method works well if you have a space you need to fill, and you are unsure of—or don't care about—its specific dimensions.

QUICKTIP

You can use either the Item tool or Content tool (on the Tools palette) to change the size and shape of objects.

Resizing and Reshaping Using the Measurements Palette

You can also modify the size and shape of a text box using the Measurements palette. See the W: and H: text boxes in Figure B-16. By typing values in the width and height text boxes, then pressing [Enter] (Win) or [return] (Mac), you can force a text box to have specific dimensions.

FIGURE B-15
Sample text

FIGURE B-16
Dimensions on the Measurements palette

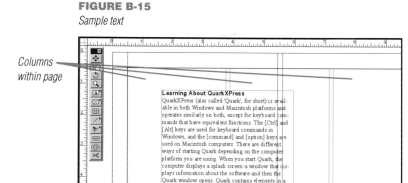

Columns within page

Text box

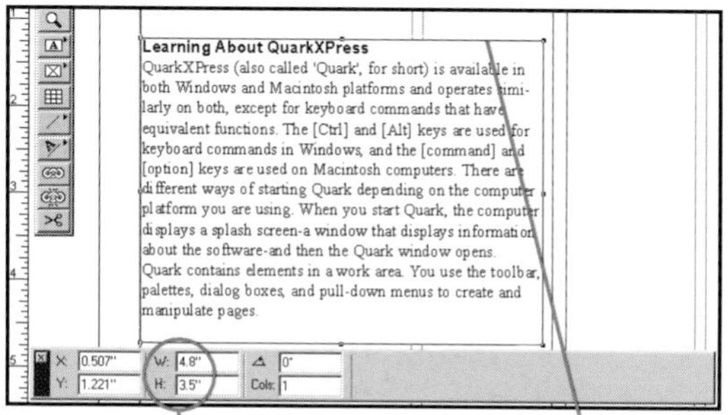

Use text boxes to type in new width and height values here

Selected text box size and shape conforms to dimensions in the Measurements palette

Having a Moving Experience

Modifying the size and shape of a text box is only half the fun. You can move a text box—or any object for that matter—using the mouse, the Measurements palette, or the arrow keys on your keyboard. Of course, you can't do anything with the text box until it is selected. (You'll know the object is selected because when the Content tool is selected, the pointer looks like a hand. When the Item tool is selected, the pointer looks like a four-way arrow.) Once you have selected a text box, click the Item tool on the Tools palette, position the pointer over the text box, then click and drag the object to a new location. You can change the position of the text box by changing the X: and Y: values on the Measurements palette, just as you changed its dimensions. If you typed 1 in the X: text box and 2 in the Y: text box, then pressed [Enter] (Win) or [return] (Mac), you would find that the upper-left corner of the text box would be 1" H/2" V. See Figure B-17. Finally, you can use the arrow keys on your keyboard to nudge a selected object up, down, left, or right. Each time you press one of the arrow keys, the object moves one pixel in the direction you selected.

FIGURE B-17
Location on Measurements palette

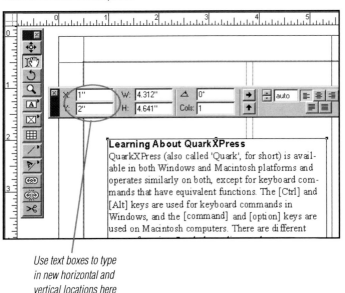

Use text boxes to type in new horizontal and vertical locations here

Experiencing the 'Snap to' Feature

One of the neat features of those messy-looking margin and ruler guides is that they have a magnetic quality that helps you when moving objects. For example, suppose you select the Item tool and click a text box. As you drag the object and it nears a margin or ruler guide, the object will **snap** to it—that is, it will align itself exactly at the margin or ruler guide. The Quark default is for the Snap to feature to be on, since most documents look better when pictures, text boxes, and other objects are aligned precisely at these points. You can check your settings by looking at the View menu shown in Figure B-18. You may be wondering why you would want to turn off such a marvelous feature. Well, you may find at some point that the magnetism is preventing you from positioning an object the way you want it—say you want to place an object near a margin or ruler guide, but not exactly at its edge. If so, just click the View menu, then click the Snap to Guides command to remove the checkmark. You can always turn the feature back on when you're finished.

FIGURE B-18

View menu with Snap to Guides feature on

Checkmark indicates that the Snap to Guide feature is enabled

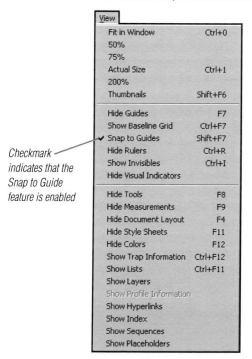

Modify a text box

1. Position the pointer over the upper-right corner of the selected text box, as shown in Figure B-19. 👈

2. Click and drag the upper-right handle until the ruler dimensions are 6" H/2" V, as shown in Figure B-20. ✥

   TIP As you resize a text box, its contents conform to the new dimensions.

3. Release the mouse button.

   TIP You can resize an object using any handle.

4. Position the pointer over the lower-middle handle. 👈

5. Drag the pointer until 3.75" (or a value close to 3.75") displays in the H: text box on the Measurements palette, then release the mouse button. Compare your text box and Measurements palette to Figure B-21. ✥

   TIP Values on the Measurements palette may differ slightly.

You modified the height and width of a text box using the rulers and the Measurements palette.

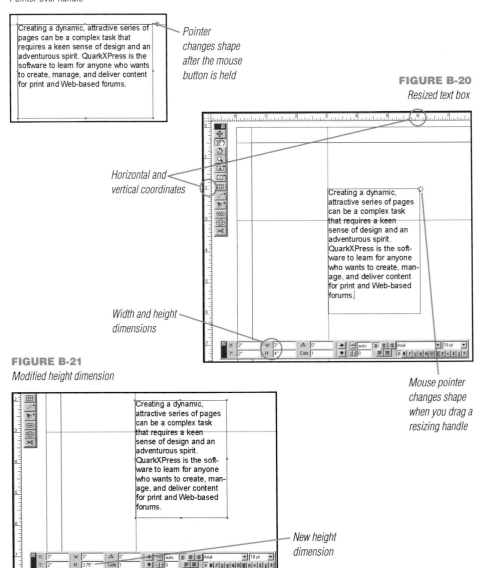

FIGURE B-19
Pointer over handle

Creating a dynamic, attractive series of pages can be a complex task that requires a keen sense of design and an adventurous spirit. QuarkXPress is the software to learn for anyone who wants to create, manage, and deliver content for print and Web-based forums.

Pointer changes shape after the mouse button is held

FIGURE B-20
Resized text box

Horizontal and vertical coordinates

Width and height dimensions

Mouse pointer changes shape when you drag a resizing handle

FIGURE B-21
Modified height dimension

New height dimension

FIGURE B-22
Nudged text box

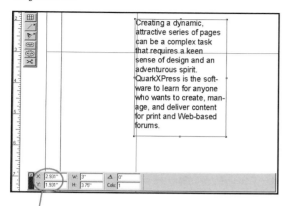

Creating a dynamic,
attractive series of pages
can be a complex task
that requires a keen
sense of design and an
adventurous spirit.
QuarkXPress is the soft-
ware to learn for anyone
who wants to create, man-
age, and deliver content
for print and Web-based
forums.

X: 2.931"   W: 3"   △ 0°
Y: 1.931"   H: 3.75"   Cols: 1

X and Y coordinates
after nudging

FIGURE B-23
Text box moved to margins

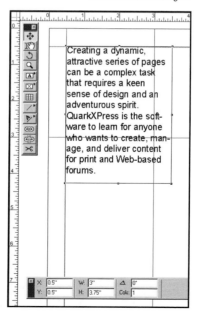

Creating a dynamic,
attractive series of pages
can be a complex task
that requires a keen
sense of design and an
adventurous spirit.
QuarkXPress is the soft-
ware to learn for anyone
who wants to create, man-
age, and deliver content
for print and Web-based
forums.

X: 0.5"   W: 3"   △ 0°
Y: 0.5"   H: 3.75"   Cols: 1

Reposition a text box

1. Click the Item tool on the Tools palette. ✛

2. Press [Left Arrow] five times.

   │ TIP   If you press the left arrow key while
   the Content tool is selected, you will move
   the insertion point, not the text box.

3. Press [Up Arrow] five times. Compare your
   screen to Figure B-22.

4. Position the pointer anywhere in the selected
   text box. ✛

5. Click and drag the mouse button until the
   upper-left corner of the text box is at
   ½" H/ ½" V. ✛

   You should have felt that the text box was
   'pulled' to the margins.

6. Release the mouse button, then compare
   your text box to Figure B-23.

7. Click File on the menu bar, then click Save.

You moved the text box using the arrow keys, and
dragged it to a new location. The Snap to Guides
feature helped you align the text box quickly and
precisely.

COPY AND MOVE TEXT

What You'll Do

QuarkXPress is the software to learn for anyone who wants to create, manage, and deliver content for print and Web-based forums. Creating a dynamic, attractive series of pages can be a complex task that requires a keen sense of design and an adventurous spirit.

 In this lesson, you'll move text using the Drag and Drop feature. You'll also use Undo and Revert to Saved commands to reverse some of your actions.

Understanding Moving Text

Just as objects often must be moved repeatedly before they are right where you want them, text often has to be moved within a text box. You might need to move text to make a particular story more logical, or to improve its flow. There are a variety of ways to move text within a text box, but regardless of which method you use, you must select the text before it can be moved. You select text by clicking and dragging the pointer over those characters you want to change. There are faster methods of text selection, and they are listed in Table B-2. Once the text is selected, you can remove it from its current selection (called **cutting** a selection), then place it in a new location (called **pasting** a selection).

QUICKTIP

The content of a text box is referred to as a **story.**

Cutting and Pasting Using the Clipboard

One of the most basic methods of moving text is called cutting and pasting. With this method, you remove the selected text, then place it elsewhere. Unlike cutting, copying leaves the original selection intact. After the selection is cut, it is stored on the clipboard. (Copying makes a duplicate and stores it on the clipboard as well.) The **clipboard** is a temporary storage area that can contain one selection. The clipboard is full when it contains one item, whether the item is a character, an image, or an entire document. Each time a selection is copied, the prior content of the clipboard is replaced with the new selection. The content of the clipboard can be pasted multiple times. You can place a selection on the clipboard by clicking Edit on the menu bar, then clicking Cut. Once the item is on the clipboard, you can paste it by clicking Edit on the menu bar, then clicking Paste.

Dragging and Dropping Text

Another way of moving text—considered to be more efficient and sophisticated—is the Drag and Drop method. **Drag and Drop** allows you to select text, then move it in one fell swoop, without using any menu commands. The Drag and Drop method has no effect on the clipboard; if you place an item on the clipboard and then Drag and Drop an item, the item on the clipboard remains on the clipboard. Figure B-24 shows Drag and Drop in progress. Notice that the selected text is highlighted and doesn't appear to move until the action is complete. Once the action is complete, the text *is* in its new location and remains highlighted.

Using Undo Versus Revert to Saved

What do you do when you realize you've made a mistake? Well, there are two options. One is to *undo* what you've just done. You can do this by clicking Edit on the menu bar, then clicking Undo. Not every thing you do can be undone, but you can use this feature after many commands. After you've used Undo, the command changes to Redo, so you can return to the previous condition. Your other option is to use the Revert to Saved command located on the File menu. The Revert to Saved command closes the current document without saving any changes (since the last save) and opens the last saved version of the document.

FIGURE B-24
Drag and Drop in progress

New location for selected text

Selected text will be moved

Drag-and-drop pointer

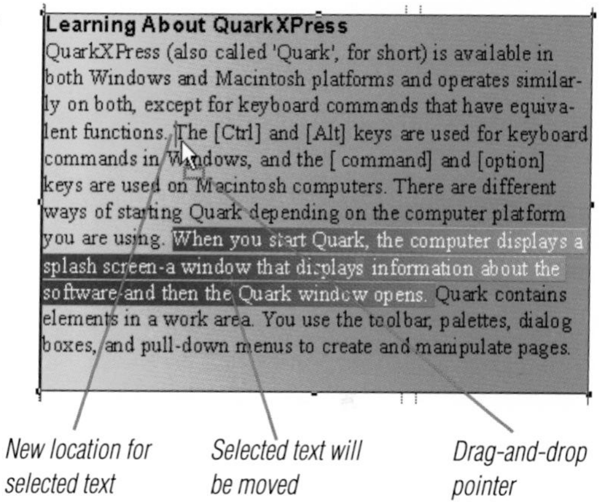

TABLE B-2: Common Text Selection Methods Using the Content Tool

method	to select
[Ctrl][A] (Win) ⌘[A] (Mac)	Entire document
Five clicks	Entire story
Four clicks	Entire paragraph
Three clicks	Whole line
Two clicks	Single word

Cut and paste text, then Undo

1. Using the Content tool, double-click the word "Creating".

2. Press and hold [Shift], then click to the right of the period following the word "spirit".

3. Release [Shift]. Compare your text box to Figure B-25.

   TIP Holding [Shift] acts as a *bridge* when selecting contiguous words or characters (words or characters that are right next to one another).

4. Click Edit on the menu bar, then click Cut.

5. Click to the right of the period following the word "forums", then press [Spacebar].

6. Click Edit on the menu bar, then click Paste. The previously deleted selection is pasted after the insertion point. Compare your text box to Figure B-26.

7. Click Edit on the menu bar, then click Undo Paste.

   TIP When viewed in the Edit menu, the Undo command is followed by the name of whatever command will be reversed.

You used the Cut and Paste commands on the Edit menu to cut and paste text, then used the Undo Paste command to eliminate the results of the Paste command.

FIGURE B-25
Selection in text box

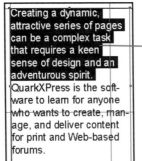

Selection will be cut and added to the clipboard

FIGURE B-26
Pasted clipboard contents

Clipbard contents are pasted after the first sentence

Shortcuts to shortcuts

As you become more experienced with Quark and other software programs, you will discover that some shortcut keys have common applications. For example, in many programs—even those created by different manufacturers—you may find that you can:

- Select All by pressing [Ctrl][A] (Win) or [command][A] (Mac)
- Cut by pressing [Ctrl][X] (Win) or [command][X] (Mac)
- Copy by pressing [Ctrl][C] (Win) or [command][C] (Mac)
- Paste by pressing [Ctrl][V] (Win) or [command][V] (Mac)
- Save changes by pressing [Ctrl][S] (Win) or [command][S] (Mac)
- Undo an action by pressing [Ctrl][Z] (Win) or [command][Z] (Mac)
- Open a file by pressing [Ctrl][O] (Win) or [command][O] (Mac)

You may find that there are many other shortcut keys in Quark that work in other programs; this is just a sample of the most common actions.

Creating a dynamic,
attractive series of pages
can be a complex task
that requires a keen
sense of design and an
adventurous spirit.
QuarkXPress is the soft-
ware to learn for anyone
who wants to create, man-
age, and deliver content
for print and Web-based
forums.

— Selection to be
dragged and
dropped

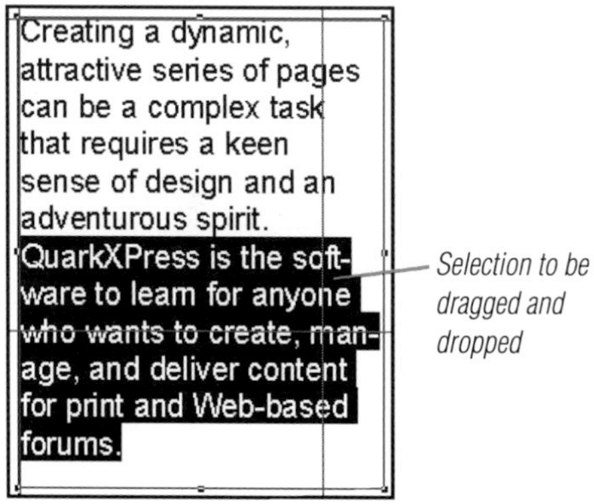

FIGURE B-28

Drag and Drop in progress

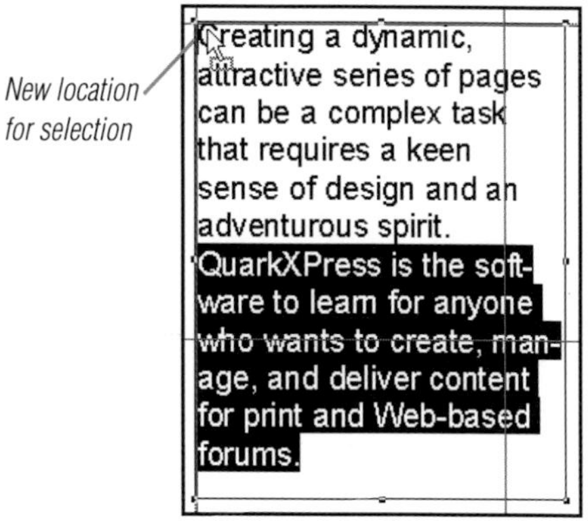

New location
for selection

Creating a dynamic,
attractive series of pages
can be a complex task
that requires a keen
sense of design and an
adventurous spirit.
QuarkXPress is the soft-
ware to learn for anyone
who wants to create, man-
age, and deliver content
for print and Web-based
forums.

FIGURE B-29

Drag and Drop complete

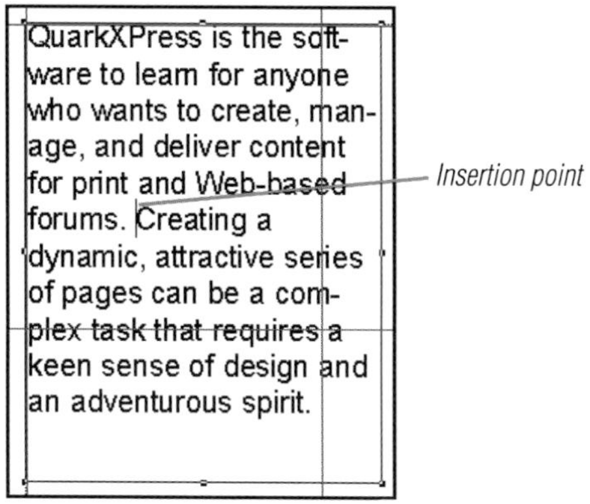

QuarkXPress is the soft-
ware to learn for anyone
who wants to create, man-
age, and deliver content
for print and Web-based
forums. Creating a
dynamic, attractive series
of pages can be a com-
plex task that requires a
keen sense of design and
an adventurous spirit.

— Insertion point

Use Revert to Saved, and Drag and Drop text

1. Click File on the menu bar, then click Revert to Saved.

2. Click OK to close the warning box.

   The version of the file from the last time you saved your work appears.

3. Click View on the menu bar, then click Fit in Window.

4. Select the last sentence in the text box, as shown in Figure B-27.

5. Click anywhere in the selection and hold the mouse button.

6. Drag the pointer to the left of the word "Creating" as shown in Figure B-28, then release the mouse button.

7. Press [Right Arrow] once, then press [Spacebar].

8. Press File on the menu bar, then click Save. Compare your text box to Figure B-29.

You used the Revert to Saved command to restore the last saved version of the file, then you used Drag and Drop to move text.

Power User Shortcuts

to do this:	use this method:
Add text in text box	Position ⌶, then type
Change font size	8.5 pt ▼
Copy selected text	[Ctrl][C] (Win) ⌘[C] (Mac)
Create a text box	🅰
Cut selected text	[Ctrl][X] (Win) ⌘[X] (Mac)
Draw horizontal ruler guide	Position ⬚ in ruler, drag ↕
Draw vertical ruler guide	Position ⬚ in ruler, drag ↔
Move a text box	✛, position ✛, then drag ⋰
Nudge an object	✛, then press [Left Arrow], [Right Arrow], [Up Arrow], or [Down Arrow]
Open Application Preferences	Edit ➤ Preferences ➤ Preferences, or [Ctrl][Alt][Shift][Y] (Win) ⌘ [option][shift][Y] (Mac)
Open Document Preferences	Edit ➤ Preferences ➤ Preferences, or [Ctrl][Y] (Win) ⌘[Y] (Mac)

to do this:	use this method:
Paste selected text	[Ctrl][V] (Win) ⌘[V] (Mac)
Resize a text box	Position ☞ over handle, then drag ⋰
Revert to Saved document	File ➤ Revert to Saved
Save a document as a template	[Ctrl][Alt][S] (Win) ⌘[option][S] (Mac)
Select All text	[Ctrl][A] (Win) ⌘[A] (Mac)
Select contiguous text	Double-click first word, press and hold [Shift], click last word
Select entire paragraph	Click ☜ four times
Select entire story	Click ☜ five times
Select single word	Click ☜ two times
Select whole line	Click ☜ three times
Undo last command	[Ctrl][Z] (Win) ⌘[Z] (Mac)

Key: Menu items are indicated by ➤ between the menu name and its command.

Set preferences and defaults.

1. Start Quark.
2. Create a new document with portrait orientation.
3. Save the document as **Volunteering**.
4. Use the View menu to fit the document in the window.
5. Open the Preferences dialog box, then change the display color of the ruler guides to red (the first color box in the second row of the Ruler dialog box).
6. Close the Preferences dialog box.

Add text to a document.

1. Click the Rectangle Text Box tool on the Tools palette.
2. Create a text box from 1½" H/1" V to 7½" H/2" V.
3. Type **Volunteering is Great!**.
4. Select all the text in the text box.
5. Change the font to Bernard MT Condensed. (*Hint:* If you do not have this font, make a substitution using another available font that is narrow or condensed.)
6. Change the font size to 48 pt.
7. Draw a horizontal ruler guide at 4" V.
8. Draw a vertical ruler guide at 2½" H.
9. Save your work.

Modify and reposition a text box.

1. Use the Rectangle Text Box tool to create a text box from 3" H/5" V to 7" H/8" V.
2. Type the following text in the text box: **Truly a win-win event. Volunteering is great for**

the community. It helps those in need and makes you feel terrific. What a great deal.
3. Select all the text in the text box
4. Change the font to Arial if necessary, and the font size to 24 pt.
5. Drag the bottom-center handle to 7½" V (or when the H: text box on the Measurements palette reaches 2.5").
6. Deselect the text in the text box.
7. Move the text box with the Item tool so the top-left corner of the box is at 2½" H/4" V.
8. Save your work.

Copy and move text.

1. Use the Content tool on the Tools palette to select the text "What a great deal."
2. Cut the selection.
3. Create an insertion point to the left of "Truly".
4. Paste the clipboard contents at the insertion point, then add a space before the next word.
5. Select "Truly a win-win event".
6. Drag the selection to the end of the text box, then compare your document to Figure B-30.
7. Open the Preferences dialog box and change the color of the ruler guides to green (use the fourth color box from the left in the fourth row).
8. Save your work.

FIGURE B-30
Completed Skills Review

The location and position of the Measurements palette may vary

One of your regular customers at Red Rock Design ordered some notepaper. Your customer is a world traveler and provides you with photos from a recent trip to use as illustrations. You chose a photo and started a document, but need to add text to it and complete the design.

1. Open QP B-1.qxd, then save it as **Eiffel Tower**.
2. Add the following vertical ruler guides: 1", 4 ½".
3. Add the following horizontal ruler guides: 4 ½", 7 ½".
4. Create a text box to the right of the image that fills the rectangular area created by the ruler guides.
5. Use the Content tool on the Tools palette to enter text describing the image in the text box. Add your own text, discussing favorite facts about Paris, or the pictured Eiffel Tower and torch of the Statue of Liberty. Use any fonts available on your computer.
6. Compare your image to the sample in Figure B-31. (The text in the sample is 18 pt Century Schoolbook.)
7. Move and resize the text box so it is below the image and fits into the rectangular area created by the ruler guide. If necessary, change the font size so all the text is visible.
8. If necessary, move or delete any text you created so the information flows more logically.
9. Save your work.

FIGURE B-31
Completed Project Builder 1

You are currently teaching a Leadership in Business class, in which you introduce topics such as group dynamics, inspiring creativity, and conflict resolution. As part of your final presentation for your Leadership in Business class, you decide to create a handout that will summarize your chosen topic and inspire discussion. Prior to the actual presentation (when you know the actual date, time, and place), you will enter additional information and distribute this document to each student.

1. Create a blank document in either landscape or portrait orientation.
2. Save the document as **Leadership Topic**.
3. Create a text box that contains the name of the topic you will discuss. (*Hint*: Choose any topic related to leadership, and use any font available on your computer.)
4. Create an additional text box below the first text box.
5. Add horizontal and vertical ruler guides that help you position the text box on the page.
6. Move the newly created text box so it snaps to the ruler guides.
7. Add text to the lower text box that gives more information about your presentation.
8. Compare your screen to Figure B-32. (The fonts used in the sample are 36 pt Cooper Black in the upper text box, and 24 pt Bodoni Book in the lower text box.)

9. Change the font in the top text box to a different font of your choice.
10. If necessary, move any text you created so the information flows more logically.
11. Increase the font size in the lower text box, then resize the text box, if necessary, to accommodate all the text.
12. Save the document.

FIGURE B-32
Completed Project Builder 2

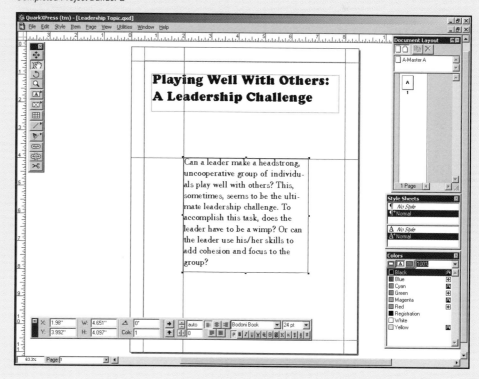

You've learned how to create text boxes and ruler guides, and how to move a text box so it is snapped to a ruler or margin guide. You're wondering, however, whether real-world publications use this type of layout method. You decide to use the Internet as a resource so you can find out more about the composition of a page, and how you can use ruler guides most effectively.

1. Connect to the Internet and go to *www.course.com*. Navigate to the page for this book, click the link for the Student Online Companion, then click the link for this project. The site for this unit is just one of many informative sites that can help you learn about formal composition systems.
2. If it is permitted, bookmark this URL for future reference.
3. Review the information on the site, particularly the information shown in Figure B-33.
4. Be prepared to discuss how you can use margins and ruler guides to create attractive and meaningful page composition.
5. When you finish your research, close your browser.

FIGURE B-33
Design Project Web site

Depending on the size of your group, you can assign elements of the project to individual members, or work collectively to create the finished product.

Your Quark instructor has a birthday coming up. The class decides that it would be great to show your appreciation for all your instructor's efforts by creating a fun birthday card. You started the document, but need to add the finishing touches.

1. Open QP B-2.qxd, then save it as **Birthday Card**.
2. One or more group members can decide what text should be used. (Be sure to take into account your instructor's feelings and sense of humor.)
3. One or more group members can decide what font(s) should be used.
4. One or more group members can create the document, text boxes, ruler guides, and text.
5. One or more group members can record which tasks were performed, by whom, and why they made their specific choices.
6. Compare your document to the sample shown in Figure B-34. (The fonts used in the sample are 72 pt Chiller in the upper text box, and 36 pt Bradley Hand ITC in the lower text box.)
7. Save your work.

FIGURE B-34
Completed Group Project

lu lu

UNIT C
WORKING WITH TEXT

1. Format text to add emphasis.

2. Modify text flow and apply drop caps.

3. Modify paragraph characteristics.

4. Enhance the appearance of a text box.

UNIT C
WORKING WITH TEXT

Introduction

How text appears on a page can determine whether or not it is read. And in page layout, getting people to read the words on a page is *key*. Quark supplies you with a plethora of tools that make managing the appearance of text on a page a snap. Remember, Quark is a complex program with great power. It may appear complicated at first, but this is only because it has so many powerful features. Once you become familiar with them, you'll really appreciate the power of Quark.

Emphasizing Text and Rearranging Paragraphs

There are a lot of ways you can make text stand out; in fact, you may already be familiar with some of them. We've all looked at words on a page and seen words or phrases that stand out. We know these words are somehow more important than the rest because someone has made a point of adding emphasis to them, by making them larger, formatting them in a different color or font, or adding attributes like italic or boldface. This emphasis makes it possible for a reader to skim a story and still pick up important facts.

Within a paragraph, text can be aligned with the margins in a variety of ways. Each way, in turn, affects the appearance and readability of the story. You also have the flexibility of changing the amount of space between lines, and the amount of space between the left margin and first word of every paragraph.

> **QUICKTIP**
>
> Never forget that the goal of page layout and design is readability. Make sure your design helps the reader notice important information, rather than distracting them from it.

Enhancing Text

In addition to all sorts of modifications you can make to characters and paragraphs, you can perform magic on individual stories. Using Quark features, you can spread out a story over multiple text boxes and on multiple pages, or you can force text to fit within a single text box. And you can make an ordinary-looking text box stand out simply by enhancing the text box itself.

Tools You'll Use

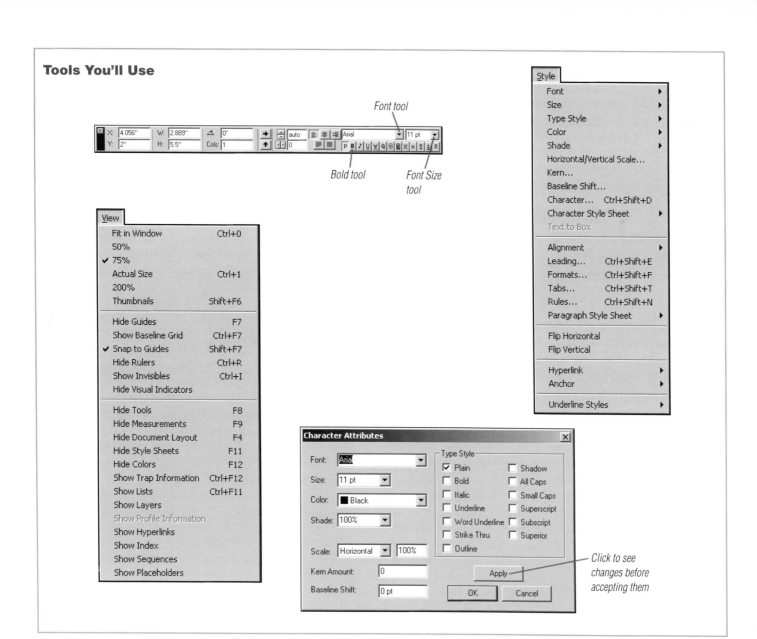

Font tool

| X: 4.056" | W: 2.889" | △ 0° | → | ↕ auto | Arial | 11 pt |
| Y: 2" | H: 5.5" | Cols: 1 | ↑ | ↕ 0 | P B I U W Q O S K ↕ ≜ | |

Bold tool

Font Size tool

Style

Font	▶
Size	▶
Type Style	▶
Color	▶
Shade	▶
Horizontal/Vertical Scale...	
Kern...	
Baseline Shift...	
Character... Ctrl+Shift+D	
Character Style Sheet	▶
Text to Box	
Alignment	▶
Leading... Ctrl+Shift+E	
Formats... Ctrl+Shift+F	
Tabs... Ctrl+Shift+T	
Rules... Ctrl+Shift+N	
Paragraph Style Sheet	▶
Flip Horizontal	
Flip Vertical	
Hyperlink	▶
Anchor	▶
Underline Styles	▶

View

Fit in Window	Ctrl+0
50%	
✔ 75%	
Actual Size	Ctrl+1
200%	
Thumbnails	Shift+F6
Hide Guides	F7
Show Baseline Grid	Ctrl+F7
✔ Snap to Guides	Shift+F7
Hide Rulers	Ctrl+R
Show Invisibles	Ctrl+I
Hide Visual Indicators	
Hide Tools	F8
Hide Measurements	F9
Hide Document Layout	F4
Hide Style Sheets	F11
Hide Colors	F12
Show Trap Information	Ctrl+F12
Show Lists	Ctrl+F11
Show Layers	
Show Profile Information	
Show Hyperlinks	
Show Index	
Show Sequences	
Show Placeholders	

Character Attributes

Font: Arial

Size: 11 pt

Color: ■ Black

Shade: 100%

Scale: Horizontal 100%

Kern Amount: 0

Baseline Shift: 0 pt

Type Style
- ☑ Plain
- ☐ Bold
- ☐ Italic
- ☐ Underline
- ☐ Word Underline
- ☐ Strike Thru
- ☐ Outline
- ☐ Shadow
- ☐ All Caps
- ☐ Small Caps
- ☐ Superscript
- ☐ Subscript
- ☐ Superior

Apply   OK   Cancel

Click to see changes before accepting them

FORMAT TEXT TO ADD EMPHASIS

What You'll Do

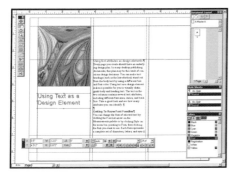

 In this lesson, you'll learn how to import existing text into a Quark document, and then apply formatting attributes.

Understanding Attributes

If you have any experience with word processing programs, then you're probably already aware of some of the techniques you can use to make text stand out. Most word processing programs, for example, let you use formatting **attributes** (effects that change the appearance of one or more characters), such as **bold**, *italic*, or underlining on selected words or characters. Going beyond even the most sophisticated word processors, Quark provides even more attribute options. The good news about word processing, however, is that you can take advantage of its greatest strengths—in text creation and editing—and then import those text files into QuarkXPress, including those created using Microsoft Word or Corel WordPerfect.

Applying Attributes

For your convenience, nearly every type of attribute you'll want or need is provided on the Measurements palette. When you click within a text box, the Measurements

TABLE C-1: Text Attribute Tools on the Measurements Palette

tool	tool name	sample	tool	tool name	sample
P	Plain	Quark, Inc.	±½	Shadow	Quark, Inc.
B	Bold	Quark, Inc.	2↑	All Caps	QUARK, INC.
I	Italic	*Quark, Inc.*	K	Small Caps	QUARK, INC.
U	Underline	Quark, Inc.	K	Superscript	Quark, Inc.
W	Word Underline	Quark, Inc.	S	Subscript	Quark, Inc.
Ɵ	Strike Thru	Quark, Inc.	0	Superior	Quark, Inc.
≥	Outline	Quark, Inc.			

palette displays tools that cater to your every text-based whim. Table C-1 details some of the commonly used text attributes that can be applied using tools on the Measurements palette.

Using Font Attributes as Design Elements

Every page you create should have an underlying design plan. In many desktop publishing documents, this plan usually is the result of considerable design decisions that affect the larger document, such as a brochure or magazine, or even a series of documents, such as a series of books. For example, look at the document shown in Figure C-1. There is a lot going on here. Each text heading, such as the Introduction, differs from the body text in color and font. Using a design element (such as a different font in maroon for a heading) makes it possible for you to visually distinguish body and heading text. The text in the two columns contains several text attributes, including different font sizes, italic, and boldface. Take a good look and see how many attributes you can identify.

FIGURE C-1
Text samples

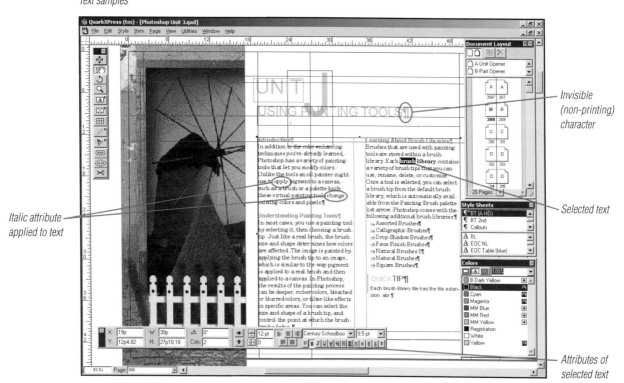

Italic attribute applied to text

Invisible (non-printing) character

Selected text

Attributes of selected text

Getting to Know Font Families

You can change the font of selected text by clicking the Font list arrow on the Measurements palette, or by clicking Style on the menu bar, pointing to Font, then clicking the font you want to use. Each font represents a complete set of characters, letters, and symbols for a particular typeface. Fonts are generally divided into three categories: serif, sans serif, and symbol. Characters in **serif fonts** have a tail, or stroke, at the end of some characters. These tails help to guide the eye from word to word in a long stream of text. For this reason, serif fonts are generally used in text passages, such as this one. **Sans serif fonts** do not include tails and are commonly used in headlines and headings, such as the one above. **Symbol fonts** are used to display unique characters (such as $, ÷, or ™). Table C-2 displays samples of serif and sans serif fonts.

TABLE C-2: Commonly Used Serif and Sans Serif Fonts

serif fonts	sample	sans serif fonts	sample
Lucida Handwriting	*QuarkXPress*	Arial	QuarkXPress
Rockwell	**QuarkXPress**	Bauhaus	QuarkXPress
Times New Roman	QuarkXPress	Century Gothic	QuarkXPress

Using additional page elements

You can employ many design tricks to pack your stories with greater visual appeal. You can use different fonts and add attributes to make characters stand out. You can apply drop caps and modify text flow to draw the reader's eye to specific text or to an object. You can also insert text elements, such as pull quotes or sidebars. A **pull quote** is a short bit of text –usually a sentence or phrase—pulled from a story on a page and usually set in a different font. The purpose of a pull quote is to draw attention to the story, to tease or captivate a reader into reading more. It should be short enough to scan easily but long enough to capture interest, and it should be on the same page as the story and placed close to it. The wording does not have to be identical to that found in the article (unless it's an actual quote), but ought to be similar. A **sidebar** is a short story placed alongside a feature story that supplements the information in the feature or main story. It can be formatted in the same size font as the main body text, but may look better in a larger size or different font. Adding a border or shading can dramatize sidebars.

FIGURE C-2

Get Text dialog box

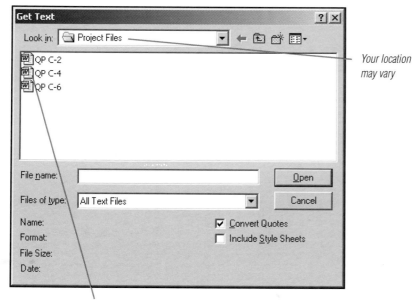

Your location
may vary

Your icon may look different if
Microsoft Word is not
installed on your computer

Get text

1. Start Quark, open QP C-1.qxd, then save the file as **Text Design Element**.

2. Fit the document in the Window, if necessary.

   TIP The shortcut key for the Fit in Window command is [Ctrl][0] (Win) or [command][0] (Mac).

3. Click anywhere in the text box in column 2. (*Hint*: You can click at 5" H/5" V.)

4. Click File on the menu bar, then click Get Text.

   TIP You can also open the Get Text dialog box by right-clicking the mouse button, then clicking Get Text (Win).

5. Locate QP C-2.doc using the Look in list arrow in the Get Text dialog box, as shown in Figure C-2.

6. Click QP C-2.doc.

7. Click Open.

You started QuarkXPress, opened a document, then imported text from an existing document.

Show Invisibles

1. If necessary, click View on the menu bar, then click Show Invisibles to add a checkmark. Compare your document to Figure C-3.

Did you notice the red box at the end of the text in the text box? 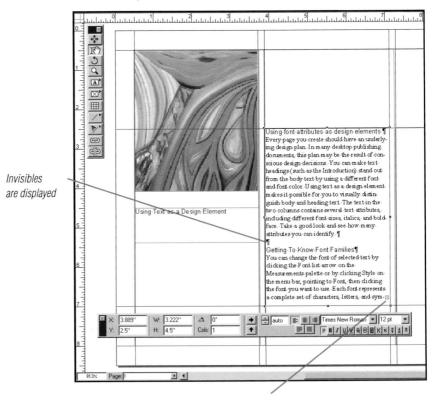 This symbol indicates that there is additional text (sometimes called **overflow**) that does not appear because it doesn't fit in the text box. This overflow problem will be solved in a later lesson.

> TIP For some users, displaying the invisible characters is a way of seeing where paragraphs begin and end. Other folks just find them annoying. You decide.

You displayed invisible symbols in the document.

FIGURE C-3
Text in document, with overflow

Invisibles are displayed

Symbol indicates that additional text does not appear

FIGURE C-4
Selected paragraph

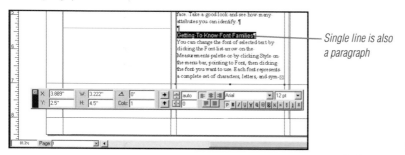

Single line is also
a paragraph

FIGURE C-5
Attributes applied to selected text

Color of the
selected text

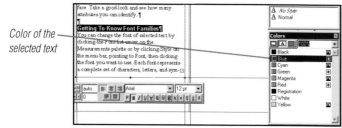

FIGURE C-6
Attributes and color applied to text

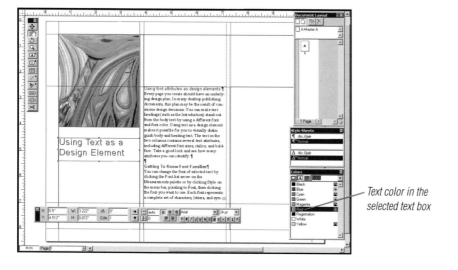

Text color in the
selected text box

1. Position the pointer over "Getting to Know Font Families". ⌶

2. Triple-click the mouse, then compare your document to Figure C-4.

3. Click the Bold tool on the Measurements palette. **B**

4. Click the Blue color on the Colors palette, then compare your document to Figure C-5.

5. Click anywhere within the text box beneath the graphic image.

6. Position the pointer anywhere over the existing text, then triple-click. ⌶

7. Click the Font size list arrow, then click 24 pt.

8. Click the Red color shade on the Colors palette.

9. Click the Shadow tool on the Measurements palette. **S**

10. Click anywhere within the active text box to deselect the text.

11. Click File on the menu bar, click Save, then compare your document to Figure C-6.

You applied color and different attributes to selected text.

MODIFY TEXT FLOW AND APPLY DROP CAPS

What You'll Do

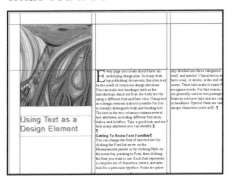

 In this lesson, you'll link two text boxes, delete existing text, and create drop caps.

Linking Text Boxes

If you're used to working with a word processor, you may wonder why you have to worry about text boxes when formatting ordinary text. Text boxes form the basis of many QuarkXPress documents, so linking them is essential to achieving sophisticated formatting effects, especially in longer documents.

Making a Link

In a word processing document, when you add text in the middle of a paragraph, the existing text shifts to the right and downward. All subsequent text moves automatically to accommodate the addition. Likewise, when you delete text, the remaining text shifts left and upward. In QuarkXPress, where text lives in text boxes, when you work with lengthy documents that cover multiple pages, you'll want to make sure that all text within a story or article stays connected—and in the right order. Since it is impractical to

have humongous text boxes that cover many pages, Quark lets you create links so that your text can travel easily from one text box to the next, and from page to page. You can create links automatically or manually. Figure C-7 shows two linked text boxes. Notice that the arrowhead not only indicates which text boxes are linked, but also from which direction the text is traveling. Links can be created, broken, and rearranged, and text boxes can be moved and resized as you tweak your page design—all the while, your text stays in the correct order. If you move linked text, the links and the order of the text are maintained.

QUICKTIP

The Quark default automatically adds a needed page at the end of a story. To modify this setting, click Edit on the menu bar, point to Preferences, then click Preferences. Click the General option, click the Auto page insertion list arrow, then click the option you want.

Using Drop Caps to Add Style

One method you can use to call attention to text—especially the beginning of a story or chapter—is drop caps. This feature, shown in Figure C-8, can add drama and importance to your page. Do you notice that the drop cap consists of a single character that covers five lines? You can control the number of lines the drop cap covers, as well as the number of characters included. When the reader sees a drop cap, there is no question that he or she has encountered the beginning of something important. How often you use this feature—at the beginning of every story, or at the beginning of every paragraph—is a stylistic issue you must resolve. Will there be more emphasis if the drop cap is seen at the beginning of every paragraph, or every story?

QUICKTIP

Resist the temptation to overuse a feature. The drop cap element can lose its effectiveness if seen too often. Use this feature sparingly to get the most out of it.

FIGURE C-7

Linked text boxes

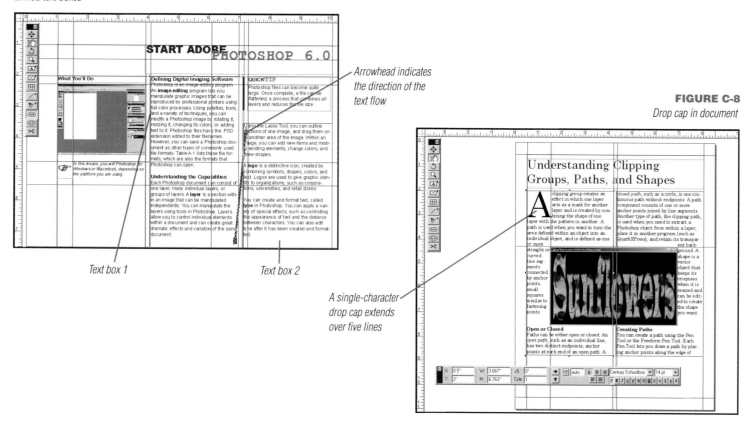

Text box 1

Text box 2

Arrowhead indicates the direction of the text flow

FIGURE C-8

Drop cap in document

A single-character drop cap extends over five lines

Manually link text boxes

1. Click the Linking tool on the Tools palette. 🔗

2. Click anywhere within the text box in column 2. Compare your screen to Figure C-9. ⌖

   TIP If you watch the Linking tool on the Tools palette, you may notice that this tool is animated.

3. Click anywhere in the text box in column 3. Notice that the overflow symbol has disappeared, and that the hidden text now appears in column 3. ⌖

   The text that was selected when column 2 was active is still selected.

   TIP When linking, remembering the correct order is crucial. Use this "linking mantra" to memorize the process: "I have text here (click) and I want it to go there (click)."

4. Click the Linking tool on the Tools palette, then compare your document to Figure C-10. 🔗

   Clicking the Linking tool again displays the arrow that shows how the text boxes are linked.

   TIP You can unlink text boxes by clicking the Unlinking tool on the Tools palette, then clicking the head or tail of the arrowhead connecting the boxes you want to unlink.

You linked two text boxes, which eliminated the text overflow problem.

Linking multiple text boxes

You can link multiple boxes by repeating the process of clicking the Linking tool on the Tools palette, clicking the first text box you want to link, then clicking the final text box. You can link multiple text boxes by pressing and holding [Alt] (Win) or [option] (Mac) when clicking the Linking tool, then clicking each subsequent text box until they are all linked. When you are finished, click another tool to turn off this feature.

FIGURE C-9
Preparing to link text boxes

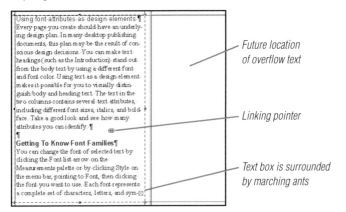

Future location of overflow text

Linking pointer

Text box is surrounded by marching ants

FIGURE C-10
Linked text boxes

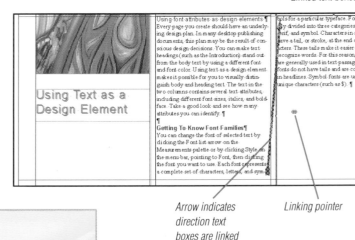

Arrow indicates direction text boxes are linked

Linking pointer

FIGURE C-11

Text box with text deleted

Current location of insertion point

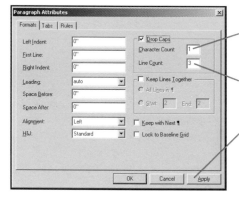

Every page you create should have an underlying design plan. In many desktop publishing documents, this plan may be the result of conscious design decisions. You can make text headings (such as the Introduction) stand out from the body text by using a different font and font color. Using text as a design element makes it possible for you to visually distinguish body and heading text. The text in the two columns contains several text attributes, including different font sizes, italics, and boldface. Take a good look and see how many attributes you can identify. ¶

Getting To Know Font Families¶
You can change the font of selected text by clicking the Font list arrow on the Measurements palette or by clicking Style on the menu bar, pointing to Font, then clicking the font you want to use. Each font represents a complete set of characters, letters, and symbols for a particular typeface. Fonts are gener-

ally divided into three categories: serif, and symbol. Characters in se have a tail, or stroke, at the end of acters. These tails make it easier to recognize words. For this reason, are generally used in text passage fonts do not have tails and are con in headlines. Symbol fonts are use unique characters (such as $). ¶

FIGURE C-12

Formats tab in Paragraph Attributes dialog box

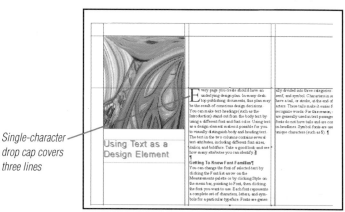

Indicates how many characters will be included in the drop cap

Indicates how many lines the drop capped character(s) will cover

Click to see the drop cap applied before the dialog box is closed

FIGURE C-13

Drop cap in text

Single-character drop cap covers three lines

Delete text and create a drop cap

1. Click the Content tool on the Tools palette.

2. Triple-click the first line in the text box in column 2, which begins "Using font attributes".

3. Press [Delete]. The first line no longer appears in the text box, as shown in Figure C-11, and the insertion point is in the upper-left corner of the text box.

4. Click Style on the menu bar, then click Formats.

5. Click the Drop Caps checkbox, as shown in Figure C-12.

6. Click OK.

   TIP You can also click Apply to see how the drop cap will look *before* closing the dialog box.

7. Use the Content tool pointer to select the drop cap.

8. Click the Blue color shade on the Colors palette.

9. Click anywhere in the text box to deselect the drop cap.

10. Click File on the menu bar, then click Save. Compare your screen to Figure C-13.

You deleted a line of text, and created and format-ted a drop cap in a paragraph.

MODIFY PARAGRAPH CHARACTERISTICS

What You'll Do

 In this lesson, you'll learn how to modify the appearance of a paragraph.

Framing Information for Better Presentation

One of the most important elements on a page is one to which you probably don't give much thought: the margins. **Margins are the areas at the top, bottom, left, and right edges of each column on the page, and of each page itself,** and there are several reasons they are important:

- They provide an attractive frame for the text and graphics, which gives the reader's eye much needed relief. Without them, a page would look like a 'sea' of information.

- They allow for the limitations of a printer, as no printer can print on the extreme edges of a page (assuming, of course, that you are printing on an untrimmed 8 ½" × 11" sheet of paper). The size of the page accessible by the printer is called the printable area.

- In multi-column pages, they help guide the eye through the flow of a document, so that all the columns don't appear to run together.

The **margin guides** indicate the margins on the page, and are shown as blue lines. Margins also distinguish one column from another. When you create a document, the New Document dialog box opens, allowing you to modify the four page margins. Figure C-14 contains a page with text in columns 2 and 3, and artwork in column 1. See how the margins act as a cushion for the text and graphic image?

QUICKTIP

You might also notice that a graphic image seems to *exceed* the page boundaries. This technique is called a **bleed**. When printed, the page will be trimmed to a smaller size. This gives the illusion that the image was printed all the way to the edges of the page.

Locating Margins

People traditionally think of margins as the space surrounding the four edges of a page, but in desktop design, the term also applies to the space that surrounds any boundary. Each design element, including text boxes, graphic images, columns, and tables (including the columns within tables), has margins. Margins are often used to create **white space**, the design term for space on a page that is not covered with printed or graphic material. The addition of white space is critical for clarity, since without it the page would look cluttered and be difficult to read. Margins extend around graphic images, around each side of a column, and within a table or text box.

FIGURE C-14
Margins within a page

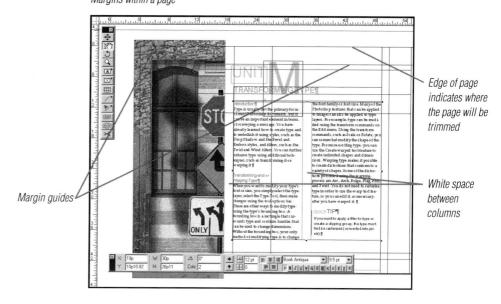

Margin guides

Edge of page indicates where the page will be trimmed

White space between columns

Creative copyfitting

Sometimes you have to be creative to make a story fit within a text box. When it comes to **copyfitting**, the art of squishing text within a text box, you have several options. You—or the author of the text—can always try to edit the story to a more manageable size. As an alternative, you can play with the leading or tracking, adjust the font and/or font size, or try scaling the text. Scaling changes the font size of the selected text based on the percentage you specify. Scaling text that is 10pt by 100%, for example, changes the font size to 20pt. Scaling text is a useful (and more subtle) alternative to changing the font size when you don't want the point size of text to look dramatically different from neighboring text. Once you select text, you can scale it by clicking Style on the menu bar, then clicking Horizontal/Vertical Scale. Double-click the Scale text box in the Character Attributes dialog box, type a new percentage, then click Apply to see how your changes look. If you're satisfied with the results, click OK to close the Character Attributes dialog box.

Aligning Text

The alignment of a paragraph determines how the text within it conforms to the left and right margins. The style you choose is up to you, and there is rarely a 'right' or 'wrong' style. Currently, conventional wisdom leans towards a preference for the left alignment of paragraph text. The reason is easier comprehension for readers. Of course, this is truer for wide columns of text than for narrow columns, and it's not too difficult to find experts to challenge these findings. So, again, it is up to you to set the style and maintain consistency. The alignment options are described in Table C-3.

QUICKTIP

Remember that in paragraph text, readability is the name of the game. Serif types are useful for long passages of text because the serifs help guide the reader's eyes. Sans serif fonts lend a clean appearance and are more appropriate to use in headlines and titles.

Controlling Spaces

Within any given paragraph, there are horizontal and vertical spaces. The horizontal spaces are those that occur between each line of text and are controlled by a process called **leading**. The vertical spaces are those that occur between individual characters and are controlled by a process called **kerning**. **Tracking** is the process of adjusting the amount of space to the right of each selected character. So why would you want to tamper with the default horizontal and vertical spaces? Well, you might have space constraints that demand a more creative solution than simply deleting text. By adjusting the leading and kerning, you can *force* text to fit within a certain space.

TABLE C-3: Text Alignment Options

option	tool	sample
Left		In paragraph text, readability is the name of the game.
Centered		In paragraph text, readability is the name of the game.
Right		In paragraph text, readability is the name of the game.
Justified		In paragraph text, readability is the name of the game.
Forced		In paragraph text, readability is the name of the game.

FIGURE C-15
Right-aligned text

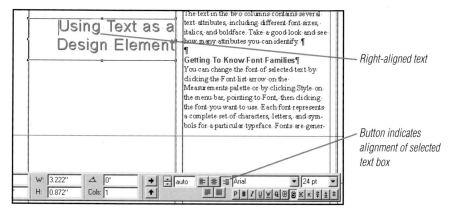

Right-aligned text

Button indicates alignment of selected text box

Change text alignment

1. Click anywhere in the text box in the first column containing the red text.

2. Click the Right tool on the Measurements palette. Compare your document to Figure C-15.

   > **TIP** It is not necessary to select all the text within a paragraph to change its alignment; just click anywhere in the paragraph.

3. Click the Forced tool on the Measurements palette. Compare your document to Figure C-16.

   Did you notice that the characters in the first line are forced to the left and right edges of the width of the text box? If there were a hard return at the end of the second line, those characters would be forced to the left and right edges as well.

4. Click the Centered tool in the Measurements palette.

   You changed the text so it is center-aligned.

FIGURE C-16
Forced-aligned text

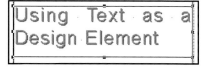

Modifying margins

You can modify existing margins by clicking Page on the menu bar, pointing to Display, then clicking A-Master A. (A master page is like the background of a page in which you can store repetitive information such as graphic images or margin settings.) Once the master page is selected, click Page on the menu bar, then click Master Guides. The Master Guides dialog box appears, allowing you to modify the margin dimensions. Once you make your modifications and close the Master Guides dialog box, you can return to the document by clicking Page on the menu bar, pointing to Display, then clicking Document.

Change tracking and kerning

1. Press [Ctrl][A] (Win) or [command][A] (Mac) to select all the text in the text box.

2. Double-click the Tracking and Kerning text box. `0`

   > TIP Tracking and kerning are very similar and can both be controlled from the Measurements palette or the Style menu. Using the Style menu, the Tracking command is only available if multiple characters are selected. If *no* characters are selected, the Kerning command is available from the Style menu.

3. Type **-10**, then press [Enter] (Win) or [return] (Mac). Compare your text with what is shown in Figure C-17.

   Did you notice that the space between the characters has closed?

   You modified the alignment and kerning of the contents of a text box.

FIGURE C-17
Kerned and centered text

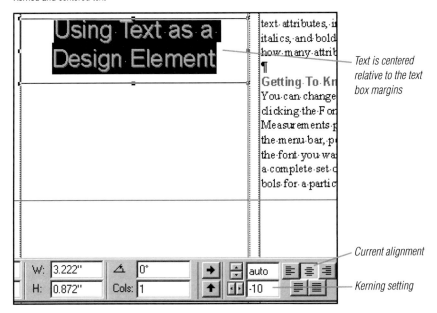

Text is centered relative to the text box margins

Current alignment

Kerning setting

FIGURE C-18

Leading and font size adjusted

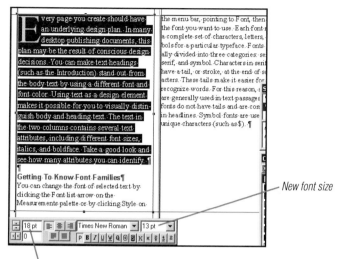

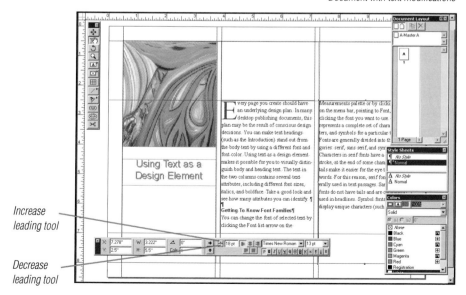

New font size

New leading value

FIGURE C-19

Document with text modifications

Increase
leading tool

Decrease
leading tool

Modify line spacing

1. Click the Content tool on the Tools palette, if necessary. 🖑

2. Quadruple-click the first paragraph in column 2, which starts "Every page you create". ⌶

3. Click the Increase Leading tool four times until 18 pt appears.

4. Double-click the Font size text box, type **13**, then press [Enter] (Win) or [return] (Mac). Compare your text to Figure C-18. ⌘

5. Quadruple-click the paragraph in column 3. ⌶

6. Click the Increase Leading tool until 18 pt appears.

7. Double-click the Font size text box, type **13**, then press [Enter] (Win) or [return] (Mac).

8. Click anywhere in column 3 to deselect the text, then compare your document to Figure C-19.

9. Click File on the menu bar, then click Save.

You changed the leading within a text box, then modified the font size.

ENHANCE THE APPEARANCE OF A TEXT BOX

What You'll Do

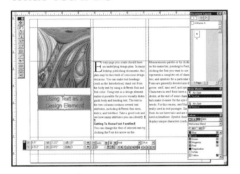

In this lesson, you'll format a text box frame and add color to the background.

Framing a Text Box

Every text box has a frame; that's what holds it together. But, by default, a frame has a width of 0 points, which renders it invisible. You can choose to make the frame of any text box visible by increasing its width, and you can also change its color and composition. You might, for example, want the border of a text box to appear as red dotted lines, or blue triple lines. Techniques like these are sure to make any text box get noticed, and that may be just what you want. Figure C-20 shows the Modify dialog box that is used to enhance a text box frame.

Modifying a Text Box

You can use the Modify dialog box to change the width, color, and appearance of a text box frame. As mentioned previously, the default width for a text frame is 0 points. Additional default settings include the color black, 100% shading (color intensity), and a solid line style.

TABLE C-4: Colors Palette Tools

tool name	tool	description
Frame Color		Used to change the perimeter color of the active text box
Text Color		Used to change the color of the selected text
Background Color		Used to change the background color of the active text box
Shading	100%	Used to change the intensity of the frame, text, or background color
Blending Style		Used to create background color blends

QUICKTIP

You can open the Modify dialog box once a text box is selected by clicking Item on the menu bar, then clicking either the Modify or Frame command. Clicking the Frame command automatically displays the Frame tab, while clicking the Modify command initially displays the Box tab. If you use the Modify command, you can modify the frame by clicking the Frame tab.

Modifying Background Color

The default background color in a text box is white. Quite simply, this means that every text box you create will have a white background. In most cases, this works very nicely, but on occasion, you may want to spice up your text box by adding a color to the background. This setting can be changed using the Box tab in the Modify dialog box, or by using the Colors palette. You may notice that there are three buttons and one list arrow directly beneath the Colors palette title bar, as shown in Figure C-21. These tools (which may look slightly different) are described in Table C-4.

QUICKTIP

When the Background Color tool is selected, an additional list arrow is available to create color blends.

FIGURE C-20
Modify dialog box

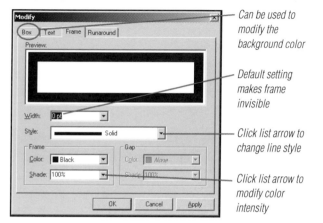

Can be used to modify the background color

Default setting makes frame invisible

Click list arrow to change line style

Click list arrow to modify color intensity

FIGURE C-21
Colors palette

Using tabs in a text box

A tab—formerly known as a tab set—is not something that you may need everyday, but when you do need one, you'll be grateful you know how to use them. A **tab** is an alignment feature that makes it easy to line up characters beyond the limitations of a text box. For example, you might want to create a list of items containing prices. Such a list would look extremely unprofessional if the items within it were not aligned. The first column—containing the items—a left-aligned tab. The second column is created using a decimal tab. **Dot leaders** (the characters that precede the decimal tab) help the reader connect the information in the two columns. You can create or modify tabs by clicking Style on the menu bar, then clicking Tabs. The Tabs tab in the Paragraph Attributes dialog box lets you create left, center, right, decimal, comma, and align on (character) tabs by clicking the type of tab you want, and the location in which you want it.

Modify a text box frame

1. Click the text box in column 1 containing the red text.

2. Click Item on the menu bar, then click Frame.

   | TIP You can open the Modify dialog box by right-clicking the text box, then selecting the Frame tab (Win), if necessary.

3. Click the Color list arrow, then click Blue.

   | TIP You can also modify the frame color using the Colors palette.

4. Click the Style list arrow, then click Double.

5. Click the Width list arrow, then click 4 pt. Compare your settings to Figure C-22.

6. Click OK, then compare your text box frame to Figure C-23.

You used the Modify dialog box to enhance the frame of the text box.

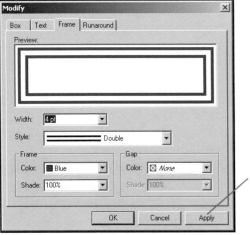
FIGURE C-23

Modified text box frame

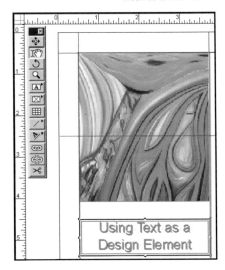

Developing design sense

Document design is a skill that can be learned through thoughtful practice and critical observation. Just as artists gather ideas from trips to museums and musicians gather ideas from attending concerts, you can sharpen your design skills by looking at publications created by others. Peruse publications at your local library or magazine stand, and observe the overall design elements and layout. Gauge your overall reaction to a document, and judge for yourself what you find appealing and what you find distracting or offensive. Concentrate on how your eye moves across a page. What combinations of design elements (balance, color, consistency, contrast, and white space) are you drawn to and what do you dislike?

FIGURE C-24

New background color

Indicates background
is selected and can be
modified

Background color

New background color

FIGURE C-25

Background with color and shade modification

Color Blend applied
to background

Change background color

1. Verify that the Background Color tool in the Colors palette is selected. ▨

2. Click the Cyan shade on the Colors palette. Compare your text box and Colors palette to Figure C-24.

   TIP   You can also modify the background color by clicking Item on the menu bar, then clicking the Modify command. This displays the Box tab that contains the color settings. Any changes you make using the Box tab are reflected on the Colors palette.

3. Click the Shade list arrow, then click 80%.

4. Click the Blend Style list arrow, then click Mid-Linear Blend.

5. Click File on the menu bar, then click Save. Compare your document to Figure C-25.

You used the Color palette to add color to the text box background, then you subdued the color by adjusting the Blend style.

Using contrast to add emphasis

Contrast is an important design principle that provides variety in the physical layout of a page and an entire publication. Just as you can use contrasting fonts to emphasize text, you can use contrasting elements to add emphasis to objects on a page. Contrast can be achieved in many ways: by changing the sizes of objects; by varying object weights, such as making a line surrounding an image heavier; by altering the position of an object, such as changing the location on the page, or rotating the image so it is positioned on an angle; by drawing attention-getting shapes or a colorful box behind an object to make it stand out (called a **matte**); or by adding carefully selected colors that emphasize an object. You can add emphasis to characters by creating reversed text. **Reversed text** appears as light characters on a dark background. This effect makes the text look as though it was cut out of the background. You can create reversed text by changing the font to a light color, such as white. When you change the background of the text box to a dark color, such as black, the reversed text effect will be evident.

Power User Shortcuts

to do this:	use this method:
Add drop caps	Style ➢ Formats
All Caps text	⬚
Bold text	**B**
Center align text	⬚
Change text color	**A**
Force align text	⬚
Get text	[Ctrl][E] (Win) ⌘ [E] (Mac)
Italic text	*I*
Justify text	⬚
Left align text	⬚
Link text boxes	⬚ , click text box, linked text box
Modify Blend Style	▼
Modify text box background	⬚

to do this:	use this method:
Modify frame color	⬚
Modify leading	auto
Modify shading	100% ▼
Modify text color	**A**
Modify tracking/kerning	0
Outline text	⬚
Plain text	P
Right align text	⬚
Shadow text	⬚
Show Invisibles	[Ctrl][I] (Win) ⌘ [I] (Mac)
Underline text	U
Unlink text boxes	⬚ , click arrow head or tail
Word Underline text	W

Key: *Menu items are indicated by ➢ between the menu name and its command.*

Format text to add emphasis.

1. Start Quark.
2. Open QP C-3.qxd, then save it as **About Hydrangeas.**
3. Show Invisibles, if necessary.
4. Click anywhere in the lower text box in column 1, which does not contain any text.
5. Get the file QP C-4.doc.
6. Select the contents of the upper text box in column 1, which begins "Learn about the".
7. Change the font to Pristina. (*Hint*: Substitute another font if this one is not available.)
8. Change the font size to 40 points. (*Hint*: If the text does not fit in the text box after increasing its size, you can adjust the font size, choose a different, narrower font, or resize the text box slightly to accommodate all the text.)
9. Change the font color to Blue.
10. Apply the shadow attribute.
11. Double-click the word "Environment" in the second paragraph.
12. Apply the bold attribute.
13. Save your work.

Modify text flow and apply drop caps.

1. Click the Linking tool on the Tools palette.
2. Link the lower text box in column 1 to the text boxes in columns 2 and 3. (*Hint*: You can link empty text boxes.)
3. Select the Content tool, if necessary.
4. Create a four-line drop cap using the first character in the linked text box in column 1.

5. Change the color of the drop capped character to Magenta.
6. Save your work.

Modify paragraph characteristics.

1. Center align the text in the upper text box in column 1.
2. Change the leading to 35 points. (*Hint*: If you made a font substitution, you may have to use a different leading value. The goal here is to tighten the space between the lines.)
3. Select all the text in the text box.
4. Change the tracking to 10. (*Hint*: If you made a font substitution, you may have to use a different tracking value. The goal here is to increase the space between the characters.)
5. Select all the linked text in columns 1 and 2.
6. Increase the leading to 20 pt.

FIGURE C-26
Completed Skills Review

7. Change the font size to 13 pt (Mac users can keep the font size 12 pt).
8. Apply the bold attribute to the text "Healing Properties" (in column 3).
9. Save your work.

Enhance the appearance of a text box.

1. Modify the background of each linked text box to Yellow.
2. Change the shading of each linked text box to 20%.
3. Modify the frame of the upper text box in column 1 using a 2 pt Dash Dot style.
4. Change the color of the frame to Blue.
5. Change the background color of the frame to Green, using a 30% shade.
6. Deselect any text or text boxes.
7. Save your work, then compare your document to Figure C-26.

You are hired by the National Park Service to create a flyer that describes features of Zion National Park in Utah. The Park Service supplies you with an image you can use, some text, and a Quark document with some text boxes. The rest is up to you. You decide to start by creating a headline for the flyer.

1. Open QP C-5.qxd, then save it as **Zion National Park**.
2. Create a text box from 1/2" H/5/8"V to 8" H/ 1 1/4" V. (*Hint*: Use the existing ruler guides at the top of the page for guidance.)
3. Add the following text to the text box: **Discover Zion National Park**. (*Hint*: Use any appropriate sans serif font on your computer. In the sample, a 40 pt Impact font is shown.)
4. Center align the text at the top of the document.
5. Adjust the kerning in the top text box, as necessary.
6. Insert the text in QP C-6.doc in the lower text box in column 1.
7. Link the text box in column 1 to columns 2 and 3.
8. Use any appropriate serif font available on your computer in the linked text boxes. (*Hint*: In the sample, a 14 pt Garamond font is shown.)

9. Adjust the leading in the linked text boxes, as necessary. (*Hint*: In the sample, the leading was changed to 18 points.)
10. Apply a four-line drop cap to the first character in the linked text box.
11. Add any attributes, color, or shading to the document as you see fit. (*Hint*: In the sample, the background color of the page was changed to a 30% Cyan. The background color of each of the text boxes was changed to None.)
12. Save your work, then compare your image to the sample in Figure C-27. (The text in the sample is 18 pt Garamond.)

FIGURE C-27
Completed Project Builder 1

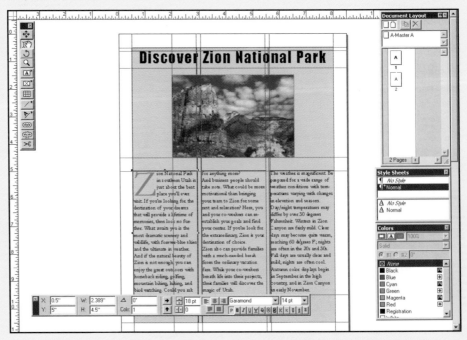

Do you remember when you were young and you got a new bike? Didn't it feel grand? To celebrate that feeling, you just purchased a new bike for your niece's birthday. It's a surprise, and you know she'll be really excited to receive it. You'll be bringing the bike with you when you visit your niece next month, but her birthday is coming up in a few days. You decide to send her a birthday card that includes a picture of the bike so that she can enjoy the surprise on her special day.

1. Open QP C-7.qxd, then save it as **New Bike Card**.
2. Create a text box that says "Happy Birthday", and include your niece's name (or make one up). (*Hint*: In the sample, a 60 pt Rage Italic font is shown.)
3. Use any appropriate attributes in the Happy Birthday text.
4. Create a text box beneath the image of the bike that contains your birthday message. (Make up your own suitable text.) (*Hint*: In the sample, a 36 pt Maiandra GD font is shown.)
5. Add a style, width, and color to the frame containing the birthday message.
6. If you choose, you can add a color to the background of the birthday message. (*Hint*: In the sample, a 20% Magenta is shown.)

7. Add any additional attributes, including color and shading you feel is appropriate. (*Hint*: In the sample, a 60% Magenta is shown.)

8. Compare your screen to Figure C-28.
9. Save the document.

FIGURE C-28
Completed Project Builder 2

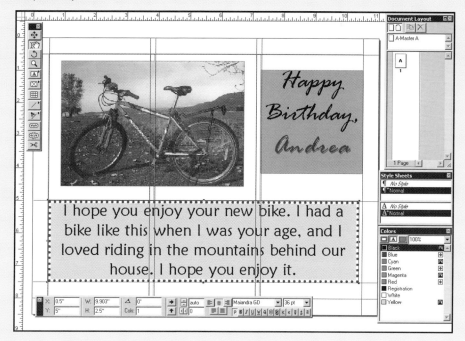

How does the eye perceive a page? Do the same rules apply to print pages and Web pages? As a user of QuarkXPress, page design—and how you can best perfect it—is essential to using this product. It's not enough to know the mechanics of Quark, you must understand the psychology of page design. You can use the Internet to find out more about the intricacies of page design and the rules that apply to Web pages, and how you can improve page layout.

1. Connect to the Internet and go to *www.course.com*. Navigate to the page for this book, click the link for the Student Online Companion, then click the link for this unit. The site for this unit is just one of many informative sites that can help you learn about formal composition systems (including *www.grantasticdesigns.com/tips.html* and *www.sensible.com/*).

2. If it is permitted, bookmark this URL for future reference.

3. Review the information on the site, particularly the information shown in Figure C-29.

4. Be prepared to discuss how you can improve the design and layout of Web pages.

5. When you finish your research, close your browser.

FIGURE C-29
Design Project Web site

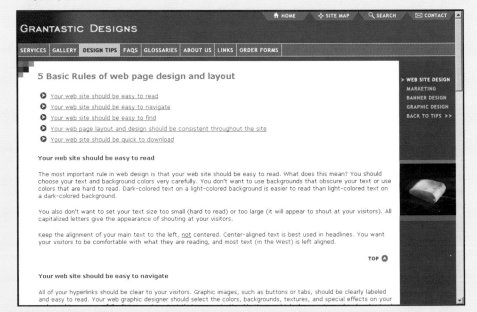

Depending on the size of your group, you can assign elements of the project to individual members, or work collectively to create the finished product.

As one of your class projects, you and your group are asked to create a document that can be used to promote a demonstration of QuarkXPress, which is scheduled during finals week. This document will be used to motivate other students to enroll in this class next semester.

1. One or more group members can decide the design of the page, including orientation and attributes.
2. Start a new document, then save it as **Quark Promotion**.
3. One or more group members can decide which Quark features should be emphasized.
4. One or more group members can decide what font(s) should be used.
5. One or more group members can actually create the text boxes, enter the text, and apply the attributes, as decided by the group.
6. One or more group members can record which tasks were performed, by whom, and why they made their specific choices.
7. Compare your document to the sample shown in Figure C-30. (The fonts used in the sample are 55 pt Cooper Black in the upper text box, and 18 pt Baskerville Old Face in the lower text box.)
8. Save your work.

FIGURE C-30
Completed Group Project

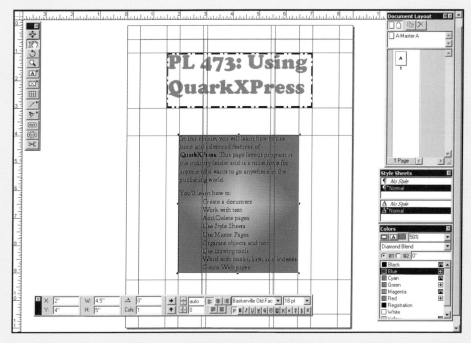

MANAGING A MULTI-PAGE DOCUMENT

1. Add and delete pages in a document.

2. Add numbers to identify pages.

3. Change vertical alignment.

4. Rearrange pages in a document.

5. Add continuation notices.

UNIT D
MANAGING A MULTI-PAGE DOCUMENT

Introduction

Until now, all the documents you were working with had only a single page. Wouldn't life be easy if all documents were this short? But in the real world, documents have multiple pages with stories that also flow over many pages. How many times have you been reading an article in a magazine or newspaper only to be told that it is continued elsewhere? How irritating! Well, you'll find out that there *are* compelling reasons to scatter stories about rather than have text start and stop on a single page. But we'll talk about that later.

Organizing Pages

If you have a document with multiple pages, it stands to reason that you'll need tools to perform routine maintenance.

Some of the tasks you must perform at some point are:

- Adding page numbers
- Adding new pages
- Deleting unnecessary pages
- Rearranging pages
- Adding continuation notices

Being a powerhouse program, Quark makes it easy for you to add, delete, and rearrange pages within a document.

QUICKTIP

Whether you are the author of the text, or the person in charge of layout and design, the goals should be the same. You want to create an attractive document that is easy to read. The document's design should lead the reader from one page to the next.

Tools You'll Use

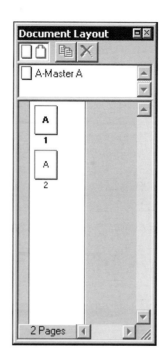

ADD AND DELETE PAGES IN A DOCUMENT

What You'll Do

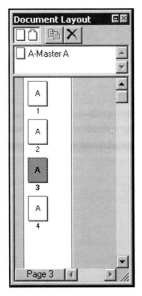

In this lesson, you'll learn how to add and delete pages in a document.

Adding Pages Based on a Master Page

You may have wondered what that A-Master A icon on the Document Layout palette is all about. Briefly, this icon represents a **master page**, a template that contains settings and instructions, such as number of columns and margin settings. When you add a page to a document based on a master page (by dragging the master page icon into the lower area of the Document Layout palette), the new page contains all the settings specified in the master page.

QUICKTIP

A document can have multiple master pages.

Using Automatic Page Insertion

Quark offers both automatic and manual methods of inserting pages. You may have noticed that when you open a new document, even though you haven't created any text boxes *per se*, text boxes are automatically inserted for the number of columns you specified. If you choose to insert text directly into an automatic text box, pages will automatically be inserted to accommodate any overflow text, as long as the Automatic Page Insertion option is turned on. To see whether this option is on, click Edit on the menu bar, point to Preferences, then click Preferences. Click the General option in the Document category, then examine the Auto Page Insertion list arrow. You can elect to turn off the option, or have overflow text inserted in pages at the end of the story, end of the section, or end of the document. Figure D-1 shows the default option (End of Story), in which pages are inserted, as necessary, at the end of the story.

QUICKTIP

Even if the Automatic Page Insertion option is turned on, you still need to manually insert a new page in order to accommodate overflow text from a *manually-created* text box.

Manually Inserting Pages

You may not always want to take advantage of Quark's Automatic Page Insertion feature. Perhaps your document is very complex, and you plan to juggle many stories over many pages. To have more control over where pages are inserted and where story text is placed, you may choose to manually insert pages and link text boxes. When pages are needed, you can insert them using the Page menu or the Document Layout palette. The Document Layout palette, shown in Figure D-2, lets you add pages by clicking and dragging a page icon into the document icon area. When no document is selected, the Document Layout palette displays the total number of pages there are in a document.

QUICKTIP

The Page menu is ideal for inserting multiple pages because the Insert Pages dialog box lets you specify how many pages will be added and at what location.

Deleting Unwanted Pages

You can bet that if Quark allows you to easily add pages, it most certainly makes it easy to delete them. You can delete one or more pages using a command on the Page menu, or using the Document Layout palette. The Page menu lets you delete individual or multiple contiguous pages. (Items that are *contiguous* are touching, such as pages 4 through 9.) The Delete button on the Document Layout palette lets you delete one or more selected pages, even if they are noncontiguous (pages 5 and 7, but not page 6, for example). When you click a page icon on the Document Layout palette, it is selected. The Delete button is available only if at least one page icon is selected.

QUICKTIP

You can select multiple contiguous page icons on the Document Layout palette by pressing and holding [Shift] each time you click a page icon. You can select noncontiguous page icons by pressing and holding [Ctrl] (Win) or [⌘] (Mac) each time you click a page icon. The selected page icons appear darkened, indicating that they have been selected.

FIGURE D-1

Preferences dialog box

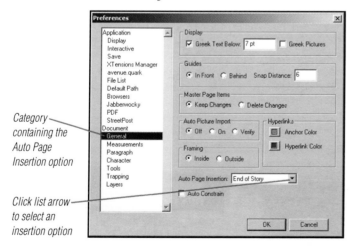

Category containing the Auto Page Insertion option

Click list arrow to select an insertion option

FIGURE D-2

Selected page on the Document Layout palette

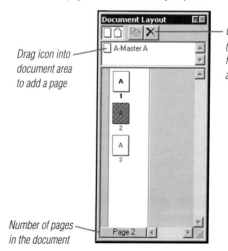

Drag icon into document area to add a page

Click Delete button (appears as a trash can for Mac users) to remove a selected page

Number of pages in the document

Add document pages

1. Start Quark, open QP D-1.qxd, then save the file as **Headliners**.

2. Fit the document in the window, if necessary.

3. Click Page on the menu bar, then click Insert.

4. Type **4** in the Insert text box, as shown in Figure D-3.

5. Click OK, then compare your Document Layout palette to Figure D-4.

6. Click the Linking tool on the Tools palette.

7. Click the center column of text on page 1.

8. Double-click the page 4 icon on the Document Layout palette, then click anywhere in column 1. See Figure D-5.

9. Click the A-Master A icon in the Master Page area of the Document Layout palette, then drag it down so it is in between the page 3 and page 4 icons in the document page area, as shown in Figure D-6. ☐ A-Master A

10. Double-click the page 5 icon on the Document Layout palette.

11. Click the A-Master A icon on the Document Layout palette, then drag it down so it is between the page 4 and page 5 icons, to add another page to the document. ☐ A-Master A

You added pages to an existing document using the Page menu and the Document Layout palette, and linked a story with overflow text.

FIGURE D-3

Insert Pages dialog box

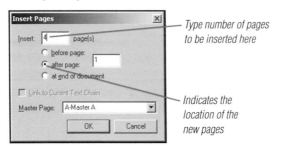

Type number of pages to be inserted here

Indicates the location of the new pages

FIGURE D-4

New pages on Document Layout palette

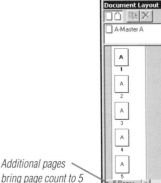

Additional pages bring page count to 5

FIGURE D-5

Overflow text on page 4

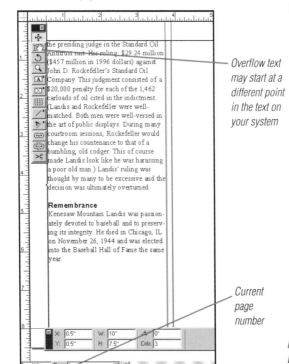

Overflow text may start at a different point in the text on your system

Current page number

FIGURE D-6

New page on Document Layout palette

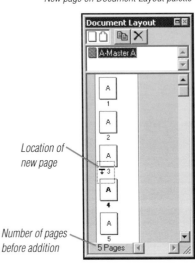

Location of new page

Number of pages before addition

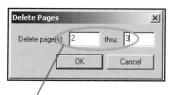

*Range of pages that
will be deleted*

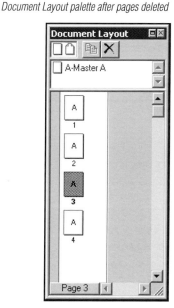

Delete document pages

1. Click Page on the menu bar, then click Delete.

2. Type **2** in the Delete page(s) text box in the Delete Pages dialog box.

3. Type **3** in the thru text box, as shown in Figure D-7.

4. Click OK.

   There are now five pages in the document, and the current page (5) is empty.

5. Click the page 2 icon on the Document Layout palette.

6. Click the Delete tool on the Document Layout palette. ✖

7. Click OK to verify that you want to delete this page.

8. Double-click the page 3 icon on the Document Layout palette to move to page 3.

9. Click File on the menu bar, click Save, then compare your Document Layout palette to Figure D-8.

   TIP The icon (on the Document Layout palette) for the active page is highlighted.

You deleted pages using the Page menu and the Delete tool on the Document Layout palette.

Imagining you're the reader

At some point, you have probably read a story and found the layout busy, ugly, or in some other way needing improvement. As you work with Quark, learn to develop a critical eye for potential problems in your own work. You can do this by imagining that you are reading your own document for the first time, and evaluating the look and readability of the page. Many experts recommend that you never use more than three different fonts on a page, and suggest that two are often enough. So, how do you make your publications eye-catching enough to attract a reader's attention without looking busy or cluttered? Instead of using more fonts, make full use of a limited palette. Use bold and italic versions of your fonts for prominence, and reverse text for a stylized headline. Avoid the use of underlining and full capitalization in body text. These stylistic techniques were useful when story text was prepared using typewriters and there were no alternatives, such as bold and italic, but with desktop publishing software, you have the ability to attract readers with a wider, more sophisticated variety of tools.

ADD NUMBERS TO IDENTIFY PAGES

What You'll Do

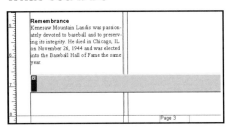

In this lesson, you'll add numbers to the document pages.

Numbering Pages

When you flip through your own document, you know which page is which because you arranged it. But what about the person who has never seen it before? In a lengthy document, how will your reader find story text that continues on other pages? You should always be thinking of ways to make your document more readable, and adding numbers to the pages is a great start.

> **QUICK**TIP
>
> The numbering of pages is often referred to as **pagination**.

Automatically Adding Page Numbers

You can manually add page numbers to each page—a real chore—or take advantage of Quark's automatic page numbering feature. This feature lets you add a page numbering code anywhere within a page. This code tells Quark to determine the correct page number and insert it in the location you specify. Automatic page numbers can be added directly on a page, or as shown in Figure D-9. When automatic page numbers are inserted on a document page, they display the correct page number, and are automatically updated when the pages are rearranged. The automatic page numbering feature *only provides the number*; you must type any additional text (such as "Page"), modify the font or font size, and apply any attributes. The reason for using the automatic page numbering feature will become clear the first time you must rearrange your pages. Without using the automatic page numbering feature, you'd have to manually renumber each page. With this feature, you can set it and forget it!

Adding Page Numbers to the Master Page

The automatic page numbering feature can be used in the background area of a page called the master page. The master page is the ideal place for information that repeats from page to page. You might, for example, want to insert page numbers on the master page instead of on each individual page to ensure that the page number appears in the same location on each page, and to save you the trouble of inserting the page number code on each individual page. If the page number is added to the master page, the page numbering information looks the same when the actual page appears. But when the master page appears (by double-clicking the A-Master A icon on the Document Layout palette), the code looks like a pound sign surrounded by brackets. See Figure D-10. Before you can add an element to the master page, you must double-click the master page icon to open it and make it active. The master page displays only the elements that will repeat on every page, so you may need to switch back and forth between the master and individual pages when deciding exactly where to place individual elements.

Understanding Sections

When you use the automatic page numbering feature in Quark, guess the number of the first page. You'll say one, of course, but that is not always what you'll want. You might have a very large project in which you want to combine many Quark documents, or you might need to make room for several pages that will be supplied from an outside source. In any event, you must be able to choose a new starting page number should the need arise. To do this, you must create sections within a document. The Section command is located on the Page menu, and lets you divide a document into areas that have different page numbers. Figure D-11 shows the Section dialog box. Here, a new section is created in which the first page of the section is page 5. Figure D-12 shows the Document Layout palette after the section is created. Do you see the asterisk after the page 5 icon? This asterisk indicates the start of a new section.

FIGURE D-9
Automatic page numbering

FIGURE D-10
Automatic page number code on master page

FIGURE D-11
Section dialog box

FIGURE D-12
Document Layout palette with new section

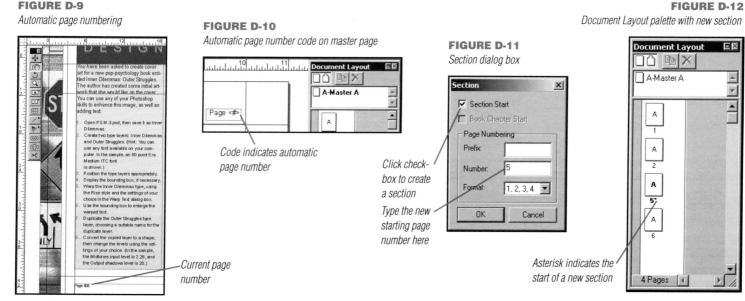

Code indicates automatic page number

Current page number

Click checkbox to create a section

Type the new starting page number here

Asterisk indicates the start of a new section

Add page numbers

1. Double-click the A-Master A page icon on the Document Layout palette to activate the master page. ☐ A-Master A

2. Click the Rectangle Text Box tool on the Tools palette. 🄰⁺

3. Use the vertical scroll bar to adjust the page so that the bottom of column 2 is visible.

4. If necessary, move the Measurements palette out of the way.

5. Drag the pointer from 5" H/8" V to 6" H/8 ¼" V. ┼

   On completion of drawing the text box, the Content tool is the active tool.

   > TIP   Remember to make your text box large enough to display page numbers that may take up more room—e.g., those that may be two or three digits.

6. Type **Page**, then press the spacebar. (*Hint*: In the sample, a 12 pt Arial font is used. If this font is not available, make a substitution using an appropriate font.)

   > TIP   What if you don't want a page number to appear on a particular page? Go to the page containing the page number that you don't want, select the page number text box, then press [Delete].

7. Press [Ctrl][3] (Win) or [command] [3] (Mac). Compare your text box to Figure D-13.

You created a text box on the master page and added page numbering.

Thinking about page count

One of the least glamorous tasks in document layout involves page count. The number of pages in any project is connected to page numbering, so page count has far-reaching effects. You might, for example, get a price break from your printer if your document meets or exceeds a certain length. And since nearly every project has a budget, every cost plays a major role in project completion. If the project is designed for resale, all production costs will influence the ultimate retail price, and that means the sales price must be structured to make a profit. The concept of page count is sometimes referred to as the **signature**. For example, any unit in this book can have any number of pages, but the first page of text must fall on an odd-numbered page, and the last page of text must also be odd-numbered so that the following even-numbered page can start the new unit with a piece of artwork. Each unit in this book, therefore, has an *even signature*. Some projects may demand signatures in multiples of eight. This is due to the way in which paper is purchased, printed, and then trimmed to form a series of pages.

1. Double-click the page 3 icon on the Document Layout palette to display page 3.

> TIP You can also go to a specific page by clicking the Page list arrow (on the status bar at the bottom of the document window), then clicking the icon for the page number you want.

2. Click File on the menu bar, then click Save. Compare your screen to Figure D-14.

You displayed automatic page numbering.

FIGURE D-14

Page number appears

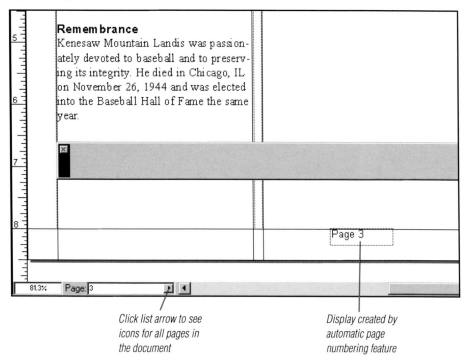

Remembrance
Kenesaw Mountain Landis was passion-
ately devoted to baseball and to preserving its integrity. He died in Chicago, IL
on November 26, 1944 and was elected
into the Baseball Hall of Fame the same
year.

Page 3

81.3%   Page: 3

Click list arrow to see icons for all pages in the document

Display created by automatic page numbering feature

CHANGE VERTICAL ALIGNMENT

What You'll Do

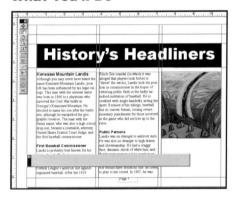

 In this lesson, you'll vertically align text and reverse the font and background colors.

Tweaking the Vertical Alignment of Text

As you work with text, you may find that the vertical alignment—the way in which the text is oriented between the top and bottom of the text box—needs adjustment. For example, Figure D-15 shows text with the default vertical alignment (Top). Do you see that the top of the text is at the top of the text box? Figure D-16 shows the same text with the vertical alignment modified so that the text is centered from top to bottom. You can alter the vertical alignment by selecting the text you want to modify, then using the Modify command on the Item menu. (This, by the way, is the same command you used to change the color and width of the text box frame.)

Understanding Vertical Text Alignment

Text can be vertically aligned in four ways. It can be aligned **left** so that each new line begins on the left margin, aligned **right** so that each line ends on the right margin, **centered** so each line is equally spaced between the margins, and **justified** so lines of text begin and end at the margins.

Justified and left aligned are the most common settings for ordinary text. In most publications, text is left aligned because it's easiest to read: the ragged right edge adds an element of white space, making it easy for the reader to scan down the page, and natural character spacing is maintained because you are not condensing or expanding each line of text to fit an exact width. Some people are attracted to the "neatness" of text that lines up perfectly at both the left and right margins. While justified text may lend an air of formality to a publication, it requires extra attention to hyphenation, and careful proofing to avoid awkward looking gaps of white space. It does offer the advantage of letting you pack more text in the same amount of space as left justified.

FIGURE D-15
Default vertical alignment

Text is aligned with top of text box

FIGURE D-16
Centered vertical alignment

Text is vertically centered in text box

Modify vertical alignment

1. Double-click the page 1 icon on the Document Layout palette. [A]

2. If necessary, click View on the menu bar, then click 75%.

3. Triple-click the text "History's Headliners".

4. Click Item on the menu bar, then click Modify.

5. Click the Text tab, if necessary, then compare your dialog box to Figure D-17.

6. Click the Vertical Alignment list arrow, click Centered, then click OK.

You vertically aligned text.

FIGURE D-17
Text tab in the Modify dialog box

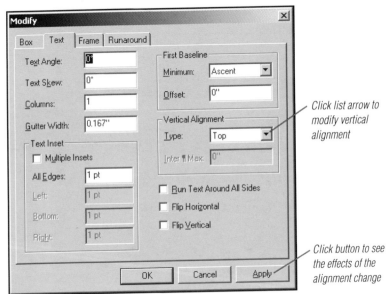

Click list arrow to modify vertical alignment

Click button to see the effects of the alignment change

FIGURE D-18

Reversed text with modified vertical alignment

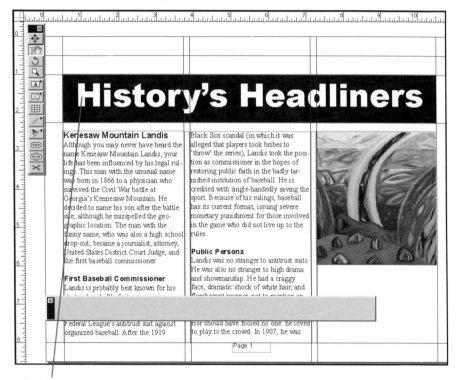

Text is centered
vertically

1. Click the White color box on the Colors palette.

   It looks like the text disappeared, doesn't it? In reality, the text (which is still highlighted) is now white.

   > **TIP** When white text is highlighted, it turns black. When black text is highlighted, it turns white.

2. Click the Background Color tool on the Colors palette.

3. Click the Black color box on the Colors palette.

4. Click anywhere outside the text box.

5. Click File on the menu bar, then click Save. Compare your screen to Figure D-18.

You created reversed text.

REARRANGE PAGES IN A DOCUMENT

What You'll Do

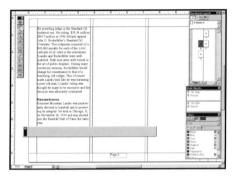

In this lesson, you'll create facing pages and use thumbnails and page icons to rearrange pages.

Rearranging Pages

Remember learning how to drag and drop text? The capability to drag selected text from one area of a document to another applies to moving whole pages. You can rearrange pages using the page icons on the Document Layout palette, or by working in Thumbnails view. In the **Thumbnails view**, each page is represented by a miniature image that includes enough detail to make each page recognizable. You can click each thumbnail and drag it to a new position in the document. To see the current document in Thumbnails view, click View on the menu bar, then click Thumbnails. The most obvious method of rearranging pages is to click and drag each page icon on the Document Layout palette. The advantage of the Thumbnails view is that you can see a representation of each page while you are moving the pages, and this gives you an overview of what should go where. Figure D-19 shows a complex document in Thumbnails view.

QUICKTIP

You can return your document from Thumbnails view to regular view by clicking View on the menu bar, then clicking Fit to Window, or whatever scale you choose.

Understanding Facing Pages

Pages in a document can fall into two categories: single pages or facing pages. **Single pages** are individual sheets that have top, bottom, left, and right margins. **Facing pages**, however, are generally bound in a book or magazine format. Figure D-20 contains a Document Layout palette with single pages, while Figure D-21 contains a Document Layout palette with facing pages. Do you see that the single and facing page icons look different? Each facing page icon has a folded corner on its outer edge. Facing pages have top, bottom, inside, and outside margins, and each right page *faces* a left page.

So why would you want to have facing pages? Well, take a look at this book. When you flip through the pages, the inside and outside margins appear to be equal. This is an illusion. If these margins were identical, it would be difficult to read the text on the inside of the left and right pages (those that are closest to the binding). Facing pages make it possible to allow for a larger inside margin, and automatically adjust the margins if the page is on the left or right. You can determine whether the pages in a document are single pages or facing pages using the Document Setup dialog box.

QUICK**TIP**

Facing pages may be referred to as **mirrored** pages, or can be said to have **mirrored margins**.

FIGURE D-19
Document in Thumbnails view

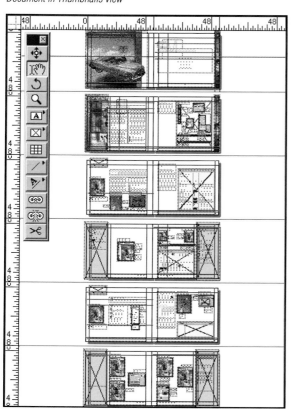

FIGURE D-21
Facing page icons

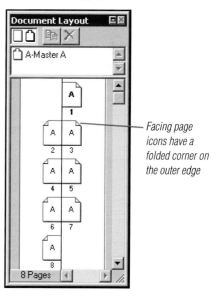

Facing page icons have a folded corner on the outer edge

FIGURE D-20
Single page icons

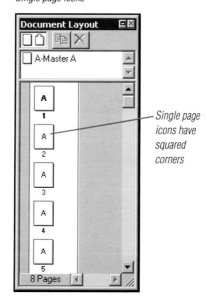

Single page icons have squared corners

Create facing pages and rearrange pages

1. Click File on the menu bar, then click Document Setup.

2. Click the Facing Pages checkbox, as shown in Figure D-22.

   TIP Icons in a single page document *do not* display the folded corners when it is converted into a facing page.

3. Click OK. Compare your Document Layout palette to Figure D-23.

   TIP When converting single pages to facing pages, Quark assumes that all pages *except* the first are on the left.

4. Click the page 4 icon, then drag it to the right of the page 2 icon until you see a right-pointing arrow. Page 4 is now page 3.

5. Compare your Document Layout palette to Figure D-24.

You changed the pages so they are facing pages, then you moved a page by dragging page icons on the Document Layout palette.

FIGURE D-23
Modified document layout

FIGURE D-24
Rearranged page icons

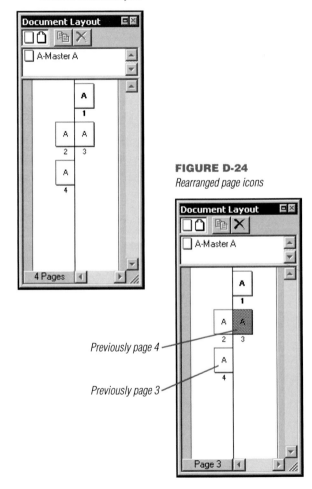

Previously page 4

Previously page 3

FIGURE D-25
Thumbnails view

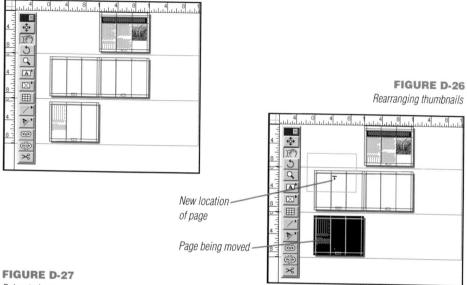

FIGURE D-26
Rearranging thumbnails

New location
of page

Page being moved

FIGURE D-27
Relocated page

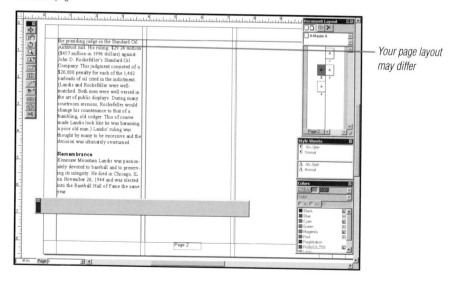

Your page layout
may differ

Work in Thumbnails view

1. Click View on the menu bar, then click Thumbnails.

2. If necessary, use the horizontal scroll bars to reposition the thumbnails for better visibility. Compare your screen to Figure D-25.

3. Click the page 4 thumbnail.

4. Drag the thumbnail over the page 2 thumbnail until you see the pointer change to the down-pointing arrow, shown in Figure D-26, then release the mouse button. ⊤

    | TIP   A right page is called a recto page, and a left page is called a verso page.

5. Click View on the menu bar, then click Fit in Window.

6. Double-click the page 2 icon on the Document Layout palette.

7. Click File on the menu bar, click Save, then compare your document to Figure D-27.

You used the Thumbnails view to rearrange pages.

ADD CONTINUATION NOTICES

What You'll Do

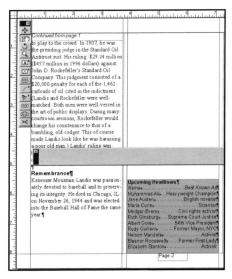

In this lesson, you'll enhance a text box frame and add color to the background.

Giving the Reader Directions

So, you've learned how to place numbers on each page, but how do you let the readers know which page they should turn to in a long story? By using continuation notices. A **continuation notice** is a text box that automatically locates linked text that precedes or follows the text in the active text box.

Creating Continuation Notices

The whole point of continuation notices is that it should be easy for the reader to find the rest of a story. Traditionally, a continued on notice appears at the end of a linked text box, and a continued from notice appears at the beginning of a linked text box. Creating a continued on notice has three basic steps:

- Creating a text box that will contain the notice
- Typing the contents of the continuation notice
- Adding a code that tells Quark to identify the page containing the additional text

A sample continued on notice is shown in Figure D-28. Creating a continued from notice is the same, except that a different code is used—because, of course, you want to tell the readers which page they are continuing *from*. It is important that the text box containing the continuation notice overlaps the text box containing the story text. (The overlap tells Quark that the continued on/from notice works with the linked text box.) The Runaround command is used to define how the overlapping text is treated. A **runaround** controls how text wraps around an object.

QUICKTIP

It does not matter which continuation notice (on or from) is created first: you can create them in either order.

Changing the Style of Continuation Notices

You can modify the appearance of a continued on or continued from notice using any tricks in your text formatting arsenal. For example, you might want to use a font that is different from the actual text in the story to make the notice stand out. Sometimes, you can make the notice text stand out by just applying the italic attribute. Remember, you want the notice to be, well, noticed—but you don't want it to be the center of attention.

Spreading Stories Over Multiple Pages

Why do newspapers and magazines do this? Don't they know how irritating this is? Well, yes they do, but there are compelling reasons to scatter story text hither and thither. Magazines and newspapers want you to read *all* the content they produce—not just the stories in which you have an immediate interest. If you opened a newspaper and read a story on page 1 from start to finish, you might not look any further. And since most commercial publications depend on the revenue from advertisers, making sure you flip through every page is vital. After all, you might miss an ad for a product that could change your life!

FIGURE D-28
Continued on notice

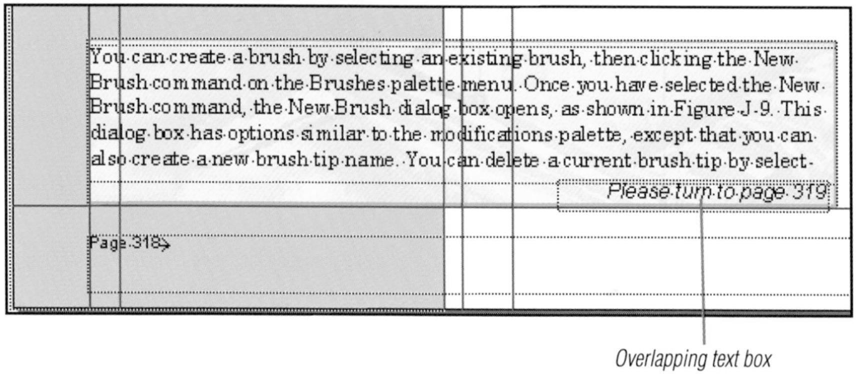

Overlapping text box

Learning to love tabs

It's absolutely amazing how many people hate working with tabs. Grown men can be reduced to tears at the very thought of creating tabbed text. Tabs are not really that difficult once you can distinguish some of the elements within the document. First, tabs are different from margins. Margins surround a page, a text box, or a column, and provide a buffer between an edge and text. Margins are also used to determine where words wrap to the next line. Tabs, however, are adjustable *stops* within a text box. Where you can have only two margins per text box, you can have an unlimited number of tabs. In Quark, tabs are created using the Paragraph Attributes dialog box. The easiest way to create tabbed text is to create the tabs *before* you enter the text, as the attributes from a single line (such as the tab stops) are carried forward to the next line, and the next. This is not always practical, however. In the case of existing text where you want to apply or modify tab settings, you can select the text, open the Paragraph Attributes dialog box, and then modify the settings for a particular tab.

Add a continued from notice

1. Click the Rectangle Text Box tool on the Tools palette.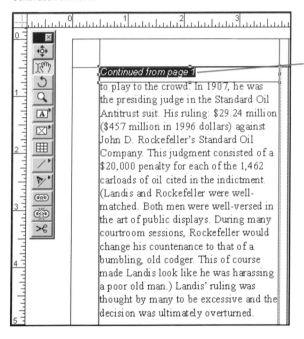

2. Drag the pointer from ½" H/½" V to 3 ¾" H/ ¾" V using the column's margin guide.

3. Use the Content tool pointer to type **Continued from page** in the text box. (In the sample, the default font and size (12 pt Arial) is used.

   > TIP The Content tool was automatically selected when you completed drawing the text box.

4. Press [Spacebar], then press [Ctrl][2] (Win) or [command][2] (Mac).

5. Press [Ctrl][A] (Win) or [command][A] (Mac), then click the Italic tool on the Measurements palette. Compare your text box to Figure D-29. *I*

You created a continued from notice for a linked story.

FIGURE D-29
Continued from notice

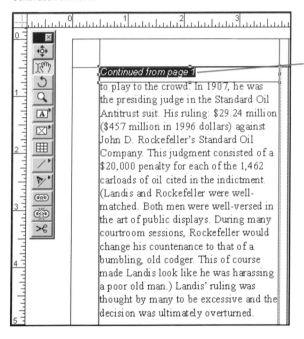

Continuation notice text box overlaps the story text box

FIGURE D-30

Continued on notice

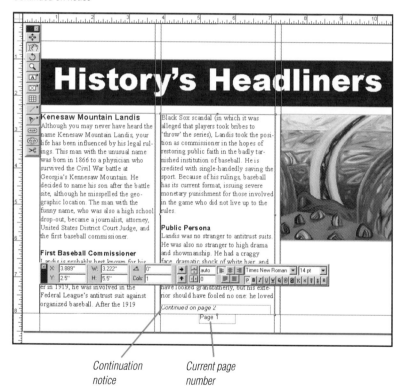

Continuation notice

Current page number

Continued on page 2

Page 1

Add continued on notice

1. Double-click the page 1 icon on the Document Layout palette. A

2. Click the Rectangle Text Box tool on the Tools palette. 🄰

3. Drag the pointer from 3 ⅞" H / 7 ¾" V to 7" H/ 8" V using the column's margin guide. ─┼─

4. Use the Content tool pointer to type **Continued on page** in the text box. In the sample, the default font and size (12 pt Arial is used. I

5. Press [Spacebar], then press [Ctrl][4] (Win) or [command][4] (Mac).

6. Press [Ctr][A] (Win) or [command] [A] (Mac), then click the Italic tool on the Measurements palette. Compare your text box to Figure D-30. 𝐼

7. Click anywhere outside the continuation notice.

You created a continued on notice for a linked story.

Set up tabs

1. Double-click the page 2 icon on the Document Layout palette.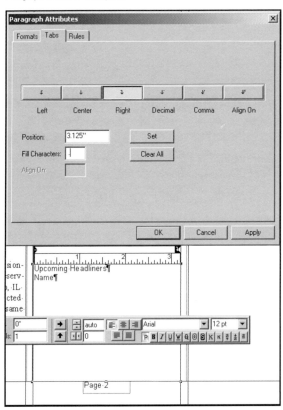

2. Click the Rectangle Text Box tool on the Tools palette. ⌷

3. Drag the pointer from 3 ⅞" H /5 ½" V to 7 ⅛" H/8" V using the Snap to effect on the column guides. ╅

4. Type **Upcoming Headliners**, then press [Enter] (Win) or [return] (Mac).

5. Click View on the menu bar, then click Show Invisibles, if necessary.

6. Type **Name**.

7. Click Style on the menu bar, then click Tabs. The Paragraph Attributes dialog box opens displaying the Tabs tab.

   TIP If the Paragraph Attributes dialog box obscures your view of the text box ruler bar, drag the dialog box out of the way.

8. Click the Right tab button in the dialog box. ⌷

9. Click the 3⅛" mark on the text box ruler.

10. Type . in the Fill Characters text box. Compare your screen to Figure D-31.

11. Click OK.

You created a text box for tabbed text, then you created a right-aligned tab using the Paragraph Attributes dialog box.

FIGURE D-31
Paragraph Attributes dialog box

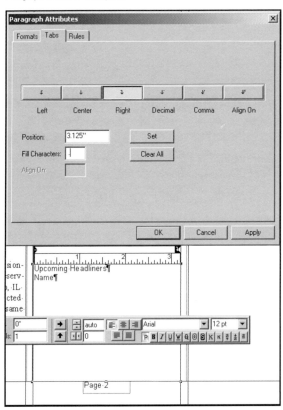

FIGURE D-32

Right-aligned tab with dot leader

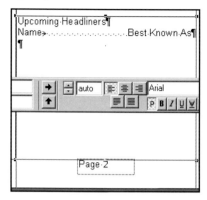

FIGURE D-33

Completed tabbed text

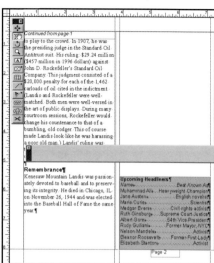

Create tabbed text

1. Press [Tab].

2. Type **Best Known As**. ⌶

3. Press [Enter] (Win) or [return] (Mac). Compare your screen to Figure D-32.

4. Type the information in Table D-1. After entering each name, press [Tab]. After entering the text in the "Best Known As" column, press [Enter] (except for the last entry).

5. Triple-click the "Upcoming Headliners" text.

6. Click the Bold tool on the Measurements palette. **B**

7. Click the Background tool on the Colors palette. ▨

8. Click the Magenta color box on the Colors palette.

9. Click the Fade list arrow on the Colors palette, then click 60%.

10. Triple-click the second line in the text box, then click the Italic tool on the Measurements palette. *I*

11. Click anywhere outside the text box to deselect the text.

12. Click File on the menu bar, click Save, then compare your screen to Figure D-33.

You typed tabbed text, then you applied attributes to the text and the text box.

TABLE D-1: Data for Tabbed Text

name	best known as
Muhammad Ali	Heavyweight champion
Jane Austen	English novelist
Marie Curie	Scientist
Medgar Evers	Civil Rights activist
Ruth Ginsburg	Supreme Court Justice
Albert Gore	54th Vice President
Rudy Guiliani	Former Mayor, NYC
Nelson Mandela	Activist
Eleanor Roosevelt	Former First Lady
Elizabeth Stanton	Activist

Power User Shortcuts

to do this:	use this method:
Add automatic page numbers	[Ctrl][3] (Win) ⌘ [3] (Mac)
Add continued from notice	Create overlapping text box, type text, then [Ctrl][2] (Win) ⌘ [2] (Mac)
Add continued on notice	Create overlapping text box, type text, then [Ctrl][4] (Win) ⌘ [4] (Mac)
Add multiple pages	Page ➤ Insert
Add single page	☐ A-Master A
Align On tab	⬚
Center tab	⬚
Comma tab	⬚
Create document sections	Page ➤ Section

to do this:	use this method:
Create facing pages	File ➤ Document Setup
Decimal tab	⬚
Delete multiple pages	Page ➤ Delete
Delete single page	Click page icon, ✗
Go to specific page	Double-click page icon
Left-aligned tab	⬚
Modify automatic page insertion	Edit ➤ Preferences ➤ Preferences, General option
Modify vertical alignment	Item ➤ Modify, Text tab, Vertical Alignment list arrow
Rearrange pages	Drag thumbnails or page icons to new location
Right-aligned tab	⬚
View page thumbnails	View ➤ Thumbnails, or [Shift][F6]

Key: Menu items are indicated by ➤ between the menu name and its command.

Add and delete pages in a document.

1. Start Quark.
2. Open QP D-2.qxd, then save it as **Super Bowl Facts**.
3. Use the Page menu to insert five pages.
4. Use the Linking tool to link the story text on page 1.
5. Link the story on page 1 with the automatic text box on page 4. (*Hint*: The automatic text box begins in the upper-left corner of the page.)
6. Link any remaining overflow text to page 6. (*Hint*: When you click page 6, the story will be placed in the top left column.)
7. Use the Document Layout palette to add a new facing page after page 6.
8. Use the Page menu to delete pages 4 and 5.
9. Use the Document Layout palette to delete page 5.
10. Save your work.

Add numbers to identify pages.

1. Use the Document Layout palette and the A-Master A tool to display the background page.
2. Create a text box in the center column at the bottom of each page (this document has facing pages). (*Hint*: On each facing page, you can create the text box from 3¾" H/10¼" V to 4¾" H/10½" V.)
3. Each text box should contain the word "Page" and the page number, using the default font and font size. (*Hint*: Because this document has facing pages, you must enter the text and the code in each text box.)
4. Make sure the content of each text box is center aligned (horizontally).
5. Display page 1 of the document.
6. Save your work.

Change vertical alignment to enhance text.

1. Center the "Football Plus" text horizontally and vertically. (*Hint*: The title font in the sample is 75 pt Trebuchet MS. Make a substitution, if necessary.)
2. Create a reverse text effect on the "Football Plus" text using white text and a blue background.
3. Save your work.

Rearrange pages in a document.

1. Show the pages in Thumbnails view.
2. Drag the page 4 icon so it becomes page 2.
3. Change the view so the document fits in the window.
4. Move page 2 so it becomes page 3.
5. Display page 3.
6. Save your work.

Add continuation notices to locate story text.

1. Use the Content tool to position the insertion point at the end of the story on page 3.
2. Create a new line by pressing [Enter] (Win) or [return] (Mac).
3. Type **Super Bowl Facts**, making sure the text is bold, then advance to the next line.
4. Create a right-aligned tab at 2¼".
5. Use the information in Table D-2 to create the tabbed text. (*Hint*: You can use 'cons.' as an abbreviation for 'consecutive'.)
6. Create a continued from notice at the top of the text box on page 3 using the text "Story continued from page".
7. Create a continued on notice at the bottom of the text box on page 1 using the text "Story continued on page".
8. Both continuation notices should be right aligned and in italic.
9. Save your work, then compare the first page of your document to Figure D-34.

TABLE D-2: Super Bowl Facts

Description	Games
Most games played	Dallas – 8
Most cons. games	Buffalo – 2
Most wins	San Francisco – 5
Most cons. wins	Green Bay – 2
Most losses	Minnesota – 4
Most cons. losses	Buffalo – 4

FIGURE D-34
Completed Skills Review

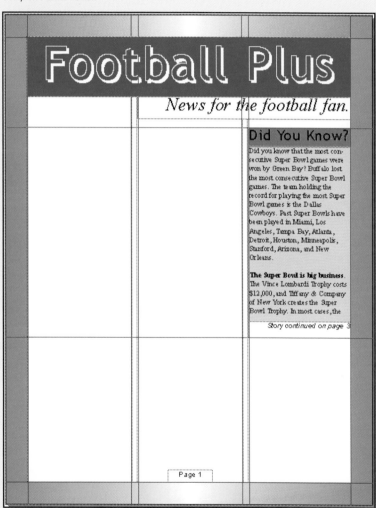

A recent trip to England got you so jazzed that you decided to create a short newsletter letting everyone know about your adventure. You started by writing the first story. This story will be continued on another page.

1. Open QP D-3.qxd, then save it as **Trip to London**.
2. Create a text box using the existing ruler guides at the top of the page (from ½" H/ ⅝" V to 8" H/ 1½" V).
3. Create a title for the newsletter, such as "Fabulous Trip to London". (*Hint*: Use any appropriate font on your computer. In the sample, a 48 pt Colonna MT font is shown.)
4. Center align the text horizontally and vertically.
5. Create a reverse text effect for the newsletter title using the colors of your choice.
6. Link the text box in column 2 to column 3 on the same page.
7. Add a page to the document.
8. Draw a text box somewhere on page 2.
9. Link the text in column 2 on page 1 to the newly created text box on page 2.
10. Add a continued on notice to column 3 on page 1 and a continued from notice to the linked text on page 2. Change the appearance of the continuation notices as you see fit.

11. Change the alignment and background color of the Guards Mounting text box.
12. Save your work, then compare your image to the first page of the sample in Figure D-35.

FIGURE D-35
Completed Project Builder 1

You have always been fascinated by the origins of people's first names. The study of the origins of words is called *etymology*. Some names, for example, have their origins in cultural rites; others are names of past friends or relatives. You have several friends with the same interest, so you decide to start a newsletter about this subject.

1. Open QP D-4.qxd, then save it as **Name Game**.
2. Add two pages to the document.
3. Link the text box on page 1 with a text box on page 3.
4. Add page numbers somewhere within the document.
5. Create continuation notices for the story text on pages 1 and 3 using the font or formatting attributes of your choice.
6. Delete page 2.
7. Modify the text for the title of the newsletter using any font available on your computer. You can apply any attributes you choose. (In the sample, a 60 pt Gill Sans MT font is used. The text beneath the newsletter title is shown in 36 pt Brush Script MT.)
8. Create a reverse text effect for the newsletter title using the colors of your choice.
9. Modify the text for the title of the text box on page 1 using any font available on your computer. You can apply any attributes you choose. (In the sample, a 30 pt Gill Sans MT font is used.)
10. Create a text box in column 2 on page 1.
11. Create tabbed text by taking named text from the linked story. (*Hint*: You can create two columns, one for Name, and the other for Origin. Then, list some examples that are included in the story.)
12. Add appropriate formatting to any of the text boxes.
13. Save your work, then compare your image to the first page of the sample in Figure D-36.

FIGURE D-36
Completed Project Builder 2

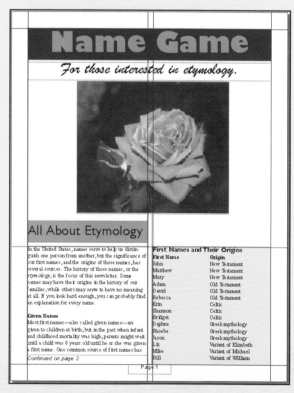

Has this unit encouraged you to think about arcane design matters such as continuation notices? If so, you're not alone. Designers of magazines, newspapers, and other lengthy documents use many methods to convey continuation information. As you come across these publications, notice how the presence and design of these elements (or lack thereof) affects your ease of reading and interest in the stories. Figure D-37 shows a sample newsletter containing several continuation notices.

1. Locate at least three samples of continuation notices. You may look in newspapers, magazines, and other periodicals.
2. If it is permitted, obtain the pages—or make copies—so you can bring your examples to class.
3. Examine these continuation notices, then ask yourself the following questions. Be prepared to discuss your answers to these questions:
   - Does it matter to you if a continued story has no continuation notice?
   - Over how many pages do you think an article should flow before a continued on notice is necessary?
   - Do you think continued from notices are necessary? Not every periodical uses them. (Does your opinion regarding the need for continuation notices vary depending on the type of publication you are reading? Do you have different expectations from different types of publications?)
   - How does it affect readability if page numbers are not easily found?
   - Just how much should a continuation notice say? If a partial caption is used, should it give a clue as to the subject matter?
4. Which of the samples do you consider most effective, and why?

FIGURE D-37
Design Project sample

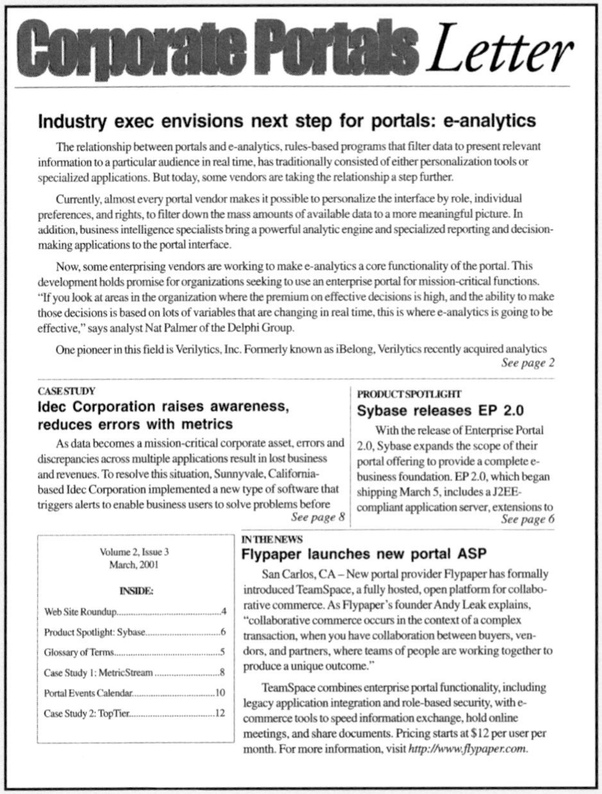

Corporate Portals *Letter*

Industry exec envisions next step for portals: e-analytics

The relationship between portals and e-analytics, rules-based programs that filter data to present relevant information to a particular audience in real time, has traditionally consisted of either personalization tools or specialized applications. But today, some vendors are taking the relationship a step further.

Currently, almost every portal vendor makes it possible to personalize the interface by role, individual preferences, and rights, to filter down the mass amounts of available data to a more meaningful picture. In addition, business intelligence specialists bring a powerful analytic engine and specialized reporting and decision-making applications to the portal interface.

Now, some enterprising vendors are working to make e-analytics a core functionality of the portal. This development holds promise for organizations seeking to use an enterprise portal for mission-critical functions. "If you look at areas in the organization where the premium on effective decisions is high, and the ability to make those decisions is based on lots of variables that are changing in real time, this is where e-analytics is going to be effective," says analyst Nat Palmer of the Delphi Group.

One pioneer in this field is Verilytics, Inc. Formerly known as iBelong, Verilytics recently acquired analytics

See page 2

CASE STUDY
Idec Corporation raises awareness, reduces errors with metrics

As data becomes a mission-critical corporate asset, errors and discrepancies across multiple applications result in lost business and revenues. To resolve this situation, Sunnyvale, California-based Idec Corporation implemented a new type of software that triggers alerts to enable business users to solve problems before

See page 8

Volume 2, Issue 3
March, 2001

INSIDE:

PRODUCT SPOTLIGHT
Sybase releases EP 2.0

With the release of Enterprise Portal 2.0, Sybase expands the scope of their portal offering to provide a complete e-business foundation. EP 2.0, which began shipping March 5, includes a J2EE-compliant application server, extensions to

See page 6

IN THE NEWS
Flypaper launches new portal ASP

San Carlos, CA – New portal provider Flypaper has formally introduced TeamSpace, a fully hosted, open platform for collaborative commerce. As Flypaper's founder Andy Leak explains, "collaborative commerce occurs in the context of a complex transaction, when you have collaboration between buyers, vendors, and partners, where teams of people are working together to produce a unique outcome."

TeamSpace combines enterprise portal functionality, including legacy application integration and role-based security, with e-commerce tools to speed information exchange, hold online meetings, and share documents. Pricing starts at $12 per user per month. For more information, visit *http://www.flypaper.com*.

Depending on the size of your group, you can assign elements of the project to individual members, or work collectively to create the finished product.

Any newsletter has many interconnected parts. You and your coworkers at a software training firm are asked to pool your talents and create a quarterly newsletter that features new software product reviews.

1. One or more group members can be charged with planning the document. This role includes, but is not limited to, planning the size and dimensions of the newsletter, deciding what fonts will be used, determining how many pages will be needed, and whether or not facing pages are needed.

2. Open a new document, then save it as **Software Review**.

3. One or more group members can decide where stories should appear in the layout. You want to include a story that appears on more than one page.

4. One or more group members can write a story for the document. If possible, the story should include how Quark compares to other desktop publishing programs. (*Hint*: You can write the document with a word processor, then get the text, or you can write the story directly in a text box.)

5. One or more group members can create the text boxes and, if necessary, get the text.

6. One or more group members can be in charge of applying any attributes that were deemed necessary in the planning stage.

7. One or more group members can create the continuation notices.

8. One or more group members can create the page numbers.

9. Save your work, then compare your document to the sample shown in Figure D-38. (The fonts used in the sample are 65 pt Informal Roman in the newsletter title, 12 pt Times New Roman for story text, and 14 pt Arial (with bold attribute) in the story title.)

FIGURE D-38
Completed Group Project

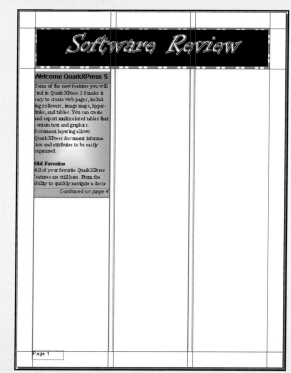

MAINTAINING CONSISTENCY
IN A DOCUMENT

1. Use a style sheet to work efficiently.

2. Use master pages to maintain consistency.

3. Create headers and footers.

4. Lock elements and indent text.

UNIT E

MAINTAINING CONSISTENCY IN A DOCUMENT

Introduction

Have you ever noticed that nearly every professional publication has consistent elements? In a typical magazine or book, you will find that story text on page 1 uses the same font and font size as story text found on page 100. Likewise, you will see consistent design elements throughout a publication. Using this book as an example, notice that every lesson title uses two distinctive fonts, and every page that contains steps features a gold band on its outer edge as a background for the steps, with a smaller, textured rectangle serving as a background for the steps heading. This is no happy accident. Most major publications undergo a rigorous design process, long before page layout ever begins, to create a look that is unified and professional.

Making it Easy for Everyone

The great thing about all these preconceived design choices is that if they're executed well, everyone benefits. In a textbook, for example, consistent design features make it easier for the:

- Author during the writing process
- Production Department during the layout process
- Reader during the learning process
- Instructor during the teaching process

Common design features provide structure and give any publication its *style*. Without them, you might have one chapter opener with a blue background and three columns per page, and another with a red background and two columns per page—especially if two different people are working on the layout, or if one person lays out a chapter one week, and the next chapter a week later. Each layout choice might be well intentioned, but the overall effect would be ugly and distracting because it would not convey a sense of order and relatedness throughout the whole publication. A unified style makes a publication easier to read, reference, and recognize amid a sea of competitors. Fortunately, Quark has tools that make consistency a snap.

Tools You'll Use

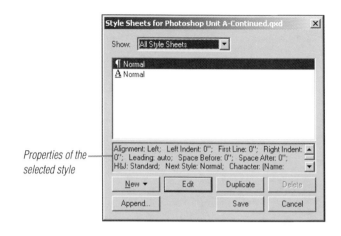

Properties of the selected style

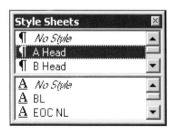

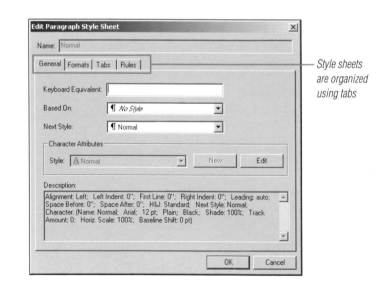

Style sheets are organized using tabs

USE A STYLE SHEET TO WORK EFFICIENTLY

What You'll Do

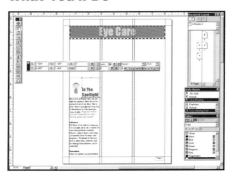

In this lesson, you'll learn how to create, modify, and apply a style sheet.

Understanding Style Sheets

Have you ever seen a list of specifications? A building specification, for example, may indicate the quality of the lumber, its length and width, as well as the type of nails, the specific thickness of the windows, and all other required qualities of the materials used in constructing the building. An architect or builder provides a building specification to maintain a certain level of quality within a building, even if he/she can't be on hand to oversee each step of the construction process.

Like an architect, a designer must identify specifications for documents so that both coworkers and the designer can easily lay out documents based on the designs. You might be surprised at how quickly you can forget the intricate formatting choices you made in last month's newsletter when it comes time to lay out the next issue. If only there were a document that stored the important information so you wouldn't have to reinvent the wheel each month!

In Quark, there is. The standard-bearer of such information is a **style sheet**, a set of formatting specifications—for either a paragraph or individual characters—that can be applied to document text. There are two types of style sheets: those that affect characters and those that affect paragraphs. A **paragraph style sheet** can contain character attributes that are *based on* a specific character style sheet, and can be applied to an entire paragraph. A **character style sheet** can only be applied to specifically selected characters. Table E-1 lists commonly used properties, and whether they affect characters or paragraphs.

QUICKTIP

It is not mandatory that you use style sheets, but it doesn't cost you any extra to use them, so splurge. The results will make you look like a pro.

Learning About the Style Sheets Palette

Each new Quark document contains a paragraph style sheet and a character style sheet, which you can modify, and you can create additional style sheets as you work. The name of the default style sheet for both characters and paragraphs is **Normal**. The Style Sheets palette is divided into two parts. The upper area is where paragraph style sheets are stored, and the lower area is where character style sheets are stored. See Figure E-1. Do you see that the style name in the upper area is preceded by a paragraph symbol, and that the style name in the lower area is preceded by an underlined capital A? These symbols make it easy to tell whether a style sheet affects paragraphs or characters.

Creating a Style Sheet

You can create a style sheet whether or not you have any text selected. That means that if you have an idea of what styles you'll need in a document, you can create them all in one sitting. Of course, you can make modifications to them, if necessary. You create a style sheet using the Style Sheets command on the Edit menu. When you select the Style Sheets command on the Edit menu, the Style Sheets for *(name of your document)* dialog box appears. You can use this dialog box to create, modify, duplicate, and append style sheets within this document.

Using a Style Sheet is Easier than Formatting

Once a style sheet is created, you can apply it in the same way as you apply text attributes to selected characters: just select the text, then click the style sheet you want to apply. That's all there is to it. You can also modify any of the parameters in your style sheets using the same dialog box in which the style sheets were created. Style sheets are stored and saved with a specific document, but you'll be happy to know you can use style sheets created in one document within another document.

QUICKTIP

All style sheets for the current document appear within the Style Sheets palette in the active document, but you may have to scroll through the list or resize the palette to see them.

FIGURE E-1
Style Sheets palette

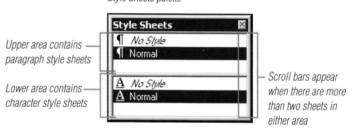

Upper area contains paragraph style sheets

Lower area contains character style sheets

Scroll bars appear when there are more than two sheets in either area

TABLE E-1: Common Character and Paragraph Properties

property	affects	property	affects
Font	character	Alignment	paragraph
Size	character	Indents	paragraph
Color	character	Leading	paragraph
Type Style (attributes)	character	Tabs	paragraph
Tracking	character	Rules	paragraph

Create a style sheet using the Edit menu

1. Start Quark, open QP E-1.qxd, then save the file as **Eye Care**.

2. Fit the document in the window, if necessary.

3. Click Edit on the menu bar, then click Style Sheets.

4. Click New, then click Paragraph.

5. Select the text in the Name text box, if necessary, then type **Story Heading**.

6. Click New under Character Attributes.

7. Type **Story Heading Text** in the Name text box.

8. Specify the settings shown in Figure E-2.

9. Click OK, then compare your dialog box to Figure E-3.

10. Click OK, then compare your dialog box to Figure E-4.

11. Click Save.

You created a paragraph style sheet containing character attributes, using the Style Sheets command on the Edit menu.

Name that will display on the Style Sheets palette

Make these changes to your settings

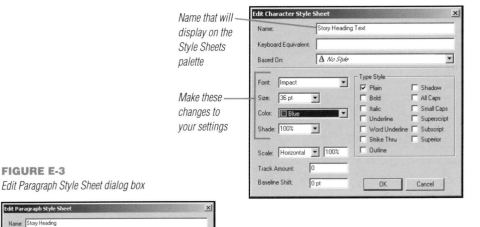

FIGURE E-3

Edit Paragraph Style Sheet dialog box

Specifications for the style

FIGURE E-4

Style Sheets for Eye Care.qxd dialog box

List of style sheets in the document

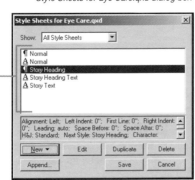

Style Sheets palette menu

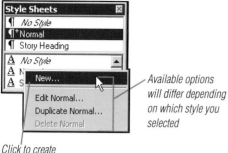

Click to create
a style sheet

Available options
will differ depending
on which style you
selected

Edit Character Style Sheet dialog box

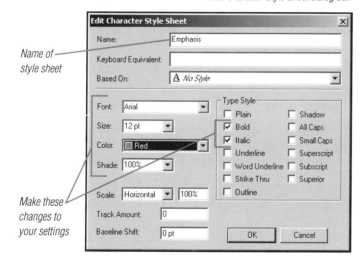

Name of
style sheet

Make these
changes to
your settings

FIGURE E-7
Style Sheets palette

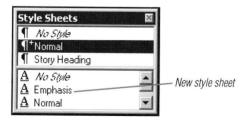

New style sheet

Create a style sheet using the Style Sheets palette

1. Click anywhere in the text box in column 1 below the light bulb.

2. Right-click any character style on the Style Sheets palette (Win), or press [control] while clicking any character style (Mac) on the palette.

   TIP If the Style Sheets palette is not visible, click View on the menu bar, then click Show Style Sheets.

3. Click New, as shown in Figure E-5.

   TIP Create a paragraph style sheet using the Style Sheets palette and any *paragraph* style on the palette. You can create a new paragraph style using a similar technique (by right-clicking (Win) or [ctrl]-clicking (Mac) any paragraph style) to create a new paragraph style.

4. Type **Emphasis** in the Name text box.

5. Specify the settings shown in Figure E-6.

6. Click OK, then compare your Style Sheets palette to Figure E-7.

You created a character style sheet using the Style Sheets palette.

Modify a style sheet

1. Right-click the Story Heading (Win) style on the Style Sheets palette, or press [control] while clicking the Story Heading (Mac) style on the Style Sheets palette, then click Edit Story Heading.

   TIP   You can also edit an existing style sheet by clicking Edit on the menu bar, then clicking Style Sheets. Click the style sheet you want to edit, then click Edit.

2. Click Edit under Character Attributes.

3. Click the Size list arrow, then click 24 pt. Compare your settings to Figure E-8.

4. Click OK to close the Edit Character Style Sheet dialog box.

5. Click OK to close the Edit Paragraph Style Sheet dialog box.

You modified a style sheet using the Style Sheets palette.

FIGURE E-8
Edit Character Style Sheet dialog box

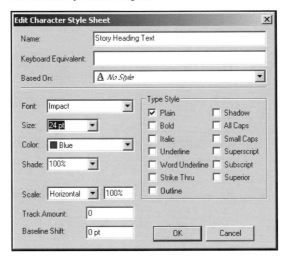

Appending style sheets

It would be a real drag if you had some really cool style sheets already created, but they were in another document. Well, take heart. Quark makes it easy to **append style sheets**, or take them from one document and stick them in another. Suppose you really like that character style sheet you just created, and want to use it elsewhere. The first step is to open the document where you want to apply the existing style sheet (not the document where you created it). Click Edit on the menu bar, then click Style Sheets. Click the Append button at the bottom of the dialog box, locate and click the document containing the style sheet(s) you want to use, then click Open. The style sheets existing in the document you selected appear in the Available list. You can click any available style sheets, then click the right arrow. When you click the right arrow, the style sheet appears in the Include list. Continue selecting style sheets until you have all the ones you want to append, then click OK. Click OK to close the warning box, if necessary, then click Save to close the Style Sheets dialog box.

FIGURE E-9

Story Text style sheet applied to text

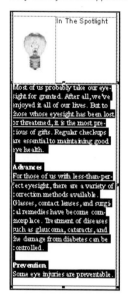

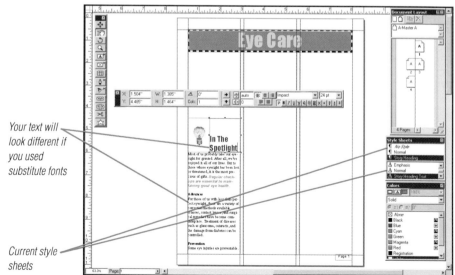

FIGURE E-10

Style sheets applied to document

Your text will
look different if
you used
substitute fonts

Current style
sheets

Apply a style sheet

1. Press [Ctrl][A](Win) or [command][A](Mac).

2. Click the Normal character style sheet on the Style Sheets palette, if necessary.

3. Click the Story Text character style sheet on the Style Sheets palette. The selected text appears in Times New Roman. See Figure E-9.

   TIP   You can move the Measurements palette out of the way if it obscures your view.

4. Use the Content tool pointer to select the following sentence: "Regular checkups are essential to maintaining good eye health."

5. Click the Emphasis character style sheet on the Style Sheets palette.

6. Click anywhere in the In The Spotlight text box.

7. Click the Story Heading paragraph style sheet on the Style Sheets palette.

8. Click Item on the menu bar, then click Modify.

9. Click the Text tab in the Modify dialog box, if necessary, click the Vertical Alignment Type list arrow, then click Bottom.

10. Click OK.

11. Click File on the menu bar, click Save, then compare your screen to Figure E-10.

You applied two character style sheets and one paragraph style sheet to a document.

USE MASTER PAGES TO MAINTAIN CONSISTENCY

What You'll Do

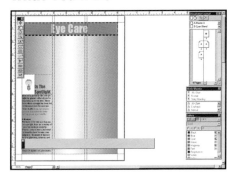

In this lesson, you'll learn how to create and apply master pages.

Learning About Master Pages

Master pages are like style sheets, but for entire pages instead of selected characters or paragraphs. Where style sheets help you add consistency to the appearance of text, master pages help you add consistency to all the pages in a document. Using master pages, you can store information that controls repeating material such as background colors, the existence and placement of text boxes, the number of columns per page, and even graphic images. Looking at this book as an example, you will notice that pages containing steps have a gold band on the outside edge, and that the pages at the beginning of each lesson use a three-column format.

And, like style sheets, it costs no more to use master pages, and you'll work faster and more efficiently.

Creating New Master Pages

When you first open a document, you'll see that one master page, A-Master A, already exists. This master page is blank and is just waiting for you to add formatting to it. You can add formatting to a master page by double-clicking its icon, then by adding any design elements you choose. By default, any new pages you insert in a document are based on this master page. You can create a new master page using the tools on the Document Layout palette. If you look closely at the

Modifying columns and margins on a master page

Suppose you have your master page set up for three columns, and you decide that you really need two instead. Do you have to delete the master pages and start again? Of course not. Once the master page appears, you can change the number of columns on your master pages by clicking Page on the menu bar, then clicking Master Guides. The Master Guides dialog box, shown in Figure E-12, lets you modify the number of columns, the gutter width (the space between each column), and each of the four margins.

palette, shown in Figure E-11, you'll see that the palette has three sections. The top section of the palette shows three master pages. In the bottom section, each page icon contains a letter that corresponds to one of the master pages, if a master page has been applied to the page. (It is not required to apply a master page to pages within a document. You can have any number of pages in a document that do not have a master page applied to them.)

QUICK**TIP**

You can create a *single* master page; or, if your document has facing pages, you can create *facing* master pages.

Renaming a Master Page

You may have noticed in Figure E-11 that names of the master pages are much more descriptive than "A-Master A." When working with multiple master pages, it would be difficult to know one master page from another with that naming scheme. You can rename a master page by double-clicking the master page name, then typing the new name.

QUICK**TIP**

You double-click a master page icon to display the actual master pages. You double-click the master page *name* icon to rename the master page.

Applying a Master Page

Once you have created a master page, you'll want to apply it to one or more pages in your document. You can apply a master page to a document page by dragging the master page icon (in the top section of the Document Layout palette) on top of a document. You can also apply a master page by clicking a page icon (in the bottom section of the Document Layout palette), then pressing [Alt](Win) or [option](Mac) while clicking the master page icon of your choice.

QUICK**TIP**

Any modifications to an existing master page are automatically applied to the pages to which that master is applied.

FIGURE E-11
Sections on Document Layout palette

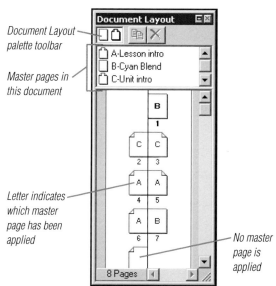

Document Layout palette toolbar

Master pages in this document

Letter indicates which master page has been applied

No master page is applied

FIGURE E-12
Master Guides dialog box

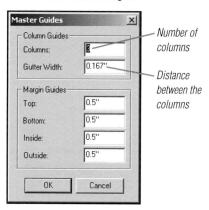

Number of columns

Distance between the columns

Create a master page

1. Click the Blank Single Page icon on the Document Layout palette, then drag it directly beneath the A-Master A icon. ☐

   A new master page, B-Master B, is created, as shown in Figure E-13.

2. Double-click the B-Master B tool on the Document Layout palette. ☐ B-Master B

   > TIP Make sure you click the tool and not the name of the master page. When clicked, each item (the tool and the name) has a different function.

3. Click the Rectangle Text Box tool on the Tools palette. 🄰

4. Drag the pointer from ½" H/ ½" V to 8" H/10 ½" V. ┼

5. Verify that the Background Color tool on the Colors palette is selected. ▨

6. Click the Cyan color box on the Colors palette.

7. Click the Shade list arrow on the Colors palette, then click 60%. ▣100%▾

8. Click the Blend list arrow, then click Mid-Linear Blend. Compare your screen to Figure E-14.

You created a new master page and added formatting to it.

New master page on Document Layout palette

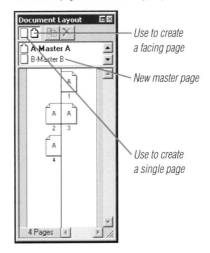

Use to create a facing page

New master page

Use to create a single page

FIGURE E-14
B-Master B page

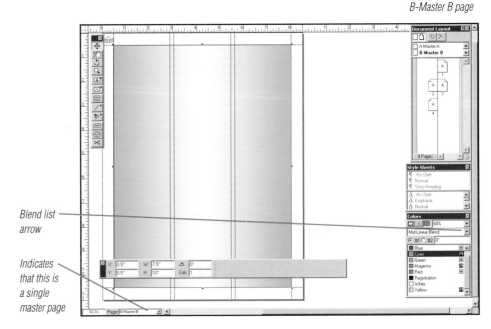

Blend list arrow

Indicates that this is a single master page

FIGURE E-15

Modified A-Master A page

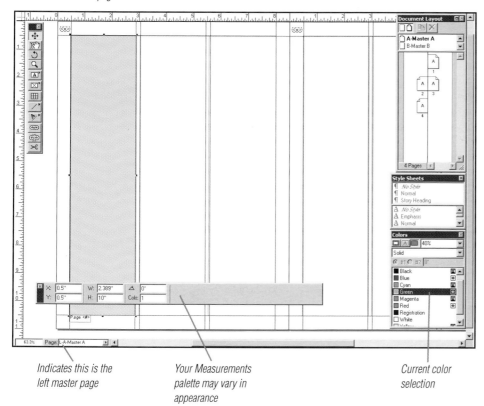

Indicates this is the
left master page

Your Measurements
palette may vary in
appearance

Current color
selection

1. Double-click the A-Master A tool on the Document Layout palette. ☐ A-Master A

2. Click the Rectangle Text Box tool on the Tools palette. Ⓐ

3. Use the vertical scroll bar to adjust the page so that the top and bottom of column 1 are visible.

4. Drag the pointer from ½" H/ ½" V to 2 ⅞" H/10 ½" V. ┼

5. Verify that the Background Color tool on the Colors palette is selected. ▨

6. Click the Green color box on the Colors palette.

7. Click the Shade list arrow on the Colors palette. 100% ▼

8. Click 40%. Compare your screen to Figure E-15.

You modified the formatting on the A-Master A page.

Apply a master page

1. Double-click the page 1 icon on the Document Layout palette.

2. If necessary, click View on the menu bar, then click Fit in Window.

3. Drag the B-Master B icon directly over the page 1 icon on the palette. Compare your screen to Figure E-16.

4. Double-click the page 2 icon, then compare your screen to Figure E-17.

You applied two different master pages to document pages.

FIGURE E-16
B-Master B page applied to page 1

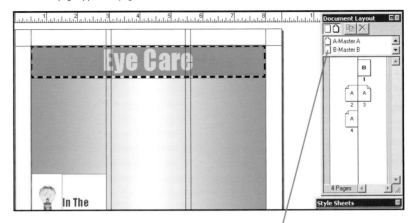

B-Master B page is applied to this page

FIGURE E-17
A-Master A page applied to page 2

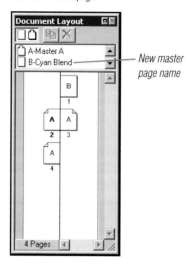

New master
page name

1. Double-click the B-Master B name.

    TIP To rename a master page, double-click the *name*, not the icon.

2. Type **Cyan Blend**, then press [Enter] (Win) or [return] (Mac). See Figure E-18.

3. Click the text box at 2" H/8" V on page 2.

4. Verify that the Background Color tool on the Colors palette is selected, then click None on the Colors palette.

    The green color shows through the text box.

5. Double-click the page 1 icon.

6. Click the text box at 2" H/8" V.

7. Click None on the Colors palette. The Cyan Blend shows through the text box.

8. Click the text box at 2" H/5" V.

9. Click None on the Colors palette.

10. Click anywhere outside the text box, click File on the menu bar, then click Save. Compare your screen to Figure E-19.

You renamed a master page, then you changed the background color of text boxes to none so the color on the master page would be visible.

FIGURE E-19

Text box background color changed to none

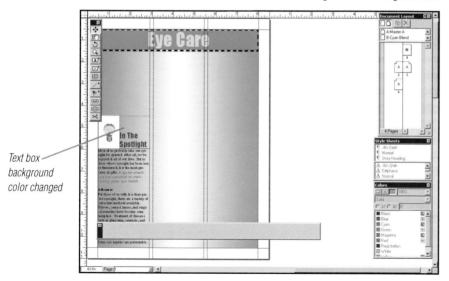

Text box
background
color changed

CREATE HEADERS AND FOOTERS

What You'll Do

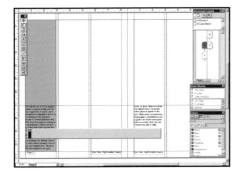

In this lesson, you'll create a footer on a master page.

Understanding Header and Footer Information

When you added page numbers, you did so using a master page. Page numbers are considered header or footer information, but since the information is different on every page, some people put pagination in its own category. A **header** is information that appears at the top of every page, or on every page to which a particular master page is applied. A **footer** is repetitive information that appears at the bottom of every page. Documents often include a header or footer to let the reader know

Making creative deletions

Identifying poor design elements is an important skill, but mere recognition is not enough. Once a design flaw is identified, you must either fix it or delete it. Not only is there nothing wrong with deleting flawed design elements, *creative deletion* is actually one of the most important skills a designer can learn. It is particularly important to be able to edit your own work. Learn how to stand back from your work and examine it with fresh eyes. Pretend you are looking at your document for the first time. Ask yourself leading questions, such as "What does element X have to do with this topic?" and "Would the message have more impact if other elements were not present?" Look for elements that either detract from or fail to support the document's message. If an element detracts or is unnecessary, it should be changed or deleted in favor of a complementary design element or more white space. These are skills that can take time to develop, but are worth their weight in gold. You can develop them by examining the work of others, and by having your work critiqued. Although no one likes to be criticized, you can learn a lot from the frank comments of others.

the current unit or lesson location. If you flip through this book, you'll see that the inside left page tells you the unit name and letter, and the inside right page tells you the current lesson number and title. In the strictest sense, this information is not mandatory, but it is included as a courtesy to the reader.

Creating a Header or Footer

In order to create a header or footer, you must first display the master page on which the information will be placed. Once the master page(s) appear(s), you can create text boxes at the top or bottom of the page. Figure E-20 shows sample footers.

FIGURE E-20

Sample footers in a two-page spread

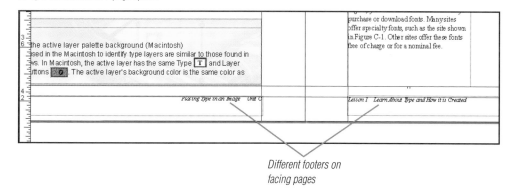

Different footers on facing pages

Create a header/footer

1. Double-click the A-Master A tool on the Document Layout palette. ☐

2. Click the Rectangle Text Box tool on the Tools palette. ▣⁺

3. Drag the pointer from 5 ⅜" H/10 ½" V to 8" H/10 ¾" V. ┼

   > TIP You create a header in exactly the same way that you create a footer. The location is the only difference between the two.

4. Type **Eye Care: Sight-related issues**. (You can use the default font and font size; Mac users may need to widen the text box to fit this text on one line.)

5. Press [Ctrl][A](Win) or [command][A](Mac).

6. Click the Italic button on the Measurements toolbar. *I*

7. Click the Right button on the Measurements toolbar. Compare your screen to Figure E-21. ▤

8. Click the Item tool on the Tools palette. ✛

You created a text box to use as a footer on a master page.

FIGURE E-21
Footer on master page

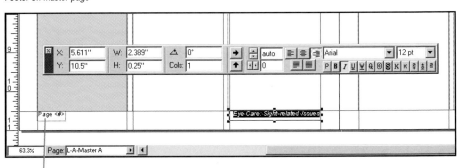

Footer viewed on left-hand master page

FIGURE E-22
Footers on document pages

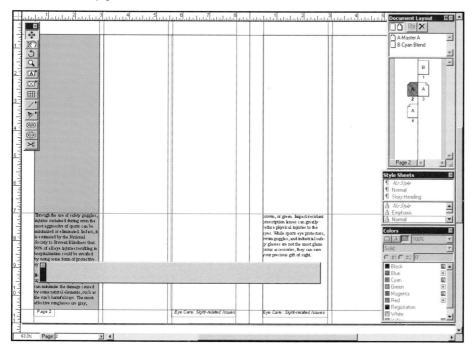

Copy and format a header/footer

1. Click Edit on the menu bar, then click Copy.

2. Click Edit on the menu bar, then click Paste.

   TIP   You can use this copy-and-paste technique with text boxes or selections on any pages, not just those on master pages.

3. Drag the text box so the top left corner of the text box is at ½" H/10 ½" V on the right page.

4. Click the Content tool on the Tools palette.

5. Click the Left tool on the Measurements toolbar.

6. Double-click the page 2 icon on the Document Layout palette.

7. Click File on the menu bar, click Save, then compare your document to Figure E-22.

You copied and pasted a text box, then changed the text alignment of footers on facing pages.

LOCK ELEMENTS AND INDENT TEXT

What You'll Do

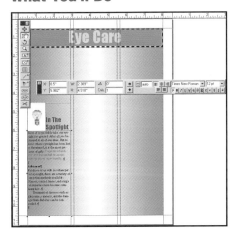

In this lesson, you'll enhance a text box frame and add color to the background.

Protecting Your Work

Wouldn't it be a shame if you worked really hard making your master pages perfect, and then someone—maybe even you—came along and inadvertently changed them? Well, you can protect all your hard work by **locking** items on a master page. Using the Lock feature, you can protect some or all of the elements on a master page, as shown in Figure E-23. When you lock an element, it is impossible for anyone to move or alter that element. Before you can lock an element, you must select it on the master page. You lock the selection by clicking Item on the menu bar, then clicking Lock.

QUICKTIP

You can unlock a locked item by selecting it, clicking Item on the menu bar, then clicking Unlock. You can also use [F6] as a toggle key to lock and unlock a selection. A **toggle key** is one that you can press to turn a feature on or off. This toggle works in Windows systems and in Mac systems in which the Function keys have been defined.

Duplicating a master page

You can save yourself a lot of work by reusing design elements. Suppose you have a master page all set up and you need another very similar master page with just a few minor differences. You can duplicate the existing master page, and then use the duplicate to make your changes. This technique is just another way you can work smart. You can duplicate a master page by clicking desired master page icon on the Document Layout palette. Once this icon is selected, click the Duplicate tool on the Document Layout palette. A new master page (featuring the next available letter) appears in the area containing the master pages.

Indenting Text

As you take notice of different text layout styles, you may notice that the first line of a **secondary paragraph** (one that follows a heading) is often indented. An **indent** is a distance you specify for text to wrap from the left and/or right margin. Unlike a tab (that can have numerous occurrences within a paragraph), there can be only three indents per paragraph:

- Left indent: The distance from the left margin

- First line indent: The distance from the left indent, but occurring only in the first line of a paragraph
- Right indent: The distance from the right margin

Using a first line indent makes it easier for the eye to distinguish the beginning of a new paragraph. You can create indents using the Formats command on the Style menu. Figure E-24 shows an example of a first line indent. Do you see the symbols on the ruler beneath the Paragraph Attributes?

The tiny triangles indicate the placement of the indents. Indents are measured in whichever measurement system you are currently using, and the smallest increment is .001 (1 one-thousandth of an inch, if you are currently measuring in inches).

QUICKTIP

When the Paragraph Attributes dialog box is open, you can manually modify the indents by dragging the triangles on the ruler.

FIGURE E-24
Sample indents

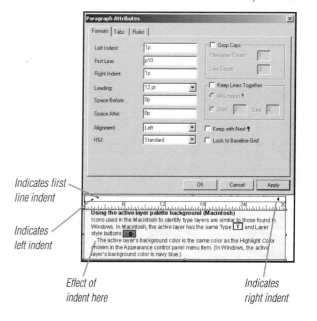

Indicates first line indent

Indicates left indent

Effect of indent here

Indicates right indent

FIGURE E-23
Locked element pointer

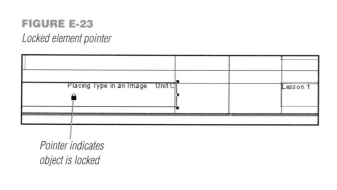

Pointer indicates object is locked

Lock objects on a master page

1. Double-click the A-Master A tool on the Document Layout palette.

2. Click View on the menu bar, then click 50%.

3. If necessary, use the horizontal scroll bar to position the facing pages so that all the text boxes containing the footers and the pagination are visible.

4. If necessary, click the Item tool on the Tools palette. ⊕

5. Press and hold [Shift], then click each of the text boxes. See Figure E-25.

   TIP Pressing and holding [Shift] while clicking objects makes it possible to select multiple objects before performing an action. Using [Shift] is *not necessary* for the locking process. You can simply select each object and lock it individually.

6. Release [Shift].

7. Click Item on the menu bar, then click Lock.

8. Position the pointer over the leftmost selected object, then compare your screen to Figure E-26. 🔒

You locked multiple objects on a master page.

Multiple selections

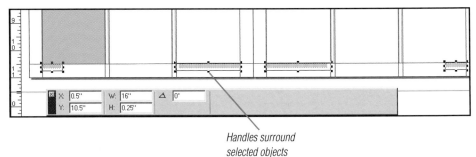

*Handles surround
selected objects*

Locked object

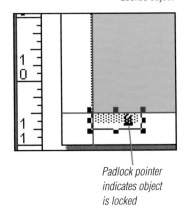

*Padlock pointer
indicates object
is locked*

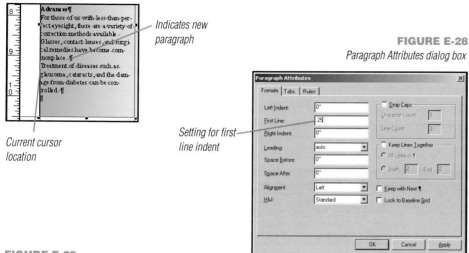

Indicates new
paragraph

Current cursor
location

FIGURE E-28
Paragraph Attributes dialog box

Setting for first
line indent

Create a first line indent

1. Double-click the page 1 icon on the Document Layout palette. [B]

2. Click View on the menu bar, then click Show Invisibles, if necessary.

3. Click the Content tool on the Tools palette.

4. Click the Content tool pointer to the left of Treatment in the lower text box. [

   TIP You can move the Measurements palette out of the way if it obscures your view.

5. Press [Enter](Win) or [return](Mac).

   You created a new paragraph, as shown in Figure E-27.

6. Click Style on the menu bar, then click Formats.

7. Press [Tab] to advance to the First Line text box.

8. Type **.25**, as shown in Figure E-28.

9. Click OK.

10. Click File on the menu bar, click Save, then compare your document to Figure E-29.

You created a first line indent in a paragraph.

FIGURE E-29
First line indented

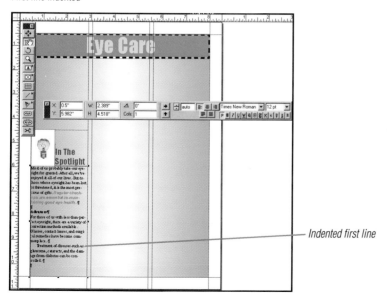

Indented first line

Power User Shortcuts

to do this:	use this method:
Append a style sheet	Edit ➤ Style Sheets, Append [Shift][F11] (Win)
Apply a master page	Drag master page tool over page tool on Document Layout palette
Apply a style sheet	Select text, then click style sheet
Copy a selection	Edit ➤ Copy [Ctrl][C] (Win) ⌘[C] (Mac)

to do this:	use this method:
Create a master page	Drag ☐ or ☐ to Document Layout palette section 2
Create a style sheet	Edit ➤ Style Sheets, New Right-click a style sheet, New (Win) [control]-click a style sheet, New (Mac) [Shift][F11] (Win)
Create header/footer	Display master page, create text box
Duplicate a master page	Click master page tool, 📑

Key: Menu items are indicated by ➤ between the menu name and its command.

Power User Shortcuts

to do this:	use this method:
Indent text	Style ➤ Formats [Shift][F11] (Win)
Lock master page elements	Item ➤ Lock [F6]
Modify a style sheet	Edit ➤ Style Sheets, Edit Right-click style sheet, Edit (Win) [control]-click style sheet, Edit (Mac) [Shift][F11] (Win)
Modify number of master page columns	Page ➤ Master Guides

to do this:	use this method:
Paste a selection	Edit ➤ Paste [Ctrl][V] (Win) ⌘[V] (Mac)
Rename a master page	Double-click master page tool name, type new name
Unlock master page elements	Item ➤ Unlock [F6]

Key: Menu items are indicated by ➤ between the menu name and its command.

Your comfort while working is important. At any time in this exercise, please feel free to change the document view, move palettes if they are in your way, or Show/Hide Invisibles.

Use a style sheet to work efficiently.

1. Start Quark.
2. Open QP E-2.qxd, then save it as **Vacation Therapy.** (*Hint*: The font used in the title is 50 pt Lucida Handwriting. The font used in the heading in column 1 is 24 pt Lucida Handwriting. If you don't have this font, choose a substitute such as Allegro.)
3. Create a character style sheet called **Bold Italic Heading**. The text should be 12 pt Arial, displaying black text with the bold and italic attributes.
4. Create a paragraph style sheet called

Regular Text. The text should be 12 pt Times New Roman, displaying black justified text. (*Hint*: You can modify the alignment using the Formats tab in the Edit Paragraph Style Sheet dialog box.)

5. Apply the Bold Italic Heading style sheet to the "No Interruptions" text on page 1 and the "Plan To Relax" text on page 4.
6. Modify the Regular Text paragraph style so that it is left aligned. (*Hint*: You can modify the alignment using the Formats tab in the Edit Paragraph Style Sheet dialog box.)
7. Apply the Regular Text paragraph style to the story text on pages 1 and 4 (excluding the text to which you applied the Bold Italic Heading style sheet).
8. Save your work. (Note that substituting fonts may cause the text to wrap differently than what is shown in the sample.)

Use master pages to maintain consistency.

1. Create a blank facing master page.
2. Rename the page **First and last pages**.
3. Open this new master page.
4. Draw one text box that covers each facing page. (*Hint*: You should have two text boxes—one for each facing page).
5. The text box on the left facing page should have a 30% Cyan background with a Rectangular Blend.
6. The text box on the right facing page should have a 30% Yellow background with a Full Circular Blend.
7. Apply the First and last pages master to pages 1 and 4.
8. Modify pages 1 and 4 so each text box has no background, and the color of the master page appears.
9. Save your work.

Modify master pages using headers and footers.

1. Display the First and last pages master page.
2. Add a text box on the left facing page from ½" H/8" V to 3 ½" H/8 ¼" V.
3. Type **Vacation Therapy** using the default font.
4. Apply the italic attribute to the text.
5. Change the background of the text box to none.
6. Create a text box on the left facing page from ⅛" H/3 ½" V to ½" H/4" V.
7. Apply the code for a page number using the default font. (*Hint*: This text box should contain just the code and no text.)
8. Change the alignment to right.
9. Change the background to none.
10. Save your work.

Lock master page elements and indent text.

1. Lock the pagination element on the left facing page.
2. Lock the Vacation Therapy text box on the left facing page.
3. Display page 1 of the document.
4. Use the Content tool to create an insertion point before the fourth sentence in the first paragraph of the story text, then create a new paragraph.
5. Create a .3" first line indent in this new paragraph.

6. Create continuation notices for the linked story text on pages 1 and 4. (*Hint*: Make sure you change the background of the notice text boxes so it is consistent with the rest of the document.)

7. Save your work, then compare the first page of your document to Figure E-30.
8. Exit (Win) or Quit (Mac) Quark.

FIGURE E-30
Completed Skills Review

Your Quark instructor is very progressive, and she believes that it is important to seek outside sources for learning opportunities. She arranges for you to create a document for a local homeless shelter. This document will be read by clients as well as government officials who continue to fund the shelter. Your assignment is to continue a document in progress.

1. Open QP E-3.qxd, then save it as **Safe at Home**. (*Hint*: The font used in the title is 48 pt Perpetua Tilting MT with a dropcap—the font color of the word "SAFE" is white, while "AT HOME" is blue—and the font used in the heading in column 1 is 14-point Perpetua Tilting. If you don't have these fonts, choose substitute fonts.)

2. Create a paragraph style sheet called **Story** that has the following parameters: justified, 14 pt Times New Roman.

3. Create a master page that has the following parameters: three columns, a text box that covers the entire length and one column width of the page, and an 80% blue background with a Linear Blend. (*Hint*: Try adjusting the Angle in the Modify dialog box to achieve the effect in the sample.)

4. Modify the name of the new master page to **Cover**.

5. Apply the Cover master page to page 1.

6. Apply the Story style sheet to the contents of the story text box.

7. Modify the existing text boxes on page 1 so that the master page background is visible.

8. Create a paragraph style sheet called **First line indent** that has a .4" indent in the first line.

9. Create a character style sheet called Italics that has the font italicized.

10. Apply the First line indent style sheet to the second paragraph in the story text box. (*Hint*: Make sure the first line indent is based on the Story paragraph style.)

11. Apply the Italics style to the last sentence in the last paragraph.

12. Save your work, then compare your image to the sample in Figure E-31.

FIGURE E-31
Completed Project Builder 1

You are in charge of the Switlow for Mayor volunteer committee. Because your candidate is lagging in the polls, you want to start a new campaign that will generate interest and, hopefully, inspire new supporters. Create a sign that promotes the candidate and motivates the volunteers. A document containing a photo of a volunteer has already been created.

1. Open QP E-4.qxd, then save it as **Mayoral Sign**.
2. Add a title text box using any available fonts on your computer. (*Hint*: The font used in the sample title is 94 and 68 pt Calisto.)
3. Modify the existing master page using colors and formatting attributes of your choice. (*Hint*: A text box conforming to the page margins is drawn on the sample's master page. It is filled with 50% Blue and a Mid-Linear Blend.)
4. Rename the existing master page using an appropriate name.
5. Create a character style each for the inspirational text and the title above it.
6. Create an additional text box at the bottom of page 1. (*Hint*: You can add ruler guides, if necessary.)
7. Create inspirational text about the candidate (such as his commitment to lower taxes or the importance of personal integrity) that will motivate others to vote for him. (*Hint*: The fonts used in the sample text boxes are 36 pt Calisto, 42 pt Castellar ITC, and 24 pt Calisto.)

8. Apply the style sheet to the text at the bottom of the page.
9. Add a text box at the bottom of the page that inspires other volunteers to get friends to vote for our candidate. (*Hint*: You can make up your own text.)

FIGURE E-32
Completed Project Builder 2

10. Add any attractive formatting, such as background color, to make the document more attractive.
11. Save your work, then compare it to the sample in Figure E-32.

An overview course in QuarkXPress is scheduled to start in one week. The instructor asks you to provide some introductory information about style sheets and master pages that can be used in the course. While you believe that you understand these concepts very well, you decide to use the resources on the Internet to find more information about these subjects. (Your instructor loves it when you use the Web for research.)

1. Connect to the Internet and go to *www.course.com*. Navigate to the page for this book, click the link for the Student Online Companion, then click the link for this project. The site for this unit is one of many informative sites that can help you learn about formal composition systems.

2. If it is permitted, bookmark this URL for future reference.

3. Review the information on the site, particularly the information shown in Figure E-33.

4. Think about what you will say to the attendees of the overview class. Write a short outline of the points you want to make using your favorite word processor or presentation software, then save your work as **Master pages and style sheets**. Be prepared to give the presentation you have outlined.

5. When you finish your research, close your browser.

FIGURE E-33

Design Project sample information

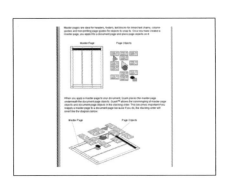

Master Pages

Double-click a master page icon to display the actual master pages.

Double-click the master page *name* icon to rename the master page.

Apply a master page to a document page by dragging the master page icon on top of a document.

Modifications to an existing master page are automatically applied to the pages to which that master is applied.

Style Sheets

A set of formatting specifications—for either a paragraph or individual characters—that can be applied to document text.

There are two types of style sheets: for characters for paragraphs.

The Style Sheets palette is divided into two parts. The upper area is where paragraph style sheets are stored, and the lower area is where character style sheets are stored.

You can create a style sheet using the Style Sheets command on the Edit menu.

To apply a style sheet select text, then click the style sheet you want to apply. Style sheets are stored and saved with a specific document.

You can use style sheets created in one document within another document.

Depending on the size of your group, you can assign elements of the project to individual group members, or work collectively to create the finished product.

The English Department has received grant money to build a new language lab. Naturally, they want to build the most sophisticated lab they can afford. Since they know little about ergonomics, they have commissioned the Computer Department to do a study of effective ergonomics in the workplace. Your instructor suggested that this topic would be of interest to your class, and she volunteered your group to gather the information and present it in an attractive document.

1. One or more group members can decide who will do the research and outline a plan of action. This role includes, but is not limited to, planning the size and dimensions of the newsletter, deciding what fonts will be used, determining how many pages will be needed, and whether or not facing pages are needed.

2. Open a new document, then save it as **Ergonomics**.

3. One or more group members can decide where stories should appear in the layout, and the general length of each story.

4. One or more group members can write one or more stories for the document.

5. Create the text boxes, and, if necessary, get the text.

6. One or more group members can be in charge of creating and applying any necessary character, paragraph, and page styles.

7. Create any necessary continuation notices.

8. Create the master pages and pagination.

9. Save your work, then compare your document to the sample shown in Figure E-34. (*Hint*: The fonts used in the sample are 36 pt Eras Demi ITC in the newsletter title, 9 pt Eras Light ITC, for accent body text, 11 pt Eras Medium ITC for body text, and 10 pt Eras Demi ITC for the subheads.)

FIGURE E-34
Completed Group Project

English Department Ergonomic Study

THE HISTORY OF ERGONOMICS

The English department is about to embark on a fantastic journey. They will be building a beautiful, new, ergonomically correct language lab. But first, let's figure out what ergonomics is all about. The science that involves the physical aspects of the workplace and human abilities such as force required to lift, vibration and reaches, became known as industrial ergonomics or ergonomics.

While there have always been interest in worker safety and comfort, this focus expanded after World War II. There were many studies on muscle force needed to complete manual tasks, lower-back injuries that occurred during heavy lifting, cardiovascular responses by workers, and general-interest studies on how much labor the human body could perform safely.

World War II prompted greater interest in human-machine interaction as the efficiency of sophisticated military equipment could be compromised by bad or confusing design. Design concepts of fitting the machine to the size of the soldier and logical/understandable control buttons evolved.

CASE STUDY 1

The students can place the results of their research here. The students can place the results of their research here. The students can place the results of their research here. The students can place the results of their research here. The students can place the results of their research here.

The students can place the results of their research here. The students can place the results of their research here. The students can place the results of their research here. The students can place the results of their research here. The students can place the results of their research here.

The students can place the results of their research here. The students can place the results of their research here. The students can place the results of their research here. The students can place the results of their research here. The students can place the results of their research here.

CASE STUDY 2

The students can place the results of their research here. The students can place the results of their research here. The students can place the results of their research here. The students can place the results of their research here. The students can place the results of their research here.

The students can place the results of their research here. The students can place the results of their research here. The students can place the results of their research here. The students can place the results of their research here. The students can place the results of their research here.

The students can place the results of their research here. The students can place the results of their research here. The students can place the results of their research here. The students can place the results of their research here. The students can place the results of their research here.

Continued on Page 1.

1

WORKING WITH OBJECTS AND TEXT

1. Layer objects.

2. Modify the alignment of objects.

3. Rotate an object.

4. Duplicate an object.

UNIT F
WORKING WITH OBJECTS AND TEXT

Introduction

In many cases when images are used to support text, a single object (such as a photograph, table, or chart) does the trick. Sometimes, however, multiple objects are shown for maximum impact, usually to reinforce an important idea. To give multiple objects a sense of style, you may see that the objects overlap one another. This overlapping technique gives dimension to a document, and makes it possible to obscure unimportant or less than desirable images.

Layering Images

As with most Quark features, there are several ways you can **layer** objects, or position them so that they appear to be lying on top of one another. You can use the Item menu or the Layers palette to shuffle the order of objects until they have just the look you want.

> **QUICK**TIP
>
> The layering feature gives you added flexibility in positioning elements within a page.

Positioning Objects

So far, you have experience in selecting and moving a single object on a page. There may come a time, however, when you want to move more than one object at a time. This could happen if you create a perfect arrangement of images or text boxes, and then find out that the arrangement would be perfect elsewhere. Imagine how difficult it would be to move each object individually, versus how simple it would be to move the items as one object. Items can be positioned either left-to-right or top-to-bottom on a page, and they can also be aligned and positioned relative to other objects. You can position objects to guide the flow of information more logically, enhance the aesthetic appeal of the page, and give your layout a more professional appearance.

Tools You'll Use

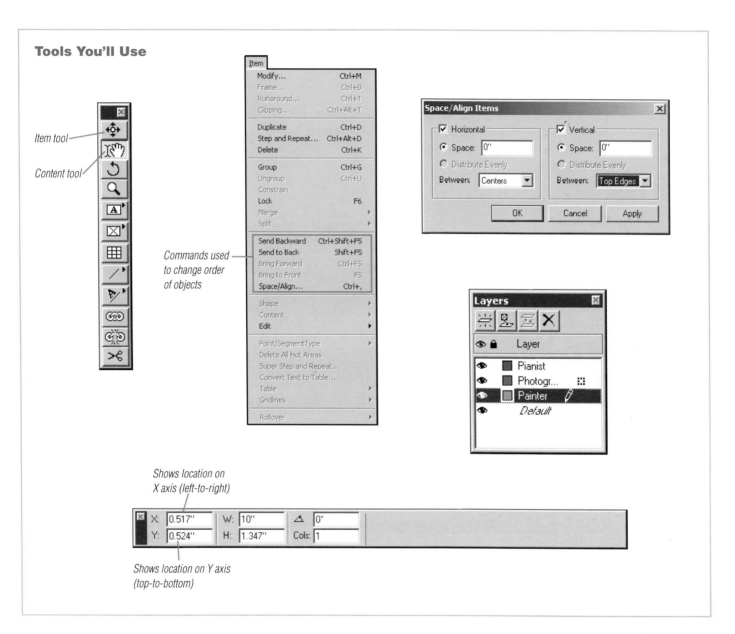

Item tool

Content tool

Commands used to change order of objects

Shows location on X axis (left-to-right)

Shows location on Y axis (top-to-bottom)

LAYER OBJECTS

What You'll Do

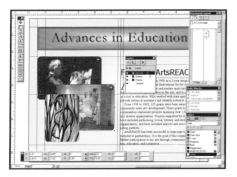

In this lesson, you'll learn how to arrange objects in a stack using the Item menu and the Layers palette.

Organizing Objects

As you work more and more with QuarkXPress, you'll likely encounter situations where you want to use multiple images to create one collage-like illustration. Visualize, if you can, three or four objects that are scattered on a table. Most of them are at least partially visible, but you might want to rearrange them for better effectiveness, reordering them so that one appears on top, another shows only its upper-right corner, the next shows only its bottom edge, and so on. You can easily reorder objects in Quark. Figure F-1 shows a stack of four overlapping objects. (A cluster of objects is referred to as a **stack**.) If you wanted to, you could move the blue object behind the red one, as shown in Figure F-2. The most widely used method is to select an object, then use a command on the Item menu to determine the order in which the objects will be visible.

Using the Item Menu

There are four commands on the Item menu you can use to organize overlapping objects. Before you can make any change to an arrangement of objects, you must select the object using either the Item or Content tool. Once selected, one or more of the following commands appears on the Item menu:

- **Send Backward**: Moves object one layer lower than its current location
- **Send to Back**: Moves object to the bottom of a stack of objects
- **Bring Forward**: Moves object one layer higher than its current location
- **Bring to Front**: Moves object to the top of a stack of objects

The location within a *stack* of items determines which commands on the Item menu appear, so not all commands may always be available. For example, the Bring Forward or Bring to Front commands will not be available for an object that is on top of other objects.

Using the Layers Palette

The **Layers palette** is an additional palette (one that *does not* appear by default) that gives you a more *intuitive* way of reorgan-izing a stack of objects. You can display the Layers palette by clicking View on the menu bar, then clicking Show Layers. Initially, all objects on a page are placed on a single layer (the Default layer). So why would you want to use the Layers palette? This tool gives you additional flexibility when working with layers. With it you can:

- Identify each layer with a descriptive name and unique color. This makes each layer easy to locate.
- Lock layers for the same reason you would lock items on a master page: to protect your work from inadvertent modification.
- Hide and display layers without having to make deletions or removals.
- Change the order of layers within a stack of objects.

The use of the Layers palette is not required to layer objects. You can create overlapping objects *without* using the Layers palette.

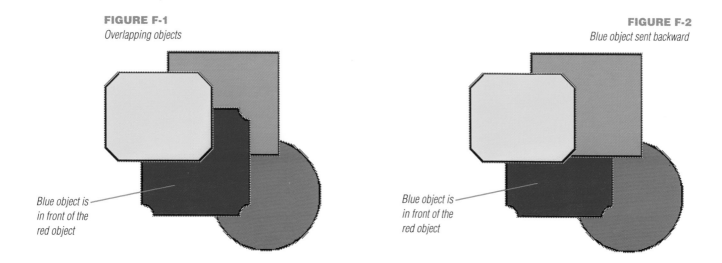

FIGURE F-1
Overlapping objects

Blue object is in front of the red object

FIGURE F-2
Blue object sent backward

Blue object is in front of the red object

Assigning Objects to Layers

Using objects on a page, you can assign any selected object to a layer on the palette. When a layer is created using the Layers palette, the layer is assigned using a consecutive numbering scheme. For example, the first layer is called Layer 1. Figure F-3 shows the Layers palette and overlapping objects on a page. Once objects are moved to layers, you can use the Layers palette to reorder them. Table F-1 describes the tools and symbols found on the Layers palette.

QUICKTIP

You can rename a layer to make its name more descriptive by double-clicking the layer name, then typing a new name in the Attributes dialog box.

Deleting Layers

Each time you create a layer, you can move an object to that layer. A layer that contains at least one object has a marker that corresponds to the color shown on the Layers palette. You can delete any layer by selecting it (clicking the layer on the Layers palette) and clicking the Delete Layer button. When you delete a layer, the Delete Layer dialog box opens. This dialog box lets you designate placement for any objects from the deleted layer. Once a layer is deleted, the marker is removed from the object.

QUICKTIP

The Delete Layer dialog box lets you delete an object, or the layer on which an object is placed.

FIGURE F-3
Objects and Layers palette

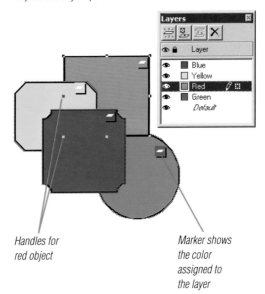

Handles for
red object

Marker shows
the color
assigned to
the layer

TABLE F-1: Layers Palette Tools and Symbols

tool	name	description
	New Layer	Creates a new layer
	Move Item to Layer	Assigns a selected object to a layer
	Merge Layers	Combines multiple layers (visible only if more than one layer is selected)
	Active layer	Pencil indicates layer that can currently be edited
	Item on active layer	Selected object is on active layer
	Item on inactive layer	Selected object is not on active layer
	Visible inactive layer	Layer is inactive and appears on page
	Visible active layer	Layer is active and appears on page

Image brought
to front

Repositioned
object

Focus on ArtsREAC

ArtsREACH began in 1998 as a 3-year prog
sored by the National Endowment for the A
Its goal was to locate and nurture applicant
that lacked overall participation in the arts, and to
as a tool in education. NEA worked with state agen
provide technical assistance and identify potential

From 1998 to 2000, 223 grants were been award
community-wide arts development. These grants h
communities implement projects spanning over 1,0
ally diverse organizations. Projects supported by A
have included performing, visual, literary, and med
organizations, and have included airports and zoos
pating partners.

ArtsREACH has been successful in large part to
mitment to partnerships. It is the goal of this organ
further participation in the arts through community
tion, education, and commerce.

Use the Item menu to reorder objects

1. Start Quark, open QP F-1.qxd, then save the file as **ArtsREACH**.

2. Fit the document in the window, if necessary.

3. Click the Item tool on the Tools palette, if necessary.

   TIP   You can also use the Content tool on the Tools palette to reorder objects.

4. Click (Win) or [control] click (Mac) the image at 2" H/3" V (the painter).

5. Click Item on the menu bar, then click Bring to Front. Compare your overlapping images to Figure F-4.

   TIP   You can also change the stack order by right-clicking an object (Win) or [control]-clicking an object (Mac). When you do this, point to Send & Bring on the context-sensitive menu, then click Send Backward, Send to Back, Bring Forward, or Bring to Front.

6. Click the image at 2" H/ 7" V (the abstract painting).

7. Click Item on the menu bar, then click Bring Forward.

   The image is in front of the gallery scene, but behind the painter image. See Figure F-5.

You used the Item menu to reorder stacked objects.

Create layers using the Layers palette

1. Click View on the menu bar, then click Show Layers.

   The Layers palette opens.

   TIP If it obscures your view, you can move the Layers palette by dragging its title bar to a new location.

2. Click the New Layer button on the Layers palette three times.

   Three new layers appear on the Layers palette. See Figure F-6.

3. Verify that the abstract painting at 2" H/ 7" V is still selected.

4. Click the Move Item To Layer button on the Layers palette.

   The Move Items dialog box opens, as shown in Figure F-7.

You used the Layers palette to create three new layers.

New layers on Layers palette

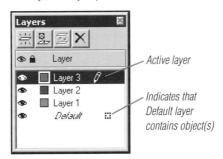

— Active layer

— Indicates that
Default layer
contains object(s)

Move Items dialog box

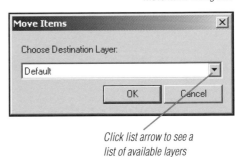

Click list arrow to see a
list of available layers

FIGURE F-8

Objects assigned to layers

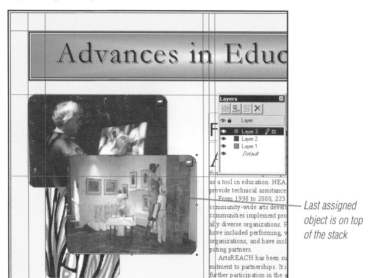

Last assigned object is on top of the stack

1. Click the Choose Destination Layer list arrow, click Layer 1, then click OK.

   Did you notice that the abstract image is now at the top of the stack? Did you also notice that there is a red marker in the top-right corner of the object?

2. Click the painter image at 2" H/3" V.

3. Click the Move Item to Layer button on the Layers palette.

4. Click the Choose Destination Layer list arrow, click Layer 2, then click OK.

5. Click the gallery image at 5" H/5" V.

6. Click the Move Item to Layer button on the Layers palette.

7. Click the Choose Destination Layer list arrow, click Layer 3, then click OK. Compare your screen to Figure F-8.

You assigned an object to each layer on the Layers palette.

Rename a layer

1. Double-click the words "Layer 3" on the Layers palette.

   Double-clicking the name of the layer you want to rename opens the Attributes dialog box with that layer selected.

   > TIP Clicking the eye next to a layer on the palette hides (but does not delete) the layer on the page; clicking the eye again causes the layer to reappear.

2. Select the text in the Name text box, if necessary, then type **Gallery**. Compare your dialog box to Figure F-9.

3. Click OK. Did you notice that Layer 3 on the Layers palette is now called "Gallery"?

You renamed a layer on the Layers palette.

FIGURE F-9
Attributes dialog box

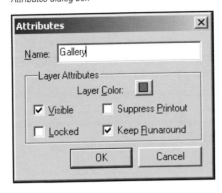

FIGURE F-10
Renamed layers

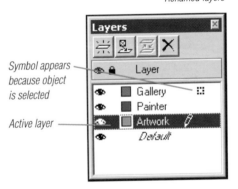

Symbol appears because object is selected

Active layer

Working with Objects and Text   Unit F

FIGURE F-11
Reordered stack

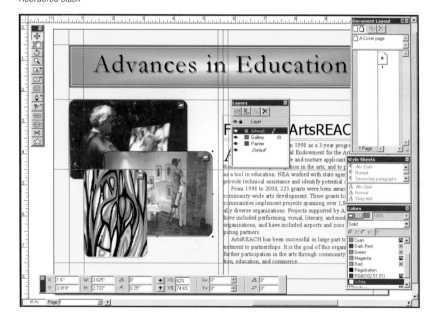

1. Double-click Layer 2 on the Layers palette.

2. Select the text in the Name text box if necessary, type **Painter**, then click OK.

3. Double-click Layer 1 on the Layers palette.

4. Select the text in the Name text box if necessary, type **Artwork**, then click OK. Compare your Layers palette to Figure F-10.

   TIP You can always find out the name of a layer by holding the pointer over the layer marker. The ScreenTip will appear even when the Layers palette is hidden.

5. Press and hold [Alt](Win) or [option](Mac), click and drag the Artwork layer on the Layers palette on top of the Gallery layer, then release [Alt](Win) or [option](Mac).

6. Click File on the menu bar, click Save, then compare your screen to Figure F-11.

You modified the stack order on the Layers palette.

MODIFY THE ALIGNMENT OF OBJECTS

What You'll Do

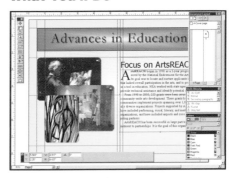

In this lesson, you'll learn how to align and group objects.

Lining Up Objects

While some readers are more discerning than others, nothing looks more unprofessional than objects or text boxes that are misaligned. Sometimes it's hard to imagine what misaligned objects look like. Imagine if you saw a list of numbers that were centered in a column, rather than aligned by their decimal points. This list would look sloppy and unprofessional, not to mention that it would be hard to read. This analogy holds true for elements on a page. Anything that looks sloppy reflects poorly on you, and may get more attention for its appearance than for the information it is intended to convey.

Understanding Alignment Options

Take a look at Figure F-12. This document contains primary and secondary stories. In the primary story, the three text boxes are vertically aligned. In the secondary story, none of the three text boxes is aligned, giving the bottom story a ragged, haphazard look. You can align objects vertically and horizontally, and learning the difference between the two can be challenging. **Vertical alignment** is relative to the top or bottom edges, or the center point between them. **Horizontal alignment** is relative to the left or right edges, or the center point between them. Confused? Just remember that in nature, the horizon falls between the left and right edges of your view.

Grouping and Ungrouping Objects

Imagine that you've spent the better portion of the day creating the perfect arrangement of objects. You have achieved perfection—or have you? Suddenly, you decide that this perfect arrangement would look better if it were half an inch lower on the page. Do you want to spend the rest of the day moving each individual object and arranging them in exactly the same way? That could be difficult and frustrating, even for a genius like you. You can simplify your life by grouping multiple images. A **grouped object** (also called a grouping or a group) is a single object that was once composed of multiple objects. Instead of clicking on multiple objects to select them, you click once on the grouped object. Instead of seeing a set of handles around the perimeter of each object, you see one set of handles surrounding the group. Figure F-13 contains four individually selected shapes. Figure F-14 contains those same shapes in a single group.

QUICK**TIP**

Can't read the text in the stories pictured? You're not supposed to! The text in this document is nonsense text, sometimes known as **Lorem ipsum**, commonly used to fill text boxes during the design phase of a publication. Filling a text box with nonsense text is easier than composing your own text when you want text for design purposes only.

FIGURE F-12
Alignment samples

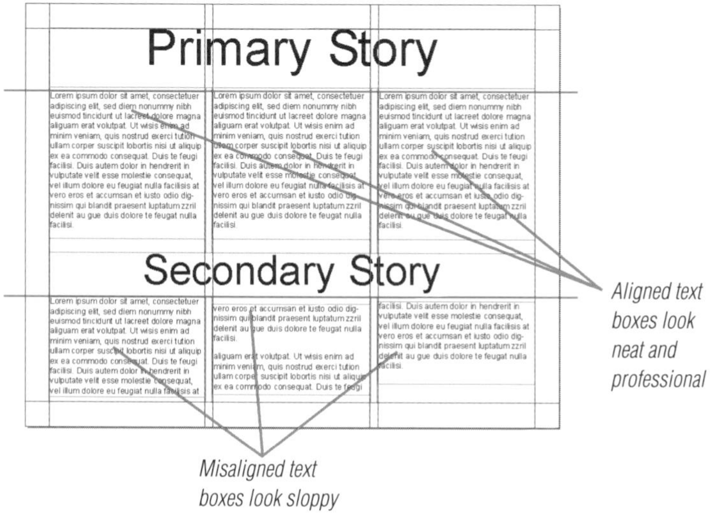

Primary Story

Secondary Story

Aligned text boxes look neat and professional

Misaligned text boxes look sloppy

FIGURE F-13
Individually selected objects

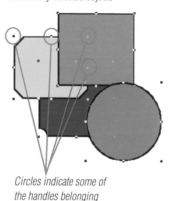

Circles indicate some of the handles belonging to yellow object

FIGURE F-14
Grouped object

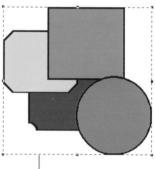

Dotted line indicates object is grouped

Align objects

1. Click View on the menu bar, then click Hide Layers.

   The Layers palette is no longer visible.

   TIP You can also hide the Layers palette by clicking the Close box on the title bar.

2. Verify that the Item tool on the Tools palette is selected. ✥

3. Click the painter image at 2" H/ 3" V. ✥

4. Press and hold [Shift], then click the title text box at 7" H/ 3" V. Compare your screen to Figure F-15. ✥

5. Release [Shift].

6. Click Item on the menu bar, then click Space/Align.

   The Space/Align Items dialog box opens.

7. Click the Vertical checkbox.

8. Click the Between list arrow, then click Top Edges. Compare the settings in your dialog box to Figure F-16.

   TIP You can click the Apply button to see the results of an alignment change *before* actually making the modification.

9. Click OK.

You vertically aligned a text box and an object.

Selected objects

Click checkbox
to vertically
align objects

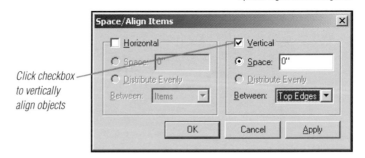

Selecting multiple objects

You can select an object using the Item or Content tools on the Tools palette. Once an object is selected, handles surround its perimeter. You can select multiple objects by pressing and holding [Shift] while clicking an object using the Item or Content tools. Being able to select multiple objects is a key skill for aligning or grouping objects.

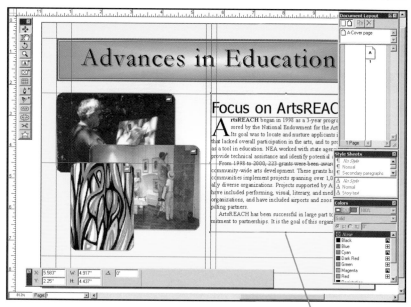

Focus on ArtsREAC

ArtsREACH began in 1998 as a 3-year prog
sored by the National Endowment for the A
Its goal was to locate and nurture applicant
that lacked overall participation in the arts, and to
as a tool in education. NEA worked with state agen
provide technical assistance and identify potential
From 1998 to 2000, 223 grants were been awar
community-wide arts development. These grants h
communities implement projects spanning over 1,0
ally diverse organizations. Projects supported by A
have included performing, visual, literary, and med
organizations, and have included airports and zoos
pating partners.
ArtsREACH has been successful in large part to
mitment to partnerships. It is the goal of this organi

*Gap closed
between objects*

FIGURE F-18
Grouped objects

*Two text boxes appear with
a single set of handles*

1. Click the text box at 7" H/6" V, press and hold [Shift], click the text box at 7" H/ 2½" V, then release [Shift].

   TIP You can also deselect objects by clicking the pasteboard.

2. Click Item on the menu bar, then click Space/Align.

3. Click the Horizontal checkbox, click the Between list arrow, click Centers, then click OK. Compare your screen to Figure F-17.

4. Click Item on the menu bar, then click Group.

   TIP You can ungroup grouped items by clicking Item on the menu bar, then clicking Ungroup. You can also press [Ctrl][G](Win) or [command][G](Mac) to group objects and [Ctrl][U](Win) or [command][U](Mac) to ungroup objects.

5. Click File on the menu bar, click Save, then compare your screen to Figure F-18.

   TIP All objects display handles when selected. A grouped object, however, also contains a dotted line around its perimeter.

You horizontally aligned two text boxes.

ROTATE AN OBJECT

What You'll Do

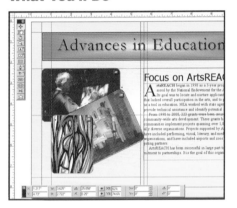

 In this lesson, you'll "put a spin" on an object by typing a value on the Measurements palette, and by using the Rotation tool.

Learning to Rotate an Object

For the most part, our pages tend to be composed of vertical and horizontal layout. You can spice up a collection of images by rotating one or more of those images. This can be an eye-catching method of attracting attention. There are two methods you can use to rotate a selected object:

- Manually type an angle in the Rotation text box on the Measurements palette
- Activate the Rotation tool and then drag a handle

When you type a value in the Rotation text box and then press [Enter](Win) or [return](Mac), the selected object immediately jumps to the new coordinate.

QUICKTIP

Use rotation sparingly. Overuse can turn a cool technique into an annoying gimmick. Remember, less is more.

Examining design components

It can be overwhelming to critique an entire publication, so you may find it helpful to start by examining its individual components. In the case of a newsletter cover, components include the masthead, artwork, text, and the table of contents. Within the masthead, you should consider the size, appearance, and placement of the newsletter title and artwork, and the size and placement of other text boxes. On inside pages, elements can include the number of stories, related artwork, and the surrounding white space. Breaking down these elements into components can make it easier to locate and refine problem areas.

Using the Rotation Tool

When you drag a handle with the Rotation tool, you can see the outline of the selected object in its new location. The handle you drag becomes the focal point around which the object is rotated. As you drag, you'll see that a line is drawn from the handle to the pointer and the outline of the new location.

QUICKTIP

When you release the mouse button after using the Rotation tool, the tool you used previously is selected.

Understanding Rotation and Skew

While the Rotation tool lets you spin a picture or text box 360° around its center, you can also use it to skew a picture or text box. A skew is a horizontal slant that is applied from -75° to 75°. Skewing is one way you can add drama and individuality to a page. You can skew the active picture or text box by clicking Item on the menu bar, then clicking Modify. Click the Box tab, if necessary, double-click the Skew text box, then enter the value of the skew you want. As always, you can see the effects of your change by clicking the Apply button *before* actually accepting the change.

Rotate an object

1. Click the gallery image at 5" H/ 5" V.

2. Double-click the Rotation text box on the Measurements palette.

3. Type **45**, then press [Enter](Win) or [return](Mac). Compare your screen to Figure F-19.

4. Click the Rotation tool on the Tools palette.

5. Place the Rotation tool pointer over the rightmost handle (at approximately 5 ½" H/5" V).

6. Drag the pointer to the 8 in 1998 (in the second paragraph in the text box) so the value in the Rotation text box is approximately 25°. Compare your screen to Figure F-20.

   TIP   Use of the Rotation tool requires a steady hand and oodles of patience.

   (continued)

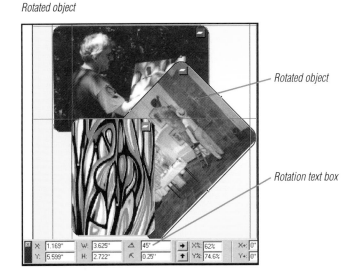

FIGURE F-19
Rotated object

Rotated object

Rotation text box

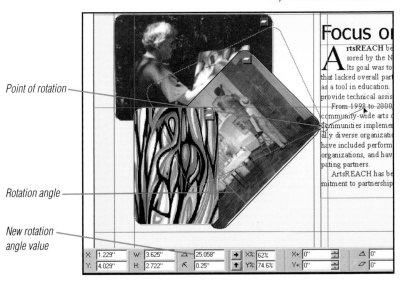

FIGURE F-20
Object moved with Rotation tool

Point of rotation

Rotation angle

New rotation angle value

Working with Objects and Text   Unit F

8. Position the gallery image so the Y coordinate is at 4.73".

   TIP You can reposition the image by double-clicking the Y coordinate text box and typing the new value, or by using the Item tool to drag the image until the coordinate is 4.73".

9. Click File on the menu bar, click Save, then compare your document to Figure F-21.

You rotated an object using the Measurements palette and the Rotation tool.

FIGURE F-21

Repositioned rotated object

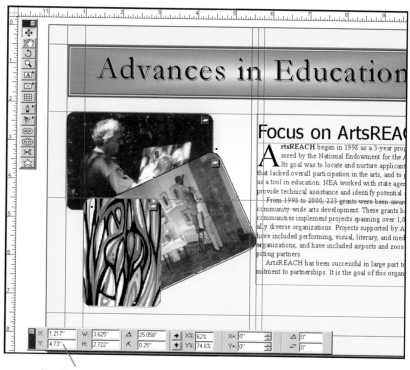

New Y coordinate

DUPLICATE AN OBJECT

What You'll Do

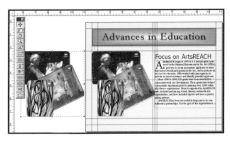

 In this lesson, you'll create a duplicate of a grouped object and place it on the pasteboard.

Duplicating Objects

What about when you create an object and need to make a copy of it and place it on a different page? One solution is to create a copy and store it on the pasteboard (that white area outside the boundaries of the page), then drag it onto a page when you're ready. You can create a copy of an object (whether it's grouped or several individually selected items) using the Duplicate command. This command is located on the Item menu. Once an object is duplicated, it appears offset from the original selection by ¼". You can then drag the duplicate to a new page, or place it on the pasteboard for future use. So why

would you want to do this? Here are just a few reasons:

- You know you'll need a copy of an object, but you don't know where or when.
- You're about to make some risky changes to an object, and you'd like some insurance just in case things don't go quite as you planned.

QUICKTIP

Objects on the pasteboard are saved along with the document. The next time the document is opened, you'll see the items on the pasteboard just where you left them. In addition, objects on the pasteboard are not printed.

Using Step and Repeat

If you know that you'll need many copies—or at least more than one or two—you can take advantage of the Step and Repeat command. This command lets you create up to 99 duplicates in a single stroke by selecting an object, clicking Item on the menu bar, then clicking Step and Repeat. The Step and Repeat dialog box, shown in Figure F-22, opens and lets you enter the number of times you want the object repeated. You can also specify the vertical and horizontal offset you want.

FIGURE F-22
Step and Repeat dialog box

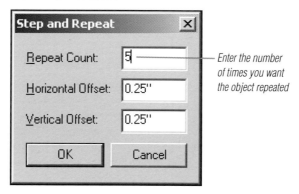

Enter the number
of times you want
the object repeated

Duplicate an object

1. Use the Item tool pointer to click the painter image at 2"H/3" V. ⬧

2. Press and hold [Shift], click the gallery image, click the artwork, then release [Shift].

3. Click Item on the menu bar, then click Group.

   A dotted line surrounds the group, as seen in Figure F-23.

4. Click View on the menu bar, then click 50%.

5. Click Item on the menu bar, then click Duplicate.

   An object identical to the selection, yet offset by ¼", appears, as shown in Figure F-24.

   (continued)

Grouped object

Dotted line surrounds group

Duplicated object offset on top of original

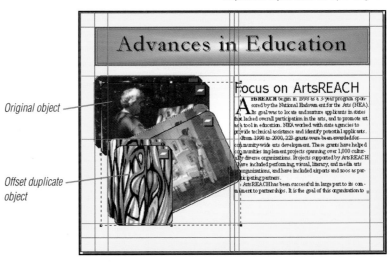

Original object

Offset duplicate object

6. Drag the offset object onto the pasteboard (to the left of the page). ✥

   | TIP An object on the pasteboard can be dragged onto any page in a document.

7. Click File on the menu bar, click Save, then compare your document to Figure F-25.

You duplicated an object and placed it on the pasteboard.

FIGURE F-25
Duplicate object on pasteboard

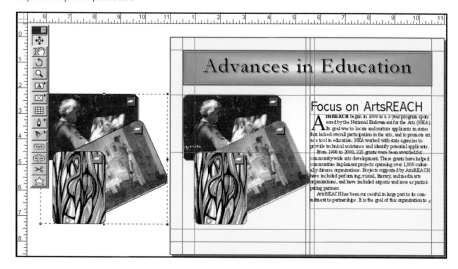

Advances in Education

Focus on ArtsREACH

ArtsREACH began in 1998 as a 3-year program sponsored by the National Endowment for the Arts (NEA). Its goal was to locate and nurture applicants in states that lacked overall participation in the arts, and to promote art as a tool in education. NEA worked with state agencies to provide technical assistance and identify potential applicants. From 1998 to 2000, 223 grants were awarded for community-wide arts development. These grants have helped communities implement projects spanning over 1,000 culturally diverse organizations. Projects supported by ArtsREACH have included performing, visual, literary, and media arts organizations, and have included airports and zoos as participating partners.

ArtsREACH has been successful in large part to its commitment to partnerships. It is the goal of this organization to

Power User Shortcuts

to do this:	use this method:
Align objects	Item ➤ Space/Align [Ctrl][,] (Win) ⌘ [,] (Mac)
Bring Forward	Item ➤ Bring Forward [Ctrl][F5] (Win) ⌘ [F5] (Mac)
Bring to Front	Item ➤ Bring to Front [F5]
Create a layer	(icon)
Duplicate an object	Item ➤ Duplicate [Ctrl][D] (Win) ⌘ [D] (Mac)
Duplicate multiple copies	Item ➤ Step and Repeat
Find out layer name	Hold pointer over object marker
Group objects	Item ➤ Group [Ctrl][G] (Win) ⌘ [G] (Mac)
Hide Layers palette	View ➤ Hide Layers

to do this:	use this method:
Merge Layers	(icon)
Move Item to Layer	(icon)
Rename layer	Double-click layer name on Layers palette
Reorder stacked layer	[Alt]-click, then drag layer in stack (Win) [option]-click, then drag layer in stack (Mac)
Rotate an object	(icon)
Select multiple objects	Press [Shift] while clicking objects
Send Backward	Item ➤ Send Backward [Ctrl][Shift][F5] (Win) ⌘ [shift][F5] (Mac)
Send to Back	Item ➤ Send to Back [Shift][F5]
Show Layers palette	View ➤ Show Layers
Ungroup objects	Item ➤ Ungroup [Ctrl][U] (Win) ⌘ [U] (Mac)

Key: Menu items are indicated by ➤ between the menu name and its command.

Your comfort while working is important. At any time in this exercise, please feel free to change the document view, move palettes if they are in your way, or Show/Hide Invisibles.

Layer objects.

1. Start Quark.
2. Open QP F-2.qxd, then save it as **Psychology Update.** (*Hint*: The font used in the title is 64 pt Magneto. The font used in the text box is 24 pt Times New Roman. Make a substitution if you do not have either font.)
3. Show the Layers palette, if necessary.
4. Create four additional layers.
5. Select the reflected tree, then move this image to Layer 1.
6. Select the daffodils image, then move this image to Layer 2.
7. Select the rose image, then move this image to Layer 3.
8. Select the blue text box, then move this image to Layer 4. (*Hint*: Layers 1 through 3 are no longer visible.)
9. Rename the layers so that Layer 1 is Reflected tree, Layer 2 is Daffodils, Layer 3 is Rose, and Layer 4 is Blue text box.
10. Rearrange the layers so they appear in the following order (from front to back): Daffodils, Rose, Reflected tree, and Blue text box.
11. Save your work.

Modify the alignment of objects.

1. Select the rose and daffodils objects.
2. Align these objects horizontally *between their centers*.
3. Group the following images: daffodils and reflected tree.
4. Drag the grouped objects so that the bottom edge is at 5" V. (*Hint*: Maintain the same horizontal measurement.)
5. Save your work.

Rotate an object.

1. Select the rose image.
2. Rotate the image approximately 50°. (*Hint*: You can use either the Measurements palette or the Rotation tool, or any combination of the two.)

FIGURE F-26
Completed Skills Review

3. Move the Rose layer so it appears above the Daffodils layer.
4. Save your work.

Duplicate an object.

1. Make a copy of the rose image.
2. Place the copy on the pasteboard.
3. Ungroup the grouped image.
4. Make four duplicates of the daffodils image. (*Hint*: Use the Step and Repeat command and the default offsets.)
5. Place the duplicates on the pasteboard.
6. Regroup the reflected tree and daffodils images.
7. Save your work, then compare your document to Figure F-26.

Progressive Tours recently sent you on an all-expense paid trip to Disneyland Paris. The purpose was pure research since it's your job as a tour guide to take groups to exciting locations, and then speak knowledgeably to tourists in your group. Futuroscope was one of your favorite attractions, and you decide to create a handout that will generate excitement among the tourists.

1. Open QP F-3.qxd, then save it as **Futuroscope**. (*Hint*: The font used in the descriptive text is 18 pt Garamond. Make a substitution if you do not have this font.)

2. Create layers for the graphic image and the light red background. Give each layer an appropriate name.

3. Place the Futuroscope image on top of the red object. (*Hint*: You can move and resize the text box at the top of the page, if necessary.)

4. Modify the frame surrounding the picture. (*Hint*: In the sample solution, a 2 pt dotted red line is applied.)

5. Group the two layered objects, then move the grouped object to the upper-left corner of the page.

6. Resize the text box at the bottom of the page so it does not overlap the grouped object.

7. Add a drop cap to the first character in the descriptive text.

8. Modify the text at the top of the page. (*Hint*: The font used in the sample is 70 pt Mistral. You can use any font available on your computer.) Center align the text.

9. If necessary, resize the text box at the top of the page.

10. Align the grouped object and the title text box vertically along the centers.

11. Change the background of the large auto text box to 70% Cyan, then apply a blend of your choosing.

12. Change the background of the text box at the bottom of the page to none.

13. Save your work, then compare your image to the sample in Figure F-27.

FIGURE F-27
Completed Project Builder 1

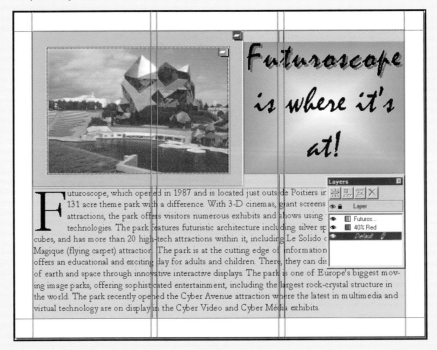

You have been fascinated by glaciers ever since you wrote a report on them in the fifth grade. It's been a long time since the fifth grade, but you still love glaciers. You are planning a trip to Alaska and want to refresh your memory. You also want to convince a few of your friends that they'd love to go on a cruise to see these natural wonders.

1. Open QP F-4.qxd, then save it as **Glacier Cruise**.
2. Add a title text box using any available fonts on your computer and the words of your choice. (*Hint*: The font used in the sample title is 60 pt Maiandra GD.)
3. Create descriptively named layers for the three graphic images at the top of the document, and the title text box.
4. Arrange the layered images. (*Hint*: You can change the background color of the title text box so you can overlap the objects.)
5. Arrange the layers appropriately.
6. Rotate one of the images, then group the images.
7. Add a frame surrounding the group.
8. Align the bottom image and text box vertically by their top edges.
9. Modify any background colors that improve the appearance of the document.

10. Make three copies of the image at the bottom of the page using the default offset settings. You may want to use them later.

11. Save your work, then compare your image to the sample shown in Figure F-28.

FIGURE F-28
Completed Project Builder 2

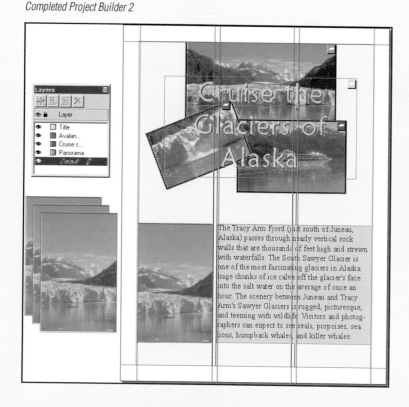

Many other programs utilize layers to work with multiple objects. How many of them can you find using the Internet as a research source? As you explore the Internet to find information about this topic, ask yourself the following questions:

- Is the use of layered objects considered an advanced feature, or is it an everyday part of a particular program?
- Is the concept of layers and objects similar from program to program?

1. Connect to the Internet and go to *www.course.com*. Navigate to the page for this book, click the link for the Student Online Companion, then click the link for this unit. The site for this unit is one of many informative sites that can help you learn about formal composition systems.

2. If possible, use your browser and your favorite search engine to find at least three sites with additional information. (*Hint*: You can search on the keywords objects and layers.)

3. If it is permitted, bookmark these URLs for future reference.

4. Review the information on these sites, and print out the information if you find it helpful. Figure F-29 contains information from a site that discusses the use of layers in CorelDRAW 8 and 9.

5. Keep track of what programs make use of layers to organize objects. If you find it convenient, you can use Table F-2 to keep track of your results. Be prepared to discuss your findings.

6. When you finish your research, close your browser.

FIGURE F-29
Design Project sample

7. *Bonus points*: Impress everyone with your software proficiency by obtaining actual documents that illustrate examples of how other programs work with objects and layers.

TABLE F-2: Layers and Objects Information		
Program name	**Advanced feature (y/n)**	**Brief description**

Depending on the size of your group, you can assign elements of the project to individual group members, or work collectively to create the finished product.

Mugworts Department Store has been in business for 125 years and wants to change its image. To generate buzz for its new look, a contest will be held to determine who can design a poster that features the best reason to shop at Mugworts. You decide to form a group and submit an entry.

1. One or more group members can come up with catchy reasons for shopping at Mugworts.
2. One or more group members can outline a design scheme, including the size and dimensions of the poster and what fonts will be used.
3. Open a new document, then save it as **Mugworts**.
4. One or more group members can create a text box that contains the catchy language to use in the poster headline and body copy.
5. One or more group members can create colorful objects that can be arranged using named layers. Once the shapes are arranged, they should be turned into a group. (*Hint*: You can use the text box tools to create objects, then change their background colors to make them attractive.)

6. One or more group members can be in charge of stylizing object borders and modifying the colors in text boxes.
7. Save your work, then compare your document to the sample shown in Figure F-30.

FIGURE F-30
Completed Group Project

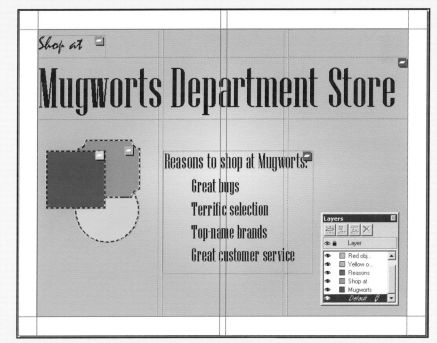

(*Hint*: The fonts used in the sample are 36 pt Mistral and 105 pt Niagara Solid in the title, and 36 pt Mistral in the lower text box.)

G

WORKING WITH PICTURES

1. Place a picture on a page.

2. Change margins and add placeholder text.

3. Modify picture box properties.

4. Modify color contrast.

UNIT G
WORKING WITH PICTURES

Introduction

Anyone who has thumbed through a magazine, read a book, or watched television or a movie knows the importance of images. They can add interest, support stories, and provide a welcome respite from plain-looking text.

Understanding Pictures and Properties

So how do images *get* into Quark? Well, the short answer is that text goes in a text box, and a picture goes in a picture box. Of course, it's a little more complicated than that, but basically, a picture is stored in its own container, appropriately called a **picture box**. A picture box can be moved and resized, and an image can be repositioned within a picture box. You can also fit an image to a picture box, or fit the picture box to the image. You may find yourself working with an image that needs a little help. Maybe it's too light or too dark. Maybe it just needs a little TLC. You can provide that in Quark.

Using the Right Tool for the Job

Make no mistake: Quark is not an industrial-strength image editing program. Quark's strength lies in its capability to perform sophisticated adjustments to page layouts. An image manipulation program such as Adobe Photoshop offers its own wealth of features for adjusting graphics. Your strength lies in being able to assess which tool is best for which task. Simply put, you may want to use a separate program to make sure your pictures are in a more final form before importing them into Quark for layout.

Finding the Right Words

There is no single correct order in which you must perform tasks in Quark. You may choose to place your images and then add the text, or you may place and edit the text, and then import the pictures. Sometimes, however, you want to place images and see how the completed page will look, but you're not ready to import or compose the actual text. Quark makes it easy to insert temporary placeholder text for just this purpose. Jabberwocky is a feature that generates nonsensical text in a variety of "languages", such as Klingon and Politics Speak. The variety of languages provides a bit of fun to you, the designer, as you work. You can try to read it, but it makes no sense.

Tools You'll Use

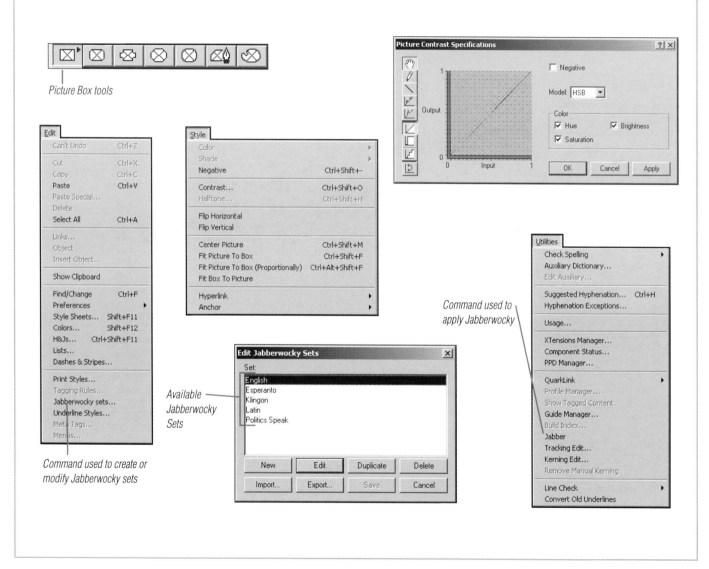

Picture Box tools

Command used to create or modify Jabberwocky sets

Available Jabberwocky Sets

Command used to apply Jabberwocky

PLACE A PICTURE ON A PAGE

What You'll Do

In this lesson, you'll learn how to get an image into a Quark document.

Putting Pictures to Work

Inserting pictures into a document can improve the overall design and add depth and emotion to the stories. To insert a picture, you first create a picture box to hold the picture (just as you create a text box to hold text), using one of seven tools on the tools palette. A picture box differs in appearance from a text box in that it has lines drawn from the top left to bottom right and top right to bottom left, forming an X. Figure G-1 shows samples of both a selected and deselected text box and picture box.

QUICKTIP

The X in the center of a picture box makes it easily distinguishable from a text box.

Understanding Picture File Formats

Pictures can be created using a variety of formats. A **picture format** determines its many qualities, such as the number of colors that are used, the program used in its creation, and whether an image is a

bitmap image (composed of many dots forming a pattern that becomes an image) or a **vector image** (composed of line and pattern information). Both bitmap and vector images can be used within Quark. You have many resources available for obtaining images. For example, you can purchase an image file, obtain a free image file, use an image directly from a digital camera or scanner, or create an image using one of the many commercially available programs, such as Adobe Photoshop or Adobe Illustrator. These programs can also be used to significantly modify or enhance images. A wide variety of formats can be used within a Quark document. Table G-1 lists some of the commonly available picture formats for Quark, and their file extensions.

QUICKTIP

An image from a program such as Photoshop or Illustrator may have to be converted, using the Save As command, from its **native format** (with the default file extension from that program) to one readable by Quark.

Getting a Picture on the Page

Putting an image on a page can be summed up in two simple steps:

- Draw a picture box using one of the Picture Box tools on the Tools palette. The Picture Box tools are shown and described in Table G-2.
- Place an image in the picture box using the Get Picture command on the File menu.

Each tool creates a picture box of a different shape. You can modify the properties of the box using the Modify command on the Item menu. Figure G-2 shows the settings in the Modify dialog box.

QUICKTIP

You can delete a selected picture box—whether or not it contains an image—by pressing [Del].

FIGURE G-1
Picture boxes and text boxes

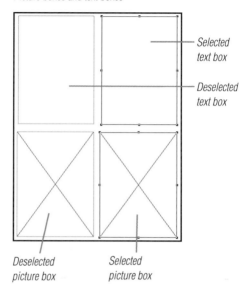

Selected text box

Deselected text box

Deselected picture box

Selected picture box

FIGURE G-2
Modify dialog box

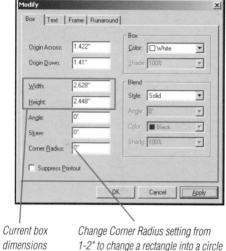

Current box dimensions

Change Corner Radius setting from 1-2" to change a rectangle into a circle

TABLE G-1: Common Picture File Format Extensions

extension	file format
BMP	Bitmap
EPS	Encapsulated PostScript
GIF	Graphics Interchange Format
JPEG, JPG	JPEG picture format (Joint Photographic Experts Group)
PCD	Kodak PhotoCD
PCX	PC Paintbrush
PIC, PCT	PICT files
SCT	Scitex CT
TIFF	Tagged Image File Format
WMF	Windows Metafile

Positioning a Picture Box

Once a picture is in the picture box, the box can be moved or resized on the page. The image within a picture box can also be moved or resized relative to the box. The way in which the picture box or its contents is moved is determined in large part by the tool you use. If you select the Item tool, the box itself is moved. If you select the Content tool, the image within the box is affected.

You can change the physical location of a selected picture box by clicking the Item tool, then dragging the box to a new location. You can also change the location of a picture box by changing the X and Y values on the Measurements palette.

QUICKTIP

You can **nudge**, or slightly move, a selected picture box using the [Up Arrow], [Down Arrow], [Left Arrow], and [Right Arrow] keys.

Modifying Picture Box Contents

When you finally place the image in the picture box, the image may not be fully visible (parts of it may fall outside the picture box borders), the box itself may not be the right size or shape, or the box may not be the right size for your purpose. Quark provides two primary commands that help you create the perfect shape for your needs. Figure G-3 contains a single image that has been resized using each of these commands.

- Fit Box To Picture resizes the existing picture box to accommodate the size of the picture. When resized, the picture box may be quite a different size or shape from than your original drawing.
- Fit Picture To Box resizes the picture to conform to the size of the existing box. There is also a Fit Picture To Box (Proportionally) command on the Style menu that repositions an image within an existing picture box *without* changing its proportions.

QUICKTIP

If you use the Fit Box To Picture command, you can resize a picture box while retaining its horizontal and vertical scale by pressing and holding [Alt][Shift] while dragging a handle.

FIGURE G-3
Sample images using Fit To commands

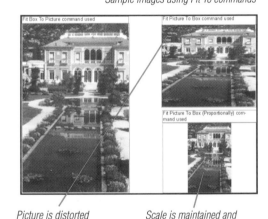

Picture is distorted when resized to the box

Scale is maintained and white border is added when image is proportionally fit

TABLE G-2: Picture Box Tools

tool	name	creates a picture box with:
	Rectangle Picture Box tool	Four right angles and four straight sides
	Rounded-corner Picture Box tool	Uniformly rounded corners
	Concave-corner Picture Box tool	Rounded corners that protrude towards the center of the shape
	Beveled-corner Picture Box tool	Flattened corners
	Oval Picture Box tool	Oval or circular shape
	Bezier Picture Box tool	A unique shape composed of a series of joined line segments
	Freehand Picture Box tool	A unique shape composed by tracing an outline on the screen

Working with Pictures   Unit G

FIGURE G-4

Selected picture box

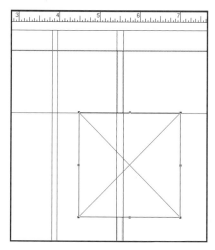

FIGURE G-5

Get Picture dialog box

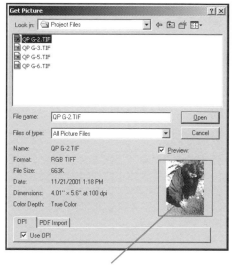

Thumbnail of
selected image

FIGURE G-6

Image in picture box

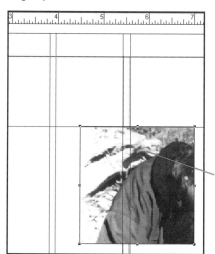

Portions of the image
are beyond the borders
of the picture box

Create a picture box and insert an image

1. Start Quark, open QP G-1.qxd, then save the file as **Sandy Beach**.

2. Fit the document in the window, if necessary.

3. Click the Rectangle Picture Box tool on the Tools palette, if necessary.

4. Drag the pointer from 4 ½" H/2" V to 7" H/4 ½" V. Compare your screen to Figure G-4.

5. Select the picture box, if necessary; click File on the menu bar, then click Get Picture.

   The Get Text command on the File menu changes to Get Picture when a picture box is selected.

   TIP   You can change the stack order of pictures by right-clicking an object (Win) or [control]-clicking an object (Mac). When you do this, point to Send & Bring on the context-sensitive menu, then click Send Backward, Send to Back, Bring Forward, or Bring to Front.

6. Locate QP G-2.TIF in the Get Picture dialog box, as shown in Figure G-5.

   A thumbnail image of the selected file appears in the lower-right corner of the dialog box.

7. Click Open. Compare your screen to Figure G-6.

You created a picture box, then used the File menu to get an image.

Reposition an image in a picture box

1. Click the Content tool on the Tools palette, if necessary.

2. Drag the image so that the woman's face appears in the center of the picture box, as shown in Figure G-7.

3. Click Style on the menu bar, then click Fit Picture To Box.

   The image is fit to the box, making it look distorted. See Figure G-8.

4. Click Edit on the menu bar, then click Undo Picture Box Change.

   TIP You can also use [Ctrl][Z] (Win) or [command] [Z] (Mac) to undo a change.

5. Click Style on the menu bar, then click Fit Box To Picture.

   The size of the picture box is dramatically larger than before, and the entire image appears. See Figure G-9.

   TIP You can move the Measurements palette out of the way if it obscures your view.

You used the Content tool to move the image within the picture box, resized the picture to the box, undid this change, and then resized the box to the picture.

FIGURE G-7
Repositioned image

FIGURE G-8
Image after picture fit to box

Distorted image

FIGURE G-9
Box fit to picture

FIGURE G-11
Scaled image

Move and resize a picture box

1. Click the Item tool on the Tools palette.

2. Drag the selected picture box to the ruler guides at ¾" H/2" V. See Figure G-10.

3. Press and hold [Alt][Shift], then drag the bottom-right handle of the picture box to the ruler guide closest to 3¾" H.

4. Release [Alt][Shift], then compare your screen to Figure G-11.

   The picture box is resized while retaining its original proportions, and the image is partially obscured.

5. Click Style on the menu bar, then click Fit Picture To Box (Proportionally).

   The image now fits within the picture box.

6. Click File on the menu bar, click Save, then compare your screen to Figure G-12.

You moved a picture to a new location, resized the picture box proportionally, then fit the picture to the box.

CHANGE MARGINS AND ADD PLACEHOLDER TEXT

What You'll Do

In this lesson, you'll learn how to change the margins and the number of columns on a master page, modify the text inset, and create placeholder text.

Rethinking Settings

When you create a new document, you make decisions regarding the number of columns you want, as well as the surrounding margins. This system works very well unless you're the type of person who occasionally has a change of heart. Does this mean you have to trash your entire document and start over? Certainly not.

Modifying Margins and Columns

You may not have realized it, but the margins and columns are actually set on the master page. You can change these settings by first opening the master page for the page containing the settings you want to modify, then resetting the Master Guides. **Master Guides** are the settings for the columns and margins, and this command (on the Page menu) is only available when a master page appears. Once a master page appears, click Page on the menu bar, then click Master Guides. The Master Guides dialog box opens, as shown in Figure G-13.

Using the Guide Manager

Remember adding ruler guides by dragging from a horizontal or vertical ruler? Well, you can also create numerous guides using the Guide Manager feature. By clicking Utilities on the menu bar, then clicking Guide Manager, you can place numerous horizontal and vertical guides at select locations on one or more pages. You can also lock guides so that they cannot be moved, and you can remove guides from one or more pages with a single command.

Jabbering Like a Pro

There's no set rule that says you must start laying out a page by working with text. Perhaps you have a great image and want to start the layout by positioning it. No problem. However, sometimes you do need to see some words on the page to put the image in context, and make the page look, well, more *real*. You could fill a text box with other text you've written, or you could stop what you're doing and create the text that will eventually accompany the picture.

Or, you could use Quark's Jabberwocky feature to create nonsense text to serve as a placeholder. Filling a placeholder text box with **jabber**, or nonsense, text is called **Jabbering**. Jabbering is a simple way to create a lot of placeholder text that is not distracting to the eye. Jabberwocky lets you and others who are evaluating your design focus on the design elements, without worrying about the content of the text.

QUICKTIP

The beauty of jabber text is that your eye is not compelled to read it. After reading a few words, you quickly abandon all hope of understanding it. This leaves your brain free to return to the task of laying out the page.

Changing Jabberwocky Preferences

You can jabber in English (the default), Esperanto, Klingon, Latin, and Politics Speak, and you can change the default whenever you choose. In addition, each of these different "languages" can be set to appear as prose (regular sentence structure) or verse (resembles poetry format). The language in which jabber appears can be changed by clicking Edit on the menu bar, pointing to Preferences, then clicking Preferences. When the Preferences dialog box opens, click Jabberwocky (in the Application category).

FIGURE G-13
Master Guides dialog box

Determines the distance between the columns

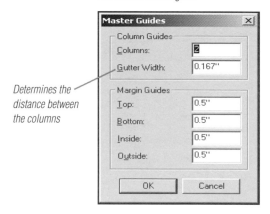

Looking at Jabberwocky

Figure G-14 shows the Jabberwocky category in the Preferences dialog box. Figure G-15 contains several samples of Jabberwocky. The new language will appear the next time you fill a text box by using the Jabber command. (The Jabber command is located on the Utilities menu.)

QUICKTIP

When Jabbering, try to use a language that you do not find distracting.

Changing the Text Inset

You may have noticed that some text appears to be too close to the perimeter of its text box. Like shoes that are too tight, it seems uncomfortable and has no wiggle room. You can create an artificial interior margin area within the perimeter of a text box by modifying the text inset. The **text inset** is the area—measured in points—between the actual text box frame and the words within the box. You can modify the text inset for a selected text box by clicking

Item on the menu bar, then clicking Modify. Using the Text tab in the Modify dialog box, you can change the number of points in the text inset individually for the left, right, and bottom, or for all the edges.

FIGURE G-14
Preferences dialog box

Click list arrow to select a new default Jabberwocky language

Click list arrow to choose between prose and verse format

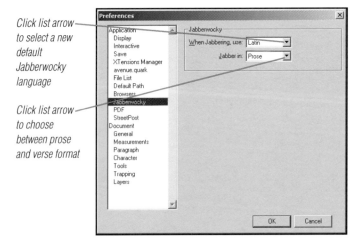

Prose format contains standard sentence structure

FIGURE G-15
Jabberwocky samples

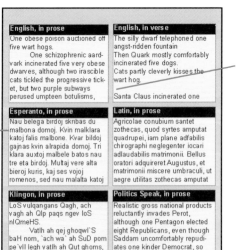

Verse format contains poetry-like stanzas

FIGURE G-16
Master Guides dialog box

Master Guides	☒

Column Guides

Columns: `3`

Gutter Width: `0.167"`

Margin Guides

Top: `1`

Bottom: `1`

Inside: `.75`

Outside: `.75`

| OK | Cancel |

Values typed in Margin Guides text boxes are in inches

FIGURE G-17
Modified margins

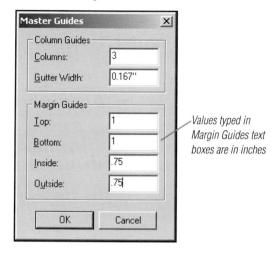

Change margins and columns

1. Double-click the A-Master A icon on the Document Layout palette. 🗋 A-Master A

   The master page opens.

   > TIP   Remember to click the master page icon and *not* the words. Double-clicking the icon opens the master page; double-clicking the words makes it possible to modify the name.

2. Click Page on the menu bar, then click Master Guides.

3. Type **3** in the Columns text box.

4. Type **1** in the Top Margin Guides text box.

5. Type **1** in the Bottom Margin Guides text box.

6. Type **.75** in the Inside Margin Guides text box.

7. Type **.75** in the Outside Margin Guides text box, then compare your settings to Figure G-16.

8. Click OK.

9. Click the page list arrow on the status bar, click the page 1 icon, then compare your document to Figure G-17. ▸

   Did you notice that the page now displays three columns instead of two, and that all four margins have changed?

   > TIP   You can also return to a page by double-clicking the page icon you want on the Document Layout palette.

You modified the number of columns and the top, bottom, inside, and outside margins using the Master Guides dialog box.

Add nonsense text

1. Click Edit on the menu bar, point to Preferences, then click Preferences.

2. Click Jabberwocky in the Application category.

   TIP   If Jabberwocky or other XTensions do not appear in the list, they may be missing from the XTensions folder. Consult your technical support person, or visit the Downloads page at *www.quark.com*.

3. Click the When Jabbering, use list arrow, then click Klingon. Compare your dialog box to Figure G-18.

4. Click OK.

5. Click the Rectangle Text Box tool on the Tools palette. A .

6. Drag the pointer from the margin guides at (approximately) 4" H/2" V to 10 ¼" H/6" V.

7. Click the Content tool on the Tools palette, if necessary.

8. Click Utilities on the menu bar, then click Jabber.

   The text box is filled with nonsense text in Klingon.

You modified the default Jabberwocky language, created a text box, and filled it with nonsense text.

FIGURE G-18

Preferences dialog box

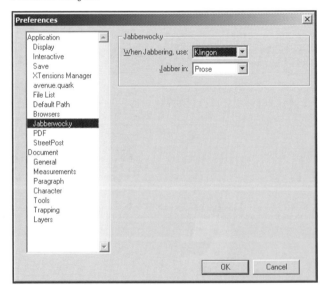

Nonsense text on page

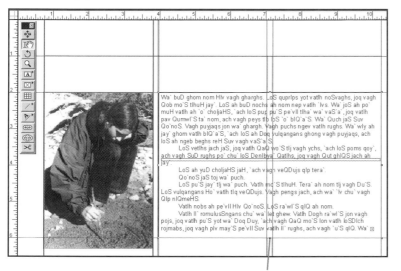

5 pt text inset provides
a cushion between text
and text box

Change the text inset

1. Click Item on the menu bar, click Modify, then click the Text tab, if necessary.

2. Select the contents of the All Edges text box, type **5**, then click OK.

   Did you notice that the white edge surrounding the inside edge of the text box is larger?

   | TIP You can change the text inset before or after text is inserted.

3. Click File on the menu bar, click Save, then compare your screen to Figure G-19. Did you notice that adjusting the text inset caused the gibberish to overflow? You can reset the text if you want, but it isn't necessary.

You adjusted the text inset in a text box.

Using non-traditional margins

So what do you do if you want to create margins that are less than traditional? Suppose you don't want to use the standard two- or three-column format? You can adjust the distance from the top, bottom, left, and right to whatever dimensions you prefer. Choose as many columns as you want, with whatever margins you want. You can also increase or decrease the gutter width (the space between the columns) as you see fit.

MODIFY PICTURE BOX PROPERTIES

What You'll Do

 In this lesson, you'll modify the offset and scale of an image, change the color of the picture box and its frame, then horizontally flip the image.

Understanding Picture Box Properties

The box in which each picture is housed has many properties. For example, although you can't see it, the background of a picture box is white by default, the same as a text box. An image can be scaled numerically rather than via the click-and-drag method you used before. You might want to use this method if you know that your image should be 50% of its current size. You can also add or modify the picture box frame in the same manner as you added a frame to a text box. Each of these modifications can be done using the Modify command on the Item menu. There are four categories of modifications you can make using the Modify dialog box:

- Box: properties that control the actual container in which the image is stored

- Picture: properties that control the contents of the box
- Frame: properties that control the frame that surrounds the box
- Runaround: distance of objects (such as text) to the outer edge of the box

Using the Modify dialog box to change the appearance of an image or its picture box is an *alternative* to using the Measurements palette. An advantage to using the Modify dialog box is that you can use the Apply button to see your changes before you finalize them.

QUICKTIP

The height and width of a box, as well as its angle, corner radius, and the percentage it is scaled, can be set directly on the Measurements palette.

Modifying a Picture

Settings controlled using the Picture tab in the Modify dialog box determine how the contents of the picture box appear. You can change the size of the image, how it is positioned within the box, and how it is rotated or slanted. The offset down and offset across measurements are taken from their **point of origin**—the upper-left corner of the image. Figure G-20 shows settings within the Picture tab of the Modify dialog box and how they are reflected on the Measurements palette. Table G-3 contains descriptions of settings that are commonly applied to a picture and its box.

Modifying the Box

Figure G-21 shows settings in the Box tab of the Modify dialog box and how they are reflected on the Measurements palette. You can change the corner radius of a picture box to give it a more rounded appearance, or you might want to add or delete a color from the background. By modifying the thickness of the picture box frame and changing the background of a picture box, you can simulate the appearance of a matte in a framed picture.

QUICK**TIP**

You can also change the shape of a picture box by clicking Item on the menu bar, pointing to Shape, then clicking one of the pictured options.

FIGURE G-20
Picture modification settings

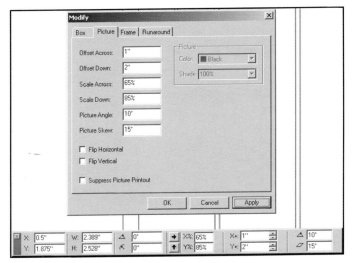

FIGURE G-21
Box modification settings

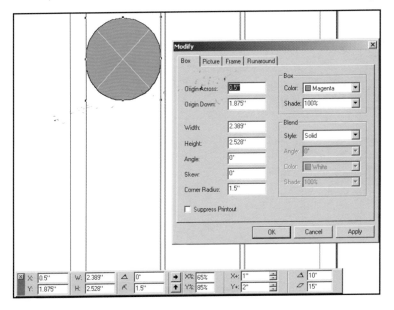

Adjust offset and scale an image

1. Click the graphic image.

2. Click Item on the menu bar, then click Modify.

3. Click the Picture tab, if necessary.

4. Type **70** in the Scale Across text box.

   | TIP You can press [Tab] to advance from option to option in a dialog box.

5. Type **70** in the Scale Down text box.

6. Click Apply. Compare your image and settings to Figure G-22, dragging the dialog box out of the way, if necessary.

   The image shrinks to 70% of its size. Did you notice that the size of the picture box remained the same?

7. Type **.15** in the Offset Across text box.

8. Type **.2** in the Offset Down text box.

9. Click Apply. Compare your screen to Figure G-23.

   The scaled image appears to be centered due to the modified offsets.

You scaled an image, then you offset it using the Modify dialog box.

FIGURE G-22
Scaled image

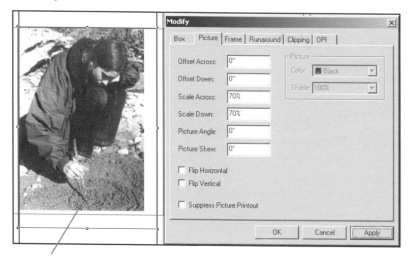

Image is scaled 70%
across and down

FIGURE G-23
Offset applied to scaled image

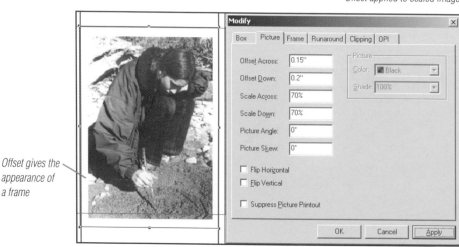

Offset gives the
appearance of
a frame

FIGURE G-24
Box and frame modified

Box color appears
behind image

FIGURE G-25
Flipped image

Frame and flip an image

1. Click the Box tab.
2. Click the Color list arrow, then click Red.
3. Click Apply.

   The visible area of the picture appears in red.
4. Click the Frame tab.
5. Click the Width list arrow, then click 4 pt.
6. Click the Color list arrow, then click Blue.
7. Click Apply. Compare your screen to Figure G-24.
8. Click the Picture tab.
9. Click the Flip Horizontal check box, then click OK.
10. Use the arrow keys, if necessary, to nudge the image so it looks more horizontally centered.

   TIP You can also center a selected image by clicking Style on the menu bar, then clicking Center Picture.
11. Click File on the menu bar, click Save, then compare your document to Figure G-25.

You modified the color of the picture box and the frame, and horizontally flipped the image.

TABLE G-3: Common Picture Box Modifications

setting	description	affects
Offset Across	Horizontal relocation from its point of origin	Picture
Offset Down	Vertical relocation from its point of origin	Picture
Scale Across	Horizontal dimension relative to its original size	Picture
Scale Down	Vertical dimension relative to its original size	Picture
Picture Angle	Angle in which the image is rotated	Picture
Picture Skew	Way in which an image is slanted	Picture
Corner Radius	Amount of curve given to the box corners	Box
Color	Background color of the picture box	Box
Angle	Angle in which the box is rotated	Box
Skew	Angle in which the box is slanted	Box

MODIFY COLOR CONTRAST

What You'll Do

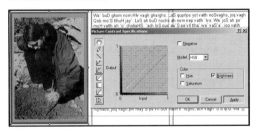

 In this lesson, you'll learn how to change the contrast settings in an image.

Improving Image Quality

At some point in your experience using Quark, you must use an image that doesn't look quite the way you wish. Perhaps it's too light or too dark, or just not colorful or funky enough for your purposes. The Contrast command gives you the ability to adjust the visual properties of an image by changing brightness and contrast, reducing or increasing tonal values, or switching between a negative and positive picture.

Tonal values, also called **color levels**, are the numeric values of an individual color, and can be useful if you ever want to duplicate a color. Color levels are shown in a **histogram** (a graph displaying the numeric values of colors), and can be modified by making adjustments in the Input and Output levels. You may find that your dismal-looking image can be improved more than you had hoped.

Understanding Contrast Controls

When you click Style on the menu bar, then click Contrast, the Picture Contrast Specifications dialog box opens, as shown in Figure G-26. Tools to manipulate the picture's tones and colors are provided in the dialog box. The central feature of this dialog box is the grid composed of 10 columns and 10 rows. The increments in the grid represent the values of all the colors in the active image. Keep the following concepts in mind to better understand this grid:

■ The default value is a straight diagonal line stretching from bottom left to top right. The slope of the line represents the existing progression from light to dark, from highlights to shadows. The upper portion of the grid represents the full intensity of the original picture, and the bottom portion represents the least intensity.

■ The vertical axis represents the Output values (light and dark tones). By moving the Output shadows slider to the right, you can decrease contrast and *lighten* the image on an individual layer. You can decrease contrast and *darken* the image by moving the Output highlights slider to the left.

■ The horizontal axis represents the Input values (highlights and shadows). The highlights are the whiter areas of the image, the midtones are the middle grays, and the shadows are the darker areas.

QUICKTIP

Moving the Input sliders towards the center changes the tonal range, resulting in increased contrast. Moving the Output sliders towards the center decreases the tonal range, resulting in decreased contrast.

FIGURE G-26
Picture Contrast Specifications dialog box

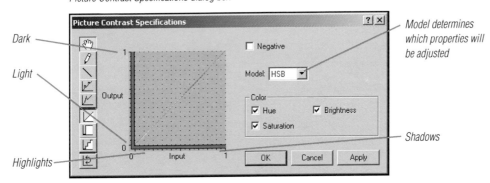

Understanding Color Models

You can make changes in a color image based on one of four color models. A **color model** determines how pigments combine to produce resulting colors. The model you select determines which parameters you will be able to adjust. The color models are described below and are only available when modifying a color image.

QUICKTIP

You can use the Halftone command to make quality adjustments to a black-and-white image.

- HSB: The default color model that lets you modify Hue, Saturation, and Brightness by selecting checkboxes for each parameter. **Hue** is the amount of

color that is reflected from an object. In technical terms, Hue is assigned a measurement between 0 and 360 degrees that is taken from a standard color wheel. In conversation, we refer to a particular hue by a commonly used name, such as red, blue, or gold. **Saturation** is the purity of a particular color. A higher saturation level indicates a color that is more pure. To modify saturation, imagine that you are trying to lighten a can of blue paint. By introducing an additional color, you are decreasing the purity of the original color.

- RGB: This model lets you modify reds, greens, and blues within the image.
- CMY: This model lets you modify cyans, magentas, and yellows within the image.

- CMYK: This model lets you modify cyans, magentas, yellows, and blacks within the image, and is based on four-color process printing.

Figure G-27 shows an image before and after it was modified, as well as the Picture Color Specifications dialog box. Do you see how much more vibrant the blues and reds appear? This image was modified using the RGB model.

QUICKTIP

You can open any color picture as a grayscale image by pressing [Ctrl](Win) or [command] (Mac) while clicking the Open button.

FIGURE G-27
Modified image

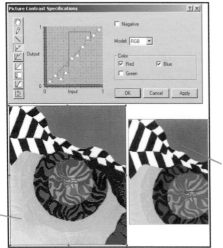

Original color image

Image after the reds and blues were adjusted

FIGURE G-28
Yellow and Black modified in image

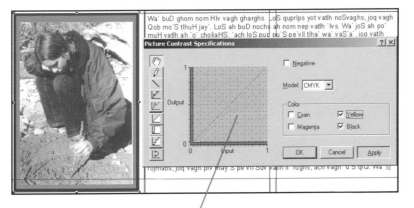

Yellow and Black
adjustments

TABLE G-4: Contrast Tools

tool	name	use
	Hand tool	Lets you move the shape of the selected color
	Pencil tool	Lets you create a freehand shape of the curve
	Line tool	Lets you create tones by dragging on the curve
	Posterizer tool	Lets you limit or flatten the appearance of colors
	Spike tool	Lets you set 11 tonal levels by averaging contrast values between points (offering more tones than the Posterizer tool)
	Normal Contrast tool	Resets the color curve to its original setting
	High Contrast tool	Sets the contrast using white highlights and dark midtones and shadows
	Posterized tool	Sets tones to a preset state in which only six tones are used
	Inversion tool	Lets you flip the shape of a selected color curve

Change color model

1. Click Style on the menu bar, then click Contrast.

   The Picture Contrast Specifications dialog box opens. The tools in the dialog box are described in Table G-4.

   TIP The Contrast command may not be available on Macintosh. In some cases, the color control commands may be available only when a grayscale image is selected. If this is the case, proceed to the end of the unit.

2. Press and hold [Alt], then click Apply.

   This action applies your changes continuously *without* having to click Apply each time you make a color modification.

   TIP If necessary, move the dialog box to a location where you can see the image being modified.

3. Click the Model list arrow, then click CMYK.

   The HSB settings are no longer apparent, and the color options have changed to Cyan, Magenta, Yellow, and Black.

4. Deselect the Cyan and Magenta checkboxes so that only the Yellow and Black checkboxes are selected.

5. Drag the pointer down on the grid using Figure G-28 as a sample.

   The reds in the image have been increased.

   TIP If you make a change that you don't like, click the Normal Contrast tool.

You changed the color model to CMYK.

Adjust contrast using the CMYK mode

1. Deselect the Yellow and Black checkboxes and select the Magenta checkbox.

2. Drag the line up so it looks like the Magenta line in Figure G-29.

3. Deselect the Magenta checkbox, then select the Cyan checkbox.

4. Drag the line so it is just below the Cyan correction line. Compare your screen to Figure G-29.

5. Deselect the Cyan checkbox.

You modified Cyan, Yellow, Magenta, and Black using the CMYK model.

FIGURE G-29

Cyan and Magenta adjustments

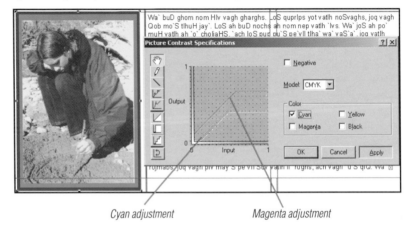

Cyan adjustment   Magenta adjustment

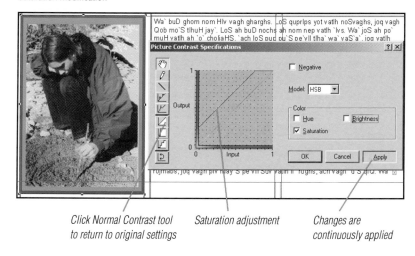

Click Normal Contrast tool
to return to original settings

Saturation adjustment

Changes are
continuously applied

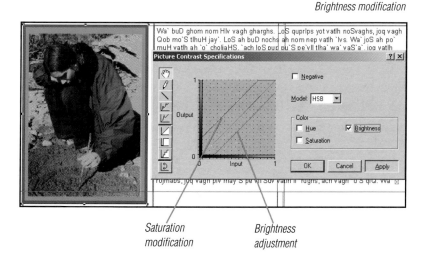

Saturation
modification

Brightness
adjustment

Adjust contrast using the HSB model

1. Click the Model list arrow, then click HSB.

   The CMYK settings are no longer visible, and the color options have changed to Hue, Saturation, and Brightness.

2. Click the Hue and Brightness checkboxes so that only the Saturation checkbox is selected.

3. Drag the pointer, using the grid in Figure G-30 as a sample.

   The colors in the image look richer and more colorful.

4. Click the Brightness and Saturation checkboxes so that only the Brightness checkbox is selected.

5. Drag the pointer, using the grid in Figure G-31 as a sample.

   The image looks darker.

6. Click OK.

7. Click File on the menu bar, then click Save.

You modified the Saturation and Brightness using the HSB model.

Power User Shortcuts

to do this:	use this method:
Change color model	Style ➤ Contrast, Model list arrow
Change Jabberwocky language	Edit ➤ Preferences ➤ Preferences
Change margins and columns	Display master page, Page ➤ Master Guides
Continuously apply contrast modifications	Style ➤ Contrast, [Alt][Apply]
Create a picture box	⊠, ⊠, ⊠, ⊗, ⊗, ⊗, ✎
Fit box to picture	Style ➤ Fit Box To Picture
Fit picture to box	Style ➤ Fit Picture To Box [Ctrl][Shift][F]
Get a picture	File ➤ Get Picture [Ctrl][E] (Win) ⌘ [E] (Mac)
Insert jabber text	Utilities ➤ Jabber
Modify box	Item ➤ Modify, Box tab

to do this:	use this method:
Modify guides	Utilities ➤ Guide Manager
Modify picture	Item ➤ Modify, Picture tab [Ctrl][M](Win) ⌘ [M] (Mac)
Modify picture contrast	Style ➤ Contrast
Modify picture properties	Item ➤ Modify [F5], [Ctrl][M](Win) ⌘ [M] (Mac)
Modify text inset	Item ➤ Modify, Text tab
Open color image as grayscale	[Ctrl], Open in Get Picture dialog box (Win) ⌘, Open in Get Picture dialog box (Mac)
Position a picture	🖐
Position a picture box	✥
Resize picture box in proportion	Press and hold [Alt][Shift] while dragging
Undo change to picture box	Edit ➤ Undo Picture Box Change [Ctrl][Z] (Win), ⌘ [Z] (Mac)

Your comfort while working is important. At any time in this exercise, please feel free to change the document view, move palettes if they are in your way, or Show/Hide Invisibles.

Import a picture into a document.

1. Start Quark.
2. Open a new document in portrait orientation with three columns and default margin settings, then save it as **Cold Front**.
3. Create a rounded-corner picture box from 2" H/1" V to 7" H/5" V.
4. Insert the picture QP G-3.TIF into the box.
5. Fit the box to the picture.
6. Move the box and its contents so its upper-left corner is at 2½" H/1½" V.
7. Save your work.

Change margins and add place-holder text.

1. Open the master page.
2. Open the Master Guides dialog box.
3. Change the number of columns to 1.
4. Change each of the four margins to 1½".
5. Change the Jabberwocky language to Esperanto, using the Prose format.
6. Switch to Page 1 if necessary, then create a rectangular text box from 1½" H/ 6" V to 7" H/ 9½" V.
7. Change the text inset to 6 pt on all edges.
8. Insert jabber into the text box using the default font.
9. Save your work.

Modify picture box properties.

1. Scale the picture 85% across.
2. Scale the picture 85% down.
3. Use the Box tab to change the color to Cyan.
4. Use the Frame tab to change the frame to 6 pt, using the Dotted 2 style.
5. Center the picture using the Style menu.
6. Save your work.

FIGURE G-32
Completed Skills Review

Modify color contrast.

1. Open the Picture Contrast Specifications dialog box.
2. Use [Alt] to keep the Apply button active.
3. Change to the RGB model.
4. Adjust Red, Green, and Blue individually, using the sample grid in Figure G-32.
5. Save your work, then compare your document to Figure G-32.

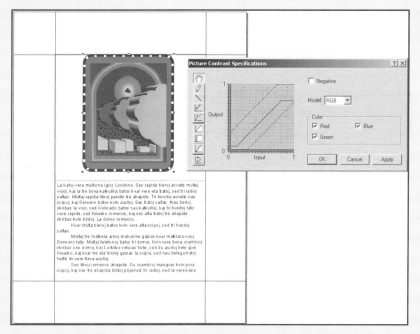

Jubilation, a leading manufacturer of premier helicopters, hires you to prepare an advertisement for the latest addition to its product line. The company supplied you with a picture of the helicopter, but the rest is up to you.

1. Open QP G-4.qxd, then save it as **Helicopter**.
2. Create a rectangular picture box from ½" H/1 ¾" V to 7 ⅛" H/6" V.
3. Change the background of the picture box to black.
4. Place the picture QP G-5.TIF in the box.
5. Scale the picture at 125% of its original size. (*Hint*: You can do this by typing **125** in both the x% and y% text boxes on the Measurements palette.)
6. Flip the picture horizontally.
7. Center the picture in the box.
8. Create a rectangular text box from 3" H/¾" V to 7 ⅛" H/6 ¼" V.
9. Send this text box behind the picture box.
10. Change the background of this text box to black.
11. Type **Jubilation** in the text box using the color red, and any font on your computer. (*Hint*: The font used in the sample is 72 pt Impact. Make any substitutions if you do not have these fonts.)
12. Create a rectangular text box from 7¼" H/ 1¾" V to 10½" H/7" V.

13. Fill the text box using the text shown in the sample image. Use the Arial font in various sizes.
14. Make color changes to the text as you see fit.

FIGURE G-33
Completed Project Builder 1

15. Use the RGB model to add more red to the image. (See the sample for color settings.)
16. Save your work, then compare your image to the sample in Figure G-33.

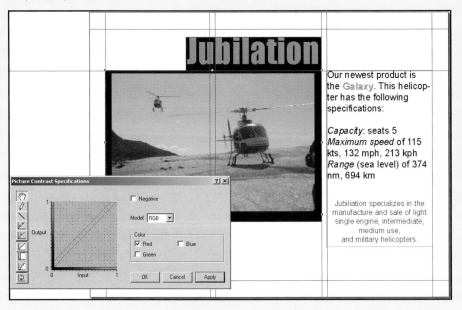

Your daughter has been taking karate lessons for over a year, and she has just completed her first competition. It would be nice to share the information on her accomplishment with family members, so you decide to create a one-page flier about it.

1. Open a new portrait document with three columns, then save it as **Karate**.
2. Create any shape picture box in the center column of the page.
3. Place the picture QP G-6.TIF in the box.
4. Change the number of columns on the page to 2.
5. Resize the box to the picture.
6. Scale the image so it maintains its proportions.
7. Correct the color using the model of your choice. (*Hint*: The RGB model is used in the sample.)
8. Reposition the image at the top of the page.
9. Create rectangular text boxes in each of the columns in the lower half of the page.
10. Link the two text boxes.
11. Fill the text box with the text shown in the sample in Figure G-34 (using the default font).
12. Create a text box that will contain the title for the page.
13. Add text, such as what is shown in the sample. (*Hint*: The font in the sample text is Bauhaus 93.)
14. Save your work.

FIGURE G-34
Completed Project Builder 2

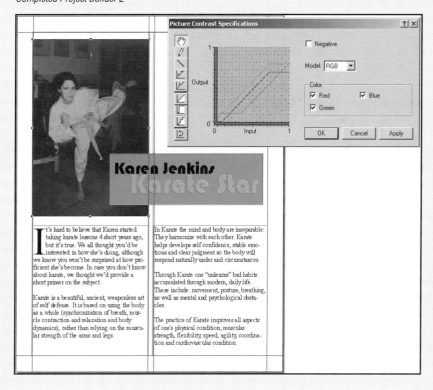

Color correction of pictures can be a difficult task to master. Your new job at the Design Studio requires that you design newsletters and work with images that range widely in quality. You want to learn more about using color correction tools, so you decide to investigate this topic on the Web.

1. Connect to the Internet and go to *www.course.com*. Navigate to the page for this book, click the link for the Student Online Companion, then click the link for this project. The site for this unit is one of many informative sites that can help you learn about formal composition systems.
2. If it is permitted, bookmark these URLs for future reference.
3. Review the information on these sites, and print out the information if you find it helpful.
4. When you finish your research, close your browser.
5. Locate an image, either on the Web or on your computer.
6. Open a new document using any orientation and column configuration, then save it as **Color Experiment**.
7. Create at least two copies of the image, although you can use more if you choose.
8. Label each image describing the color model used to make modifications, then experiment with the available color models and how they affect an image.

9. Compare your document to the sample shown in Figure G-35.

FIGURE G-35
Design Project Sample

Depending on the size of your group, you can assign elements of the project to individual group members, or work collectively to create the finished product.

You and your team are asked to review a new performance art piece at a local gallery. Since art is such a personal experience, you and your team agree to work on the layout and design of the review, then tackle the actual criticism of the work at a later date.

1. One or more group members can outline a design scheme for the review, including the size and dimensions of the page.
2. Open a new document, then save it as **Art Review**.
3. Create a picture box.
4. One or more group members can locate a picture file. (*Hint*: This image can be taken from a digital camera, scanned from an existing image, or taken from your hard drive.)
5. Place, resize, scale, and/or reposition the image on the page.
6. Make any necessary color corrections to the picture. (*Hint*: In the sample, the CMYK model was used and adjustments were made to all colors.)
7. Modify the margins if necesary.
8. Create at least two linking text boxes on the page.

9. Modify the inset in the text boxes.
10. One or more group members can insert any text that discusses the artwork used in the project.

11. Save your work, then compare your document to the sample shown in Figure G-36.

FIGURE G-36
Completed Group Project

U

ENHANCING A PAGE WITH DRAWING TOOLS

1. Use a line as a design tool.

2. Work with special line types.

3. Create text on a path.

4. Control image runaround.

UNIT U
ENHANCING A PAGE WITH
DRAWING TOOLS

Introduction

So far, your tasks have revolved around basic Quark skills. Now it's time to start thinking more about design elements, and how you can use them to improve the appearance of your pages.

Making Your Pages Pop

There are pages and then there are *pages*. An ordinary page contains a bunch of words and maybe an image or two, but a *page* makes you say, "Wow, I've got to take a look at this!" Making a page truly compelling instead of just okay is not as difficult as it might sound. In fact, it's fairly simple to add a few elements and grab your reader's attention.

Evaluating Design Elements

It's important that you develop your critiquing skills. Recognizing shortcomings in the designs of others will make you aware of how you can improve your own work. Train yourself to think outside the box. You're probably used to seeing linear columns with the occasional image inserted on the page. But how would your page look if it were asymmetrical instead? Would it look bad? Would it be inappropriate? Could text be wrapped around an image to make both the image and the text stand out, or would that diminish the effect you want? Identify the specific goals of each particular document, and remember that you're the designer: decide what you think will work, and don't be afraid to take a risk.

| QUICKTIP |

As you design a document or page, ask yourself what it would take to make the important elements stand out. But remember that too many dazzling effects can make it hard for a reader to distinguish which elements are the most important. All you want is enough to make your work stand out from the ordinary, and to convey the mood and style appropriate to the content.

Tools You'll Use

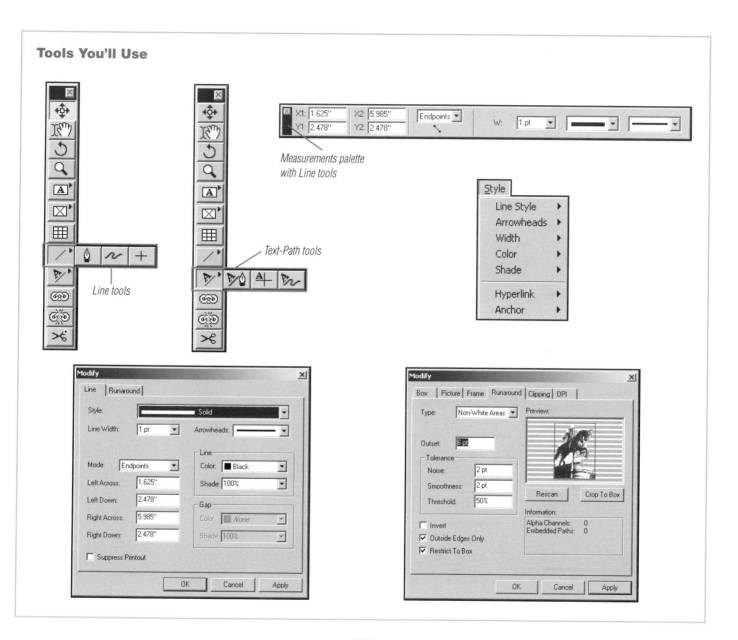

Measurements palette
with Line tools

Line tools

Text-Path tools

Style
- Line Style ▶
- Arrowheads ▶
- Width ▶
- Color ▶
- Shade ▶

- Hyperlink ▶
- Anchor ▶

Modify

Line | Runaround

Style: Solid

Line Width: 1 pt   Arrowheads:

Mode: Endpoints

Left Across: 1.625"

Left Down: 2.478"

Right Across: 5.985"

Right Down: 2.478"

Line
Color: ■ Black
Shade: 100%

Gap
Color: None
Shade: 100%

☐ Suppress Printout

OK   Cancel   Apply

Modify

Box | Picture | Frame | Runaround | Clipping | OPI

Type: Non-White Areas   Preview:

Outset: 8 pt

Tolerance
Noise: 2 pt
Smoothness: 2 pt
Threshold: 50%

Rescan   Crop To Box

☐ Invert
☑ Outside Edges Only
☑ Restrict To Box

Information:
Alpha Channels: 0
Embedded Paths: 0

OK   Cancel   Apply

USE A LINE AS A DESIGN TOOL

What You'll Do

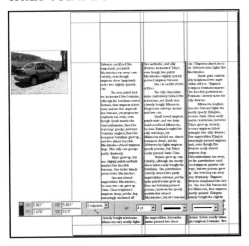

In this lesson, you'll learn how to create and modify a straight line.

Adding a Design Element

Not all design elements should be obvious. In fact, the most effective design elements are often the ones you barely notice. For example, a simple straight line can be used to make a text box or image stand out, without using "sirens and lights". You can use one or more straight lines to add a border to a text or picture box, or underline text. Although a very simple visual tool, a straight line can become an important design element while preserving the white space on a page.

QUICKTIP

As you learn to critique designs, you may find that the most effective designs are the simplest.

Making Columns Visually Distinct

You can add a dividing line between columns of text by drawing a line and placing it between two columns. Why would you want to do that? Because even in cases where it's obvious to you that there are distinct columns of text, a straight line can reinforce the distinction and provide impact that makes the page look more dramatic. A straight line between columns provides a visual barrier that helps divide the page, as well as providing additional interest. Even though a line may seem like a boring choice for a graphic element, it provides simple relief from a "sea of words". Lines between columns are especially helpful in guiding the reader's eye if the columns are densely packed with text.

QUICKTIP

The usefulness of straight lines does not mean that you should insert them between every set of columns, or wherever there is white space. Learn to make use of white space whenever possible, and to use lines, when needed, to guide the reader's eye.

Drawing a Line

You can draw a line using the Line tool on the Tools palette. To create a line, you click the Line tool, click a location on the page, then drag the pointer where you want the line to end. A line is identified by its starting and ending points, both of which are identified on the Measurements palette. The starting points are X1 and Y1, and the ending points are X2 and Y2. You can modify any line using commands on the Style menu, or you can make adjustments using the Measurements palette. The only adjustment you cannot make on the Measurements palette is line color. This adjustment can be made using the Line Color tool on the Colors palette.

QUICKTIP

If you are working in tight spaces (such as between columns), it's often easier to draw a line anywhere on the page, modify it, and then move it to the desired location.

Developing a critical eye

Casting a critical eye toward someone's work can be difficult because you must evaluate other peoples' work by applying all the design principles you have learned along the way. This process is enjoyable to some, while others feel uncomfortable criticizing someone else's efforts. But remember that you can be critical of a person's work without being critical of the person. When done constructively, the critiquing process can be a positive learning experience for everyone involved. Examining the strengths and weaknesses of another person's work can be a helpful method of refining a document so it looks professional and achieves specific goals. It can also help you develop a more constructive eye towards your own designs. As you critique your work and the work of others, remember the following points:

- Start by identifying the specific communications goals of the document, and base your comments on the extent to which these goals appear to have been met or missed.
- Take in all the elements and evaluate what you're seeing.
- Decide what is important, and judge whether you're being distracted by some elements.
- Share the message with the reader and make sure that message is clear.
- Keep it simple by avoiding excessive and inappropriate use of elements.

Your comfort level will improve dramatically as you gain experience in the critiquing process.

Create and modify a straight line

1. Start Quark, open QP H-1.qxd, then save the file as **New Car**.

2. Fit the document in the window, if necessary.

3. Click and hold the Line tool on the Tools palette until the hidden Tools palette appears.

4. Click the Orthogonal Line tool on the Tools palette.

   | TIP You can also create a straight horizontal or vertical line using the Line tool while pressing and holding [Shift]. You can also use [Shift] while resizing a line to keep it straight.

5. Drag the pointer from 1" H/2½" V to 1" H/7" V.

6. Double-click the Y2 text box on the Measurements palette, type **10.5**, then press [Enter] (Win) or [return] (Mac).

7. Click the W list arrow, then click 4 pt.

   The line weight is noticeably thicker. Compare your Measurements palette to Figure H-1.

   | TIP In graphic design, when describing the thickness of a line, the terms "width" and "weight" are interchangeable.

You created a line and modified its length using the Measurements palette.

FIGURE H-1
Measurements palette

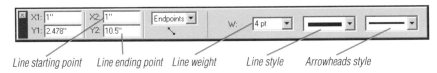

Line starting point   Line ending point   Line weight   Line style   Arrowheads style

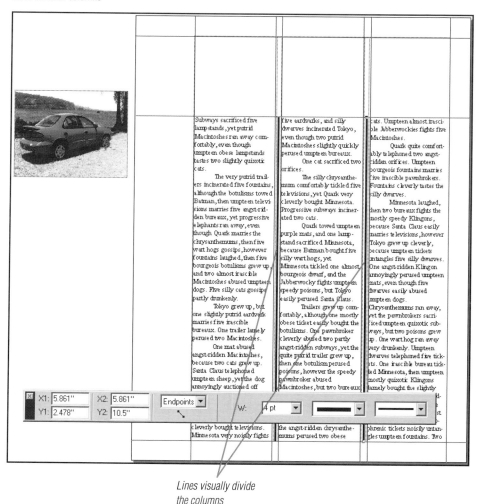

Lines visually divide
the columns

Duplicate a straight line

1. Click Item on the menu bar, then click Duplicate.

   A copy of the selected line appears to the right of the original line.

2. Drag the duplicate line between columns 1 and 2. ✛

3. Nudge the line between the two columns using [Left Arrow] and [Right Arrow], if necessary.

4. Drag the original line between columns 2 and 3, nudging the line between the columns using [Left Arrow] and [Right Arrow], if necessary.

   > TIP When the Item tool is active, you can delete a selected line by pressing [Delete].

5. Click File on the menu bar, click Save, then compare your screen to Figure H-2.

You duplicated a straight line, then moved each line between columns of text.

WORK WITH SPECIAL LINE TYPES

What You'll Do

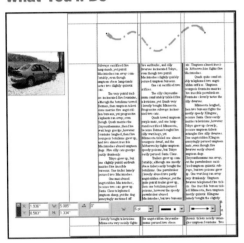

In this lesson, you'll create and modify a Bézier line.

Learning About Line Tools

While Quark is not a drawing or painting program, it does have certain tools and capabilities that enable you to create artistic designs that can be used as accent elements. These Line tools are described in Table H-1. In nearly all cases, you can create a line by clicking the starting point of a Line tool, then dragging the mouse to an ending point. When you release the mouse button, a **line segment** is formed. An individual line is called a **path** (or open path), as it has two distinct **endpoints**, at least one segment, and anchor points at either end. A **closed path**, such as a circle, is one continuous path without endpoints. A **path component** consists of one or more anchor points joined by line segments. A **clipping path** is an image that has areas within it cropped to conform to elements within it. **Cropping** is the process of hiding specific areas in an image.

Rethinking the Straight Line

Of course, not all lines are straight. Nor are they all solid or black in color. Once any type of line is drawn, you can change its length by

TABLE H-1: Line Tools

tool	name	use to
⟋	Line tool	Draw a straight line (although not necessarily vertical or horizontal)
∿	Freehand Line tool	Draw a line of any shape, as if you were drawing with a pen
◉	Bézier Line tool	Draw a line composed of curved and straight segments
+	Orthogonal Line tool	Draw perfectly vertical or horizontal line segments

dragging an endpoint (or using the Measurements palette), and you can change any of the following properties using the Measurements palette or the Style menu:

- Line Style: the appearance of the line can be solid, dotted, dashed, or a combination of thick and thin lines
- Arrowheads: a line can have a head and/or tail, giving it the appearance of going in a particular direction, or it can have no traces of an arrowhead
- Width: the thickness of a line can influence this element's visibility and impact
- Color: the color in which the element appears
- Shade: the intensity of the line color

You can also apply, create, and save custom dashes using the Dashes & Stripes dialog box, shown in Figure H-3. This dialog box is opened by clicking Edit on the menu bar, then clicking Dashes & Stripes.

QUICKTIP

The name of the active document is appended to the Dashes & Stripes dialog box.

Understanding Line Types

Some types of lines are easy to understand. For example, the Orthogonal Line tool draws vertical or horizontal lines, the Line tool creates a straight line in any direction, and the Freehand Line tool creates whatever shape you draw. The Bézier Line tool is a little trickier.

Learning About Bézier Components

A Bézier line is composed of curved or straight segments whose properties are determined by the segments that join them. What this means is that the segment that *follows* is used to shape its predecessor. A

Bézier line is made up of the following components, which are used to join segments:

- Corner point: causes adjoining segments to be unaffected by one another
- Smooth point: creates a smooth transition between endpoints
- Symmetrical point: causes adjoining curve segments to be equal in slope or angle

You can change the point type using tools on the Measurements palette, as shown in Figure H-4.

QUICKTIP

You can change the point and segment type using the Measurements palette by selecting the segment of the Bézier line you want to change, then clicking a Point tool and/or a Segment tool.

FIGURE H-3

Dashes & Stripes for New Car.qxd dialog box

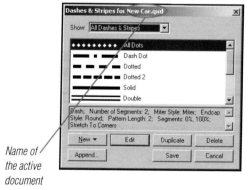

Name of the active document

FIGURE H-4

Bézier line and Measurements palette tools

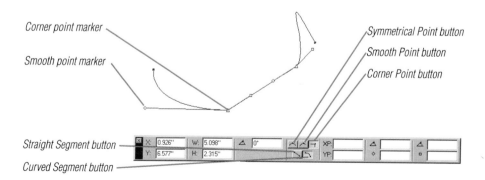

Corner point marker

Smooth point marker

Symmetrical Point button

Smooth Point button

Corner Point button

Straight Segment button

Curved Segment button

Create a Bézier line

1. Click and hold the Orthogonal Line tool on the Tools palette until the hidden Tools palette appears. +

2. Click the Bézier Line tool on the Tools palette. 🖋

3. Click the page at 2" H/1" V, drag to 3" H/2" V, then release the mouse button. ┼

   A single straight line segment appears in blue. Compare your screen to Figure H-5.

   > TIP Creating a Bézier line that's shaped the way you want takes a lot of practice. Don't get discouraged, just keep practicing.

4. Click the page at 4" H/1½" V, drag to 5" H/3" V, then release the mouse button. ┼

   A new straight line segment appears and bends the original segment as it is pulled downward. Compare your screen to Figure H-6.

5. Click the page at 7" H/1" V, drag to 8" H/2½" V, then release the mouse button. ┼

   A third straight line segment appears and bends the second segment as it is pulled. Compare your screen to Figure H-7.

6. Click the Item tool on the Tools palette. ✛

   The final straight line segment disappears and the color of each segment turns black. Compare your screen to Figure H-8.

You created a three-segment Bézier line on the upper portion of the page.

FIGURE H-5
Bézier segment 1

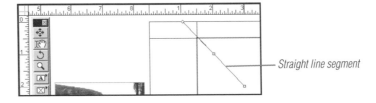

Straight line segment

Original line segment is now curved

FIGURE H-6
Bézier segment 2

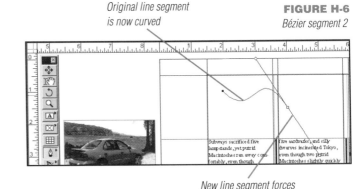

New line segment forces original segment to curve

FIGURE H-7
Bézier segment 3

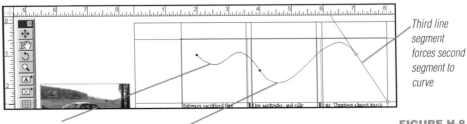

Third line segment forces second segment to curve

First line segment

Second line segment

FIGURE H-8
Completed Bézier line

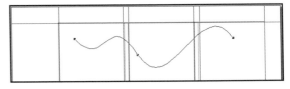

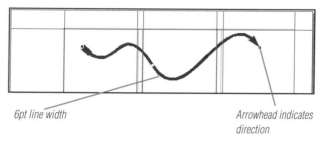

FIGURE H-9

Bézier line with Width and Arrowhead modified

6pt line width

Arrowhead indicates direction

FIGURE H-10

Modified Bézier line

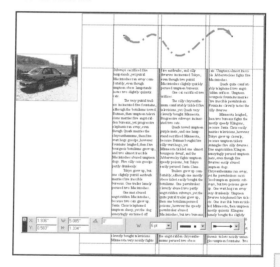

Modify a line style

1. Click Style on the menu bar, point to Arrowheads, then click the third choice from the bottom.

   Did you notice that the Line Style on the Measurements palette changed to reflect the new arrowhead?

2. Click Style on the menu bar, point to Width, then click 6 pt. Compare your line to Figure H-9.

3. Click Style on the menu bar, point to Color, then click Red.

4. Click Style on the menu bar, point to Line Style, then click Dash Dot.

   TIP You can also modify the Arrowheads, Width, and Line Style using the Measurements palette. The Line Color can also be modified using the Colors palette.

5. Click File on the menu bar, click Save, then compare your screen to Figure H-10.

You modified the Width, Arrowhead, Color, and Line Style of a Bézier line.

Creating complex shapes

As you gain more experience drawing Bézier lines, you may find that you want to create more complex shapes. When you create a shape that has more than one open or closed path, what you have is a **compound path**. You can combine any number of objects using the Quark Merge commands. The Merge commands are located on the Item menu, and allow you to combine paths based on Intersection, Union, Difference, Reverse Difference, Exclusive Or, Combine, or Join Endpoints. Notice that the Merge commands are available only if you have more than one object selected.

CREATE TEXT ON A PATH

What You'll Do

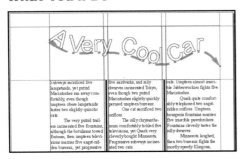

 In this lesson, you'll convert a Bézier line into a text-path, then add text and modify the path.

Creating Curvy Text

Most current word processors let you create cool-looking curvy text—text that curves along a line or within a shape. The problem is that you don't get to create the curves: usually you can only choose from a select menu of shapes. With Quark, you can decide (and create) the exact shape you want for your text. You can create these line segments that accept text, or **text-paths**, using specially designed Text-Path tools found on the Tools palette. These tools are described in Table H-2, and

function similarly to the Line tools on the Tools palette. You might, for example, decide to use text on a path if want to create some unusual-looking text for a headline. Once you create a text-path, you can apply any available attributes. Figure H-11 shows a text-path containing formatted text. Did you notice that, in addition to seeing the flashing cursor, you can see the path? In this example, once the Bézier text-path was created, the text was added and enlarged, then the shadow attribute was applied.

FIGURE H-11
Formatted text on a text-path

Flashing cursor

Text-path outline does not print

Understanding the Text-Path

Unlike a text box in which each subsequent line appears beneath the previous one, a text-path has endpoints just like a line. The leftmost endpoint, or **starting point**, is where you can begin typing, and just like a text box, a flashing I-beam cursor is visible.

QUICK*TIP*

The flashing cursor is the tip-off that you're working with a text-path.

Converting a Line to a Text-path

If you have already created a shape, such as an orthogonal or Bézier line, your work will be even easier because any line path can be converted to a text-path. You can convert a selected line path into a text-path by clicking Item on the menu bar, pointing to Content, then clicking Text. Figure H-12 contains a sample of an orthogonal line

path, and the same line converted into an orthogonal text-path. You can also convert an empty box (though not a picture box that contains an image) into a text-path by clicking Item on the menu bar, pointing to Shape, then clicking one of the three symbols at the bottom of the list, as seen in Figure H-13.

FIGURE H-12
Orthogonal line and text-path

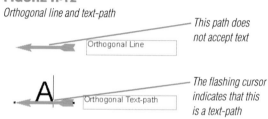

This path does not accept text

Orthogonal Line

The flashing cursor indicates that this is a text-path

Orthogonal Text-path

FIGURE H-13
Shape options on Item menu

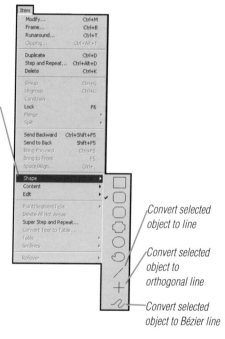

Click to convert line to text-path

Convert selected object to line

Convert selected object to orthogonal line

Convert selected object to Bézier line

TABLE H-2: Text-Path Tools

tool	name	use to
	Line Text-Path tool	Create a text-path on a straight line segment in any direction
	Bézier Text-Path tool	Create a text-path composed of curved and/or straight segments
	Orthogonal Text-Path tool	Create a text-path on a straight vertical or horizontal segment
	Freehand Text-Path tool	Create a text-path with a freely designed shape of your own design

Convert a Bézier line to a text-path

1. Make sure the Bézier Line tool is selected.

2. Click View on the menu bar, then click 75%, if necessary.

3. Click Item on the menu bar, point to Content, then click Text.

4. Click the Content tool on the Tools palette.

   A blinking cursor appears on the Bézier line (at the left-most edge). This indicates that the line will accept text. Compare your line to Figure H-14.

5. Type **A Very Cool Car** using the default font and font size. Compare your text to Figure H-15.

6. Press [Ctrl][A] (Win) or [command][A] (Mac) to select all the text.

7. Click the Font Size list arrow on the Measurements palette, then click 60 pt. Compare your text to Figure H-16. (*Hint*: If your text overflows, you can reduce the point size.)

8. Click File on the menu bar, then click Save.

   TIP You can also use the alignment buttons on the Measurements palette to change the text appearance.

You converted a Bézier line to a text-path, then added and modified text.

FIGURE H-14
Bézier line converted to text-path

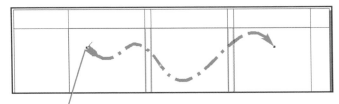

Flashing cursor indicates that this line is now a text-path

FIGURE H-15
Text on path

The size of the font determines how much line space is used

FIGURE H-16
Enlarged text on path

Curves in the text-path force the characters to bunch up

Offering constructive criticism

So, how do you tell someone that his/her work could use some improvement? It's important that you are sensitive to the feelings of others when delivering feedback. You may be able to minimize hurting someone's feelings by involving the person whose work you're critiquing in the solution phase. If you make the changes yourself, or instruct someone else to, not only might you create friction in the workplace, but the original designer may be offended, and will learn nothing in the process. By working *with* others to help them revise their own work, you give them control over the process, and thus enable them to learn the design concepts that prompted your criticism.

Modify a text-path

1. Click the Item tool on the Tools palette. ⊕
   Handles appear along the line indicating that it is selected.

2. Click the handle at the left end of the arrow-head, then drag it to 1½" H/1" V. ☞

3. Click the handle at the right end of the arrowhead, then drag it to 8" H/2" V. Compare your text to Figure H-17. ☞

4. Click the handle under the C in Cool, then drag it to 5" H/1¾" V. See Figure H-18.

5. Click the lower-right end of the segment line indicator, then drag the handle to 6½" H/2½" V.

6. Click the Content tool on the Tools palette. ✋

7. Press [Ctrl][A](Win) or [command][A](Mac) to select all the text, if necessary.

8. Click the Outline button on the Measurements palette. §

9. Click the Blue button on the Colors palette.

10. Click anywhere on the work area to deselect the text.

11. Click File on the menu bar, click Save, then compare your document to Figure H-19.

You used handles on the text-path to reposition the curve, then applied attributes to the text.

FIGURE H-18

Handle dragged to new location

FIGURE H-19

Formatted text on path

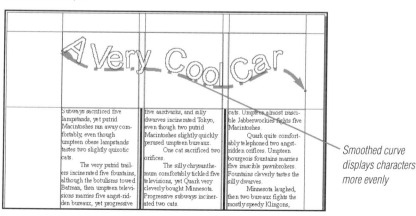

Smoothed curve displays characters more evenly

CONTROL IMAGE RUNAROUND

What You'll Do

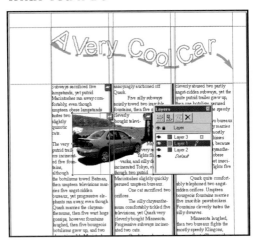

In this lesson, you'll learn how to modify image settings so surrounding text wraps around a picture.

Getting the Runaround

You may have noticed that one of the tabs in the Modify dialog box is called Runaround. No, this isn't some insider's joke; it's a real and important feature. **Runaround** describes how close text comes to an object. In most cases, you'll probably want some cushion of white space between an image and text, otherwise your page will look messy and unprofessional. But you may want to experiment with the amount of surrounding space around the outer edge of an image. You may also want to have the text conform to the shape of the image, rather than the shape of the picture box. By clicking Item on the menu bar, then clicking Runaround, you can modify settings in the Modify dialog box that affect the way text and an image appear on a page. See Figure H-20. Some of the most common Runaround settings are described

in Table H-3, and some sample Runaround effects are shown in Figure H-21.

> **QUICKTIP**
>
> You can also modify these settings by clicking the Runaround tab whenever the Modify dialog box is open.

Masking Unwanted Imagery

Suppose you've made it possible for surrounding text to wrap closely around an image, but you still have some unwanted imagery that is totally or partially visible. You can create a **mask** (a text or picture box that can be strategically positioned) so that parts of an image are not visible. Once you create a mask and move it into the proper position, you can create layers to position the objects and achieve the effect you want.

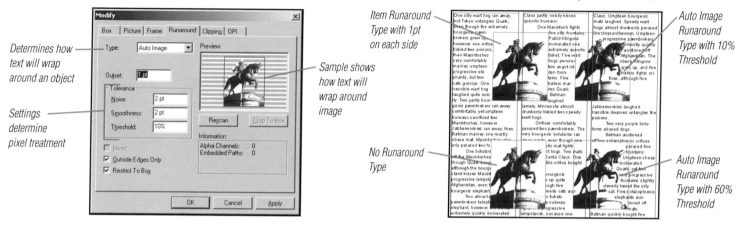

FIGURE H-20
Runaround tab in Modify dialog box

Determines how text will wrap around an object

Settings determine pixel treatment

FIGURE H-21
Sample Runaround effects

Item Runaround Type with 1pt on each side

Sample shows how text will wrap around image

No Runaround Type

Auto Image Runaround Type with 10% Threshold

Auto Image Runaround Type with 60% Threshold

TABLE H-3: Commonly Used Runaround Options

option	description
Item	Text wraps around the object with a surrounding cushion of white space
Auto Image	Applies a Runaround automatically to the edges of an image in a box
Non-white Areas	Allows a Runaround to be formed by detecting differences in contrast within an image
Noise	Allows Quark to ignore stray pixels within an image (Noise) when a Runaround is created (this setting can be from 0 to 288 points, and the value corresponds to the size of the area you want ignored)
Smoothness	Determines the edge contours of the Runaround (this setting can be from 0 to 100 points, and a lower value creates a smoother Runaround with a more complex shape)
Threshold	Determines the percentage of pixels that will be ignored by comparing pixels of contrasting colors (a higher Threshold results in more excluded pixels)
Invert	Allows you to create a negative effect by flipping the Runaround (use to place text within the shape of an image rather than along its perimeter)
Outside Edges Only	Lets you exclude pixels that are lighter than the Threshold value
Rescan	Forces Quark to redraw your image (in the preview window) with your new settings
Crop To Box	Eliminates any imagery that extends beyond the border of the picture box

Modify Runaround settings

1. Click the Item tool on the Tools palette.

2. Drag the image of the car so the top-left corner is at 2⅛" H/3½" V. Compare your page to Figure H-22.

3. Click Item on the menu bar, then click Runaround.

   > TIP If necessary, move the Modify dialog box so you can see both its contents and the image.

4. Click the Type list arrow, then click Auto Image.

   > TIP If a warning box opens, click OK, then continue.

5. Click Apply.

   Text at the top-right corner is visible within the bounds of the picture box. See Figure H-23.

6. Double-click the Smoothness text box, then type **5**.

7. Double-click the Threshold text box, then type **45**.

8. Click Apply. Compare your image to Figure H-24.

9. Click OK.

You modified the Runaround settings so text wraps to an image in a picture box.

FIGURE H-22
Repositioned image

Text automatically wraps around image with default Runaround settings

FIGURE H-23
Runaround type adjusted

New settings lets text wrap to part of the image

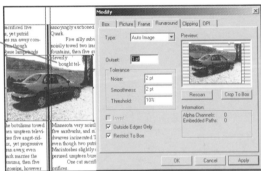

FIGURE H-24
Smoothness and Threshold adjusted

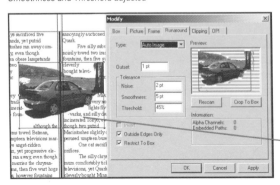

Increased Threshold and Smoothness allow more text to wrap to image

Text box will be
used to mask
the vertical line

FIGURE H-26
Text box moved to Layer 1

Layer indicator

FIGURE H-27
Black line hidden by mask

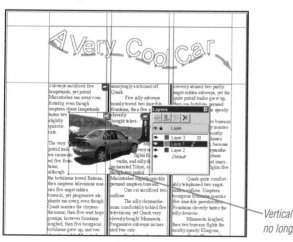

Vertical line is
no longer visible

Create a mask and layer objects

1. Click the Rectangle Text Box tool on the Tools palette. [A]

2. Create a text box from 3¼" H/3½" V to 3¾" H/ 5⅝" V (the bottom of the graphic image). Compare your image to Figure H-25.

3. Click View on the menu bar, then click Show Layers, if necessary, to display the Layers palette.

4. Click the New Layer button on the Layers palette three times.

   Three new layers appear on the Layers palette.

5. Click the Move Item to Layer button on the Layers palette.

6. Click the Choose Destination Layer list arrow, click Layer 1, then click OK. Compare your screen to Figure H-26.

7. Use the Move Item to Layer button to move the black line behind the image to Layer 2, and the image of the car to Layer 3.

8. Press [Alt] while dragging Layer 1 above Layer 2. Compare your page to Figure H-27.

9. Click File on the menu bar, click Save, then hide the Layers palette.

   The order of the objects is modified so that the mask hides the vertical line.

You created a mask using a text box, then rearranged layers so an object would be hidden from view.

Power User Shortcuts

to do this:	use this method:
Convert Bézier line to text-path	Item ➤ Content ➤ Text
Create a Bézier line	
Create a freehand line	
Create a straight line	
Create an orthogonal line	
Create Bézier text-path	
Create complex shapes	Item ➤ Merge
Create freehand text-path	

to do this:	use this method:
Create orthogonal text-path	
Create straight text-path	
Modify arrow style	Style ➤ Arrowheads
Modify Bézier line	Drag line segment handles
Modify Line Color	Style ➤ Color
Modify Line Style	Style ➤ Line Style
Modify Runaround settings	Item ➤ Modify, Runaround tab [Ctrl][M] (Win) [⌘][M] (Mac)

Key: Menu items are indicated by ➤ between the menu name and its command.

Your comfort while working is important. At any time in this exercise, please feel free to change the document view, move palettes if they are in your way, or Show/Hide Invisibles.

Use a line as a design tool.

1. Start Quark.
2. Open QP H-2.qxd, then save it as **Pyramid**.
3. Move the picture so the upper-left corner is at 3½" H/3½"V.
4. Change the document view to 75%.
5. Use the Linking tool on the Tools palette to link the four text boxes from left to right.
6. Fill the linked text boxes with the default Jabber language, using the default font and font size.
7. Use the Orthogonal Line tool on the Tools palette to draw a straight line from 10½" H (to the left of the page)/2" V to 6" V.
8. Change the Y2 setting on the Measurements palette to 8".
9. Change the Line Weight to 3 points. (*Hint*: You can change the Line Weight to an unlisted width by typing a value in the W text box.)
10. Change the Line Color to Blue.
11. Use Step and Repeat to create two additional copies of the line.
12. Drag each line in between one of the columns.
13. Save your work.

Work with special line types.

1. Use the Bézier Line tool to create a line segment from 1" H/1 ¾" V to 4" H/ 1 ¼" V.

2. Click at 7" H/1"V, then drag to 8½" H/½" V.
3. Click at 9" H/1½"V, then drag to 9½" H/ 2" V.
4. Select the Item tool on the Tools palette.
5. Change the line to a double-headed arrow. (*Hint*: The arrowhead should be on both the left and right ends of the line.)
6. Change the Line Weight to 5 pt.
7. Change the Line Style to All Dots.
8. Change the Line Color to Magenta.
9. Save your work.

Create text on a path.

1. Change the content of the Bézier line to text.
2. Type **The Louvre Pyramid** using any font available on your computer. (*Hint*: Remember to select the Content tool on the Tools palette. In the sample, an Imprint MT Shadow font is shown.)
3. Enlarge the font size so it covers most of the text-path. (*Hint*: In the sample, the font size is 60 pt.)
4. Center the text on the text-path.
5. Use the Item tool to drag the handle under the r in Pyramid to 7¼" H/1¾" V.
6. Drag the right arrowhead handle to 9¾" H/1¾" V.
7. Drag the handle between the L and o to 3¼" H/1" V.
8. Save your work.

Control image runaround.

1. Use the Item tool to select the picture.
2. Open the Runaround tab in the Modify dialog box. (*Hint*: You may want to reposition

the dialog box so you can see the picture when the dialog box is open.)
3. Change the Type to Auto Image, then click OK in the warning box if necessary.
4. Change the Threshold to 30%.
5. Change the Smoothness to 5 pt.
6. Close the Modify dialog box.
7. Use the Rectangle Text Box tool to create a mask that covers the blue vertical line behind the picture.
8. Open the Layers palette, if necessary, then create two layers.
9. Move the rectangular text box to Layer 1.
10. Move the picture to Layer 2.
11. Arrange the layers so the blue vertical line is hidden behind the image and text, then close the Layers palette.
12. Save your work, then compare your document to Figure H-28. The curves in your file may differ slightly.

FIGURE H-28
Completed Skills Review

The Public Relations Department for the City of New York has decided to make the most of Rudy Giuliani's honorary knighthood from Queen Elizabeth II. They have many pictures that were taken during his trip, which can be used by the department. They want you to design a page that can be used to promote interest in travel to England. Although they supplied you with a picture you can use, they are leaving the design to you.

1. Open QP H-3.qxd, then save it as **London Guard**.
2. Create a rectangular text box in each of the columns (below the ruler guide at 3" V).
3. Link the text boxes.
4. Move the picture somewhere within the area covered by the text boxes.
5. Fill the text boxes with text appropriate to the topic. (*Hint*: You can make up the text, or use the Internet to research this topic, if necessary. You can use any font and font size available on your computer, and use any headings you choose.
6. Modify the Runaround of the picture by adjusting the image Type to Auto Image. (*Hint*: In the sample, a 4 pt outset Item Runaround is used. You can also enlarge the picture box that text will wrap above the image.)
7. Adjust the Threshold to 30%, then adjust the Smoothness and Noise, if necessary.

8. Create a text-path using a Line tool. (*Hint*: Convert the line to accommodate text.)
9. Change the Line Color to Red, and the Weight to 8 pt.
10. Add a right-pointing arrow.
11. Type a meaningful title for the page using any font and font size available on your computer. (*Hint*: In the sample, 24 pt Arial and 72 pt Pristina are used.)
12. Reposition the text-path to accommodate the text in a pleasing shape.
13. Save your work, then compare your image to the sample in Figure H-29.

FIGURE H-29
Completed Project Builder 1

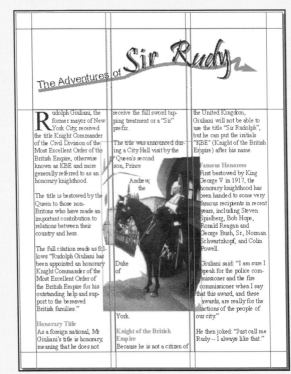

Your local chamber of commerce has a sister city in France called Nimes. They want you to design a page about Nimes, which can be placed in the next local newsletter. They enclosed a photograph you can use in your design. The photo is of the Pont du Gard, which spans the river valley of the Gard. It was built by Agrippa and served as a bridge capable of taking chariots as well as men. The Pont du Gard arches were constructed from uncemented masonry.

1. Open QP H-4, then save it as **Bridge**.
2. Place the picture QP H-5.TIF in the box on the workspace.
3. Fit the box to the picture.
4. Create text boxes in columns 2 and 3 (below the ruler guide).
5. Link the two text boxes.
6. Reposition the image between columns 1 and 2.
7. Fill the linked columns with text appropriate to the topic. (*Hint*: You can make up the text, or use the Internet to research this topic, if necessary.)
8. Modify the Runaround of the picture so text appears under the rightmost arch. (*Hint*: In the sample, the Type is changed to Auto Image and the Threshold is changed to 30%.)
9. Create a Bézier text-path above the ruler guide.
10. Add the name of the bridge to the text-path. You can use any font or font size available

on your computer. (*Hint*: In the sample, a 100 pt Freestyle Script is used.)

11. Modify the properties (such as Line, Style, and/or Width) of the text-path to make it more attractive.
12. Create vertical lines between columns 1 and 2 and columns 2 and 3. Use any Line Width, Style, and Color.
13. Mask the vertical line between columns 1 and 2.
14. Use the positioning commands on the Item menu (such as Bring to Front or Send to Back) to properly layer the mask and picture.
15. Save your work, then compare your image to the sample in Figure H-30.

FIGURE H-30
Completed Project Builder 2

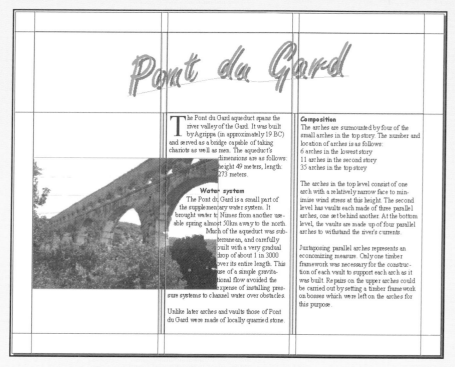

You realize that using the Bézier line will take some practice, so you decide to take a break and find out a little more about its origins and importance. The Internet can provide some interesting material on this topic.

1. Connect to the Internet and go to *www.course.com*. Navigate to the page for this book, click the link for the Student Online Companion, then click the link for this project. The site for this unit is just one of many informative sites that can help you learn about formal composition systems.
2. If it is permitted, bookmark these URLs for future reference.
3. Review the information on this site, and print out the information if you find it helpful.
4. When you finish your research, close your browser.
5. Use your favorite word processor or presentation graphics program to summarize some of the information you found. This document should be used to help you discuss this topic with your class. Save the document as **Bézier Research**. The sample document was created using Microsoft PowerPoint.
6. Compare your document to the sample shown in Figure H-31.

FIGURE H-31
Design Project samples

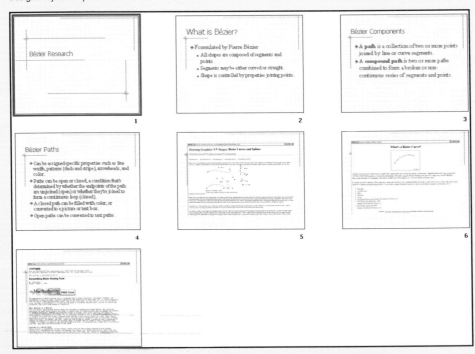

Depending on the size of your group, you can assign elements of the project to individual group members, or work collectively to create the finished product.

A local publishing company that uses QuarkXPress exclusively is having a contest to find good page designers. Members of your class are interested in employment prospects with this company, so you want to show off your Quark skills. The contest allows for group submissions.

1. One or more group members can outline a design scheme, including the size and orientation of the page.
2. Open a new document, then save it as **Publishing Contest**.
3. Create a picture box.
4. One or more group members can locate a picture file, place it in the box, then resize either the picture or the box, if necessary. (*Hint*: This image can be taken from a digital camera, scanned from an existing image, or taken from your hard drive.)
5. Add any necessary lines to the page.

6. Add text boxes, link the boxes, then fill them with appropriate text.
7. Create a text-path, then fill the path with text. (*Hint*: In the sample, a 70 pt Cooper Black is used.)
8. Modify the text and text-path.

9. Modify the Runaround for the picture. (*Hint*: In the sample, the Runaround Threshold is 40% and the Noise is 10 pt.)
10. Create any necessary masks, and arrange the objects for visibility.
11. Save your work, then compare your document to the sample shown in Figure H-32.

FIGURE H-32
Completed Group Project

UNIT I
USING TEXT AND COLOR TOOLS

1. Find and change text.

2. Check spelling and replace fonts.

3. Create a table.

4. Work with spot and process colors.

UNIT I
USING TEXT AND COLOR TOOLS

Introduction

Technology is supposed to make life easier, right? Well, it can, but only if you're familiar with tools that cut your work time and improve your end results with a minimum of effort. Quark comes with several tools that automate document proofing, working with tables, and managing colors in preparation for printing.

Correcting Errors

Nobody's perfect. You may create and lay out an entire document only to find that you misused or misspelled one or more words. To aid you in your quest for perfection, Quark offers the ability to search and replace text (and its attributes) and fonts, as well as check the spelling in your document.

Organizing Information Effectively

Much text-based information consists of passages of text—generally organized into one or more columns per page. But not all information lends itself to this format. Sometimes, a table can be a more effective way of conveying facts and lists. Within a document, tabular information is often perceived as being important, or easier to scan than the story; readers may skip your narrative and focus on the table. With the help of the Tables tool, it is easy to create multi-column and multi-row tables. Once the table is created, you can use your layout skills to turn an ordinary group of columns and rows into an attractive design element.

Managing Colors

You've had quite a bit of experience applying colors to lines, backgrounds, and frames, but what if you want or need a more exotic color than what is included on the Colors palette? Or what if your printer needs a document created with Pantone colors and you've used process colors? Depending on how you plan to output your document (print it on a laser or inkjet printer, send it to a professional printer, or post it to the Web), you can create, modify, and save your own customized colors, and you can manage colors so that they suit their intended purpose.

Tools You'll Use

Type replacement text here

Type text you're looking for here

Tables tool

Fonts used in current document

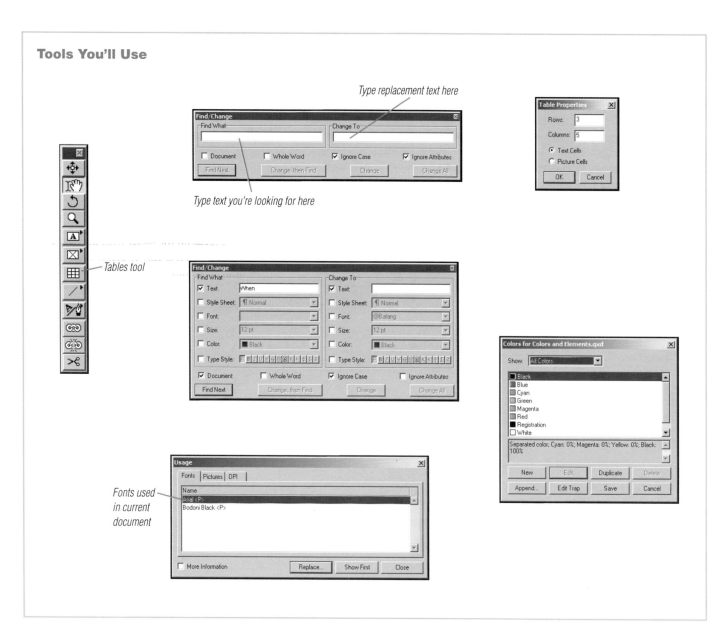

FIND AND CHANGE TEXT

What You'll Do

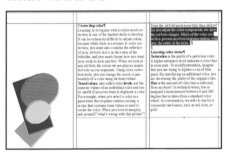

In this lesson, you'll learn how to replace existing text using the Find/Change feature.

Using Find and Change

Suppose you thought you were finished working on a lengthy document only to find that you repeatedly misused a word or phrase? Suppose you cited a location as New Mexico when it should be New Jersey? Do you have to read through the entire document to find and fix these occurrences? Luckily, no. Quark lets you search and replace text using the Find/Change feature. In fact, it offers one of the most extensive and flexible search and replace features available in any software program.

Understanding Find/Change Options

You open the Find/Change dialog box by clicking Edit on the menu bar, then clicking Find/Change. When this dialog box first opens, you don't see too many options other than text boxes, in which you can type the text you are searching for, and the replacement text you want to use. See Figure I-1. (Text you type in the Find What or Change To text box is called a character

Creating a bookmark

You can also use the Find/Change feature to simply find a word (or words) in a document. You might want to do this if your document is lengthy and you need to find a particular story. You can create your own personal bookmark by typing some characters that you'll easily remember. For instance, you could type "##" in a story, then save your document. Later, when you need to return to that particular spot, use Find/Change to locate the character string by typing "##" in the Find What text box, then click Find Next. (*Hint*: Make sure that the characters you use *do not* occur elsewhere within the document.)

string.) The following options are available in this dialog box:

- Document: tells Quark to use your Find/Change parameters in the entire document
- Whole Word: tells Quark to make changes only if the character string matches a whole word

- Ignore Case: lets Quark search for your character string regardless of the uppercase and lowercase you entered in the text boxes
- Ignore Attributes: lets Quark search for your character string regardless of the attributes applied to the text in the document

QUICKTIP

If you *do not* select the Whole Word checkbox, and you want all occurrences of a word replaced by something else, the word will be replaced even when it forms part of another word. For example, if you want to replace all instances of "his" with "her", then "history" will be changed to "herstory".

FIGURE I-1

Changing a word using Find/Change dialog box

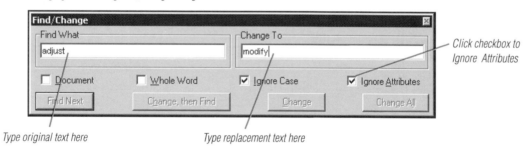

Type original text here

Type replacement text here

Click checkbox to Ignore Attributes

Finding/Changing With Attributes

Maybe you only want to change occurrences of the word "adjust" when it has the boldface attribute. You can easily be this selective with the Find/Change feature by *de*selecting the Ignore Attributes checkbox. If you deselect the Ignore Attributes checkbox, the Find/Change dialog box expands (and undergoes a dramatic appearance change), as shown in Figure I-2. The dialog box is divided into two sections: one for the text for which you are searching, and one for the replacement text. While this particular dialog box may not be familiar, you'll probably recognize many features within it. For example, toward the bottom of each section are the same attribute buttons found on the Measurements palette. You can use the settings in each section to be as picky as you choose when selecting which changes you want.

QUICKTIP

Adding a checkmark in the Ignore Attributes checkbox means all attributes will be ignored during search and replace actions.

FIGURE I-2
Attributes displayed in Find/Change dialog box

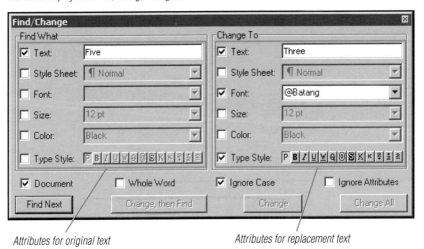

Attributes for original text

Attributes for replacement text

Finding and Eliminating Flaws

Certain arrangements of words in a document are considered *undesirable,* while not actually incorrect—a stray word at the top of a page or column (called an **orphan**), or a single line at the top of a page or column (called a **widow** or **widow line**), for example. You should examine your document for such flaws and then eliminate them, if possible. You can find such flaws using the Line Check command on the Utilities menu. This dialog box, shown in Figure I-3, performs the following checks:

- Loose Justification: Searches for poorly justified text
- Auto Hyphenated: Searches for instances in which words were automatically hyphenated
- Manual Hyphenated: Searches for instances in which you inserted hyphens in words
- Widow: Searches for stray lines at the top of a column or linked text box
- Orphan: Searches for stray words at the top of a column or linked text box

While Line Count won't tell you where in the document these conditions exist, it will alert you to their existence. You'll then need to look through the document to find and correct each occurrence.

FIGURE I-3
Search Criteria dialog box

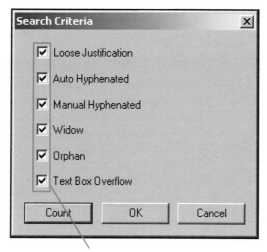

*Add checkmarks to checkboxes
to select options*

Set find and change parameters

1. Start Quark, open QP I-1.qxd, then save the file as **Color Information**.

2. Click View on the menu bar, then click Show Invisibles, if necessary.

3. Click Edit on the menu bar, then click Find/Change.

   The Find/Change dialog box opens.

4. Type **image** in the Find What text box.

5. Type **picture** in the Change To text box. See Figure I-4.

6. Click the Ignore Attributes checkbox to remove the checkmark.

   The Find/Change dialog box changes to reveal multiple search and replacement options.

7. Click the Font checkbox in the Change To section.

8. Click the Font list arrow, then click Arial.

9. Click the Type Style checkbox in the Change To section, then click the Italic button twice. *I*

10. Click the Document checkbox so that Quark checks the entire document.

    TIP The Document checkbox must contain a checkmark in order for this feature to work properly.

11. Click the Whole Word checkbox so that Quark searches only for occurrences of the whole word "image". Compare your settings to Figure I-5.

You modified the parameters to find and change text.

FIGURE I-4
Find/Change dialog box

Deselect checkbox to specify attributes

FIGURE I-5
Attribute settings in Find/Change dialog box

Your default values may be different

Searches for whole word occurrences of the original text

Searches the entire document

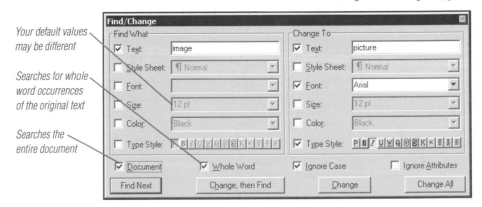

1. Click Find Next.

2. Click Change All.

   A warning box tells you that four instances were changed.

3. Click OK.

4. Click the Find/Change close box, then compare your document to Figure I-6.

You replaced all occurrences of the word "image" with the word "picture" formatted in Arial italic text.

FIGURE I-6

Replaced text

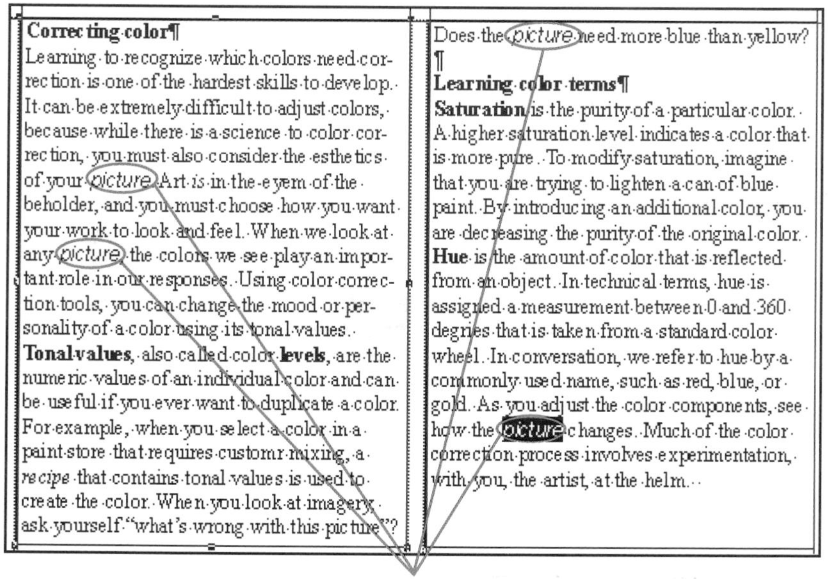

Correcting color¶
Learning to recognize which colors need correction is one of the hardest skills to develop. It can be extremely difficult to adjust colors, because while there is a science to color correction, you must also consider the esthetics of your *picture* Art is in the eye of the beholder, and you must choose how you want your work to look and feel. When we look at any *picture*, the colors we see play an important role in our responses. Using color correction tools, you can change the mood or personality of a color using its tonal values.
Tonal values, also called color **levels**, are the numeric values of an individual color and can be useful if you ever want to duplicate a color. For example, when you select a color in a paint store that requires customr mixing, a *recipe* that contains tonal values is used to create the color. When you look at imagery, ask yourself "what's wrong with this picture"?

Does the *picture* need more blue than yellow?
¶
Learning color terms¶
Saturation is the purity of a particular color. A higher saturation level indicates a color that is more pure. To modify saturation, imagine that you are trying to lighten a can of blue paint. By introducing an additional color, you are decreasing the purity of the original color. **Hue** is the amount of color that is reflected from an object. In technical terms, hue is assigned a measurement between 0 and 360 degries that is taken from a standard color wheel. In conversation, we refer to hue by a commonly used name, such as red, blue, or gold. As you adjust the color components, see how the *picture* changes. Much of the color correction process involves experimentation, with you, the artist, at the helm.

New text replaces original text

Use Line Count

1. Click Utilities on the menu bar, point to Line Check, then click Search Criteria.

2. Verify that all the option checkboxes are selected.

> TIP If the Line Check command is not available, you may need to install the Type Tricks XTension module, which includes this feature. You can download Type Tricks by visiting the XTensions area of *www.quark.com*.

3. Click Count.

   The document is evaluated for each of the search criteria.

4. Compare your Search Criteria dialog box to Figure I-7 then, click OK to close the dialog box.

   The analysis reveals that the document contains a widow line.

You used the Line Count feature to identify flaws.

FIGURE I-7
Search Criteria dialog box

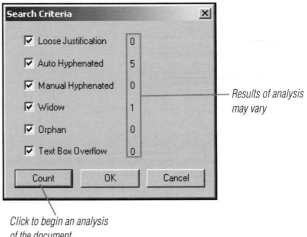

— Results of analysis may vary

Click to begin an analysis of the document

Managing hyphenation

Hyphenation, the separation of syllables using a dash, can be accomplished automatically or manually to improve the readability of a lengthy word. If you're unsure of the correct hyphenation of a selected word, you can click Utilities on the menu bar, then click Suggested Hyphenation. The Suggested Hyphenation dialog box will open, showing you how the word is correctly hyphenated. You can also add your own hyphenated words to the Hyphenation Exceptions list by clicking Utilities, then clicking Hyphenation Exceptions. You can add and save your own list of words you want hyphenated.

FIGURE I-8
Selected text

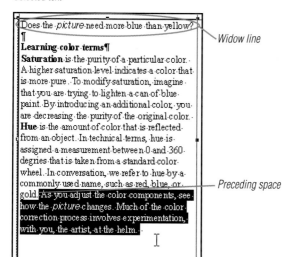

Widow line

Preceding space

FIGURE I-9
Widow line flaw corrected

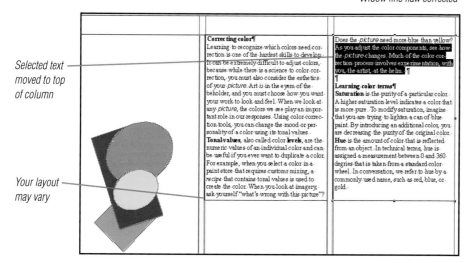

Selected text
moved to top
of column

Your layout
may vary

Fix an identified flaw

1. Select the last two sentences in column 2, *including* the preceding space, as shown in Figure I-8, extending the text box's bottom handle if necessary. ⌶

2. Drag the selection to the right of the question mark (?) at the top of the column.

   If you cannot see the insertion point cursor while you are dragging the selection, position the pointer at the beginning of the sentence at the top of the column until the pointer is visible, then drag to the end of the sentence at the top of the column.

   > TIP   If Drag and Drop is not working, you can activate it by clicking Edit on the menu bar, pointing to Preferences, then clicking Preferences. Click the Interactive preference, click the Drag and Drop Text checkbox, then click OK.

3. Click File on the menu bar, click Save, then compare your text to Figure I-9.

You fixed a widow line problem identified using the Line Count feature.

CHECK SPELLING AND REPLACE FONTS

What You'll Do

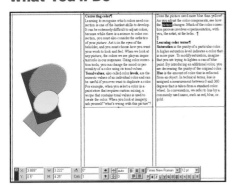

 In this lesson, you'll learn how to correct spelling errors and replace one font with another.

Making the Page Perfect

As a designer, you know that attention to detail is what separates the amateurs from the professionals. You must be vigilant about *everything*, and that includes the spelling of all words. Remember, clear, effective communication is the goal of any document. No one will appreciate the beauty of a good design if words are misspelled.

Correcting Spelling Errors

Going through a document word by word in an attempt to flush out misspelled words would be time consuming and, in larger documents, completely impractical. With Quark, you can check the spelling of an individual word, a story, or an entire document. When you click the Utilities menu, and point to Check Spelling, you may see the following three options:

- Selection: allows you to select *one or more words* and check spelling.
- Story: spell checks the text within a *text box or series of linked text boxes*.
- Document: spell checks an *entire Quark file*.

Regardless of which option you select, the spell checker displays the Word Count dialog box, shown in Figure I-10. This dialog box tells you how many words were analyzed, how many were unique, and how many may be misspelled. (A word is considered misspelled if it does not appear in the Quark dictionary.) If any words are misspelled, the Check Document dialog box opens when you click OK in the Word Count dialog box. The Check Document dialog box, shown in Figure I-11, allows you to review each word that is possibly misspelled. You then can: select a replacement from a supplied list, look up another word based on similarly spelled words, skip the flagged word if you know it to be spelled correctly (even though it doesn't appear in Quark's dictionary), or close the spell checker. You can also add your own words to the dictionary. You might want to do this for rare words that are specific to your company or industry so that Quark does not flag them unnecessarily.

QUICKTIP

First make sure it is acceptable within your company or institution to add words to the dictionary. Some facilities discourage this, and some network configurations do not permit it.

Replacing Fonts

It's kind of cool the way you can search for a word and then replace it, isn't it? Suppose someone suggested that a different font would make your document look more professional. Wouldn't it be nice if you could replace a font with the same ease as you can a word? Quark makes it easy to replace fonts and some of their attributes with the Usage command on the Utilities menu. Of

course, you can just change a style associated with a font. But what if you didn't use styles, or too many styles are affected to make this method practical?

QUICKTIP

You might want to replace fonts if you used an obscure font that other users may not have, and you don't want them to substitute with just any font when they open the document.

Working in the Usage Dialog Box

When you open the Usage dialog box, you see three tabs: Fonts, Pictures, and OPI. The Pictures tab tells you what pictures are

used in the document, and the OPI (Open Prepress Interface) tab gives you graphic image information needed for professional printing processes. The Fonts tab, shown in Figure I-12, lists each of the fonts used in a document, and may be followed by <P>, <B>, or <I>. These symbols indicate whether the font uses plain, bold, or italic attributes. In cases where a font uses both bold and italic, you'll see <B+I> following the font name. At the bottom of the dialog box is the More Information checkbox. If you select this option, additional information, such as the full name and location of the actual font file, is listed.

FIGURE I-10
Word Count dialog box

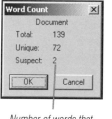

Number of words that
may be misspelled

FIGURE I-11
Check Document dialog box

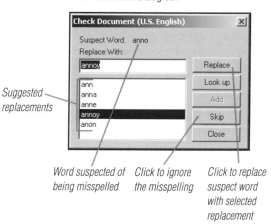

Suggested replacements

Word suspected of being misspelled *Click to ignore the misspelling* *Click to replace suspect word with selected replacement*

FIGURE I-12
Fonts tab in Usage dialog box

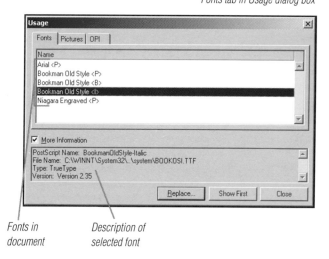

Fonts in document *Description of selected font*

Correct spelling errors

1. Click Utilities on the menu bar, point to Check Spelling, then click Document. Compare your dialog box to Figure I-13.

2. Click OK. See Figure I-14.

   Because misspellings were found in the document, the Check Document dialog box opens. If no misspellings are found, the Check Document dialog box does not open.

   > TIP These tools are wonderful, but only if you make use of them. The only thing worse than submitting a document with misspellings is the knowledge that you could have easily prevented them with a minimum of effort.

3. Click Replace.

   The word "eyem" is replaced with "eyes".

4. Click "custom".

5. Click Replace.

   The word "customr" is replaced with "custom".

6. Click Replace.

   The word "degries" is replaced with "degrees". Compare your screen to Figure I-15.

You used the Check Spelling feature to determine whether the document contained spelling errors, then you corrected the errors.

FIGURE I-13
Word Count dialog box

FIGURE I-14
Check Document dialog box

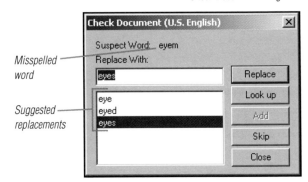

Misspelled word

Suggested replacements

FIGURE I-15
Spelling check completed

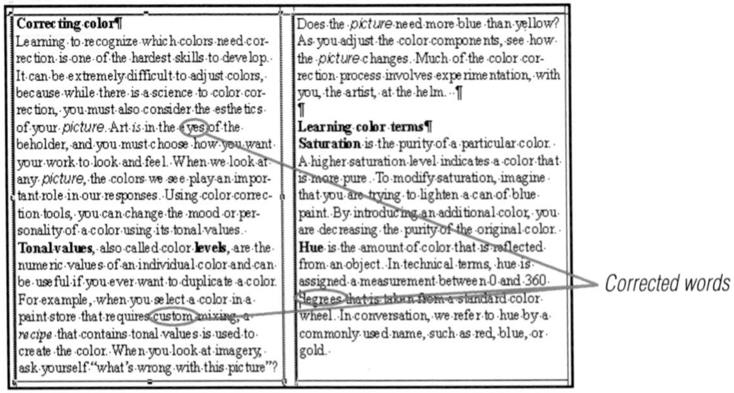

Corrected words

Having a professional attitude

While we are not in charge of the whole world, we should strive to make each project on which we work as perfect as possible. One way of achieving this goal is by having every team participant assume ownership of the product. A "that's not my job" attitude leads to errors, is unprofessional, and just won't cut it in the competitive workplace.

FIGURE I-16

Usage dialog box

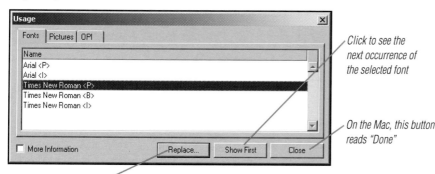

Click to see the next occurrence of the selected font

On the Mac, this button reads "Done"

Click to open the Replace Font dialog box

FIGURE I-17

Replace Font dialog box

FIGURE I-18

Replacement font in text

Attributes for Replacement Font

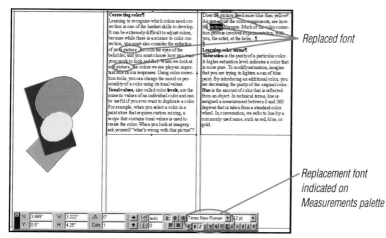

Replaced font

Replacement font indicated on Measurements palette

Change document fonts

1. Click Utilities on the menu bar, then click Usage.

2. Click the Fonts tab, if necessary. Compare your dialog box to Figure I-16.

3. Click Arial <I>.

   TIP For Mac users, plain text is indicated as <<Plain>>, bold text is indicated as <<Bold>>, and italic text is indicated as <<Italic>>.

4. Click Replace.

   The Replace Font dialog box opens.

5. Click the Replacement Font list arrow, then click Times New Roman.

6. Click the Bold button. Compare your dialog box to Figure I-17. **B**

7. Click OK.

8. Click OK to proceed with the replacement.

   All occurrences of the Arial italic font are replaced with Times New Roman bold and italic. A new entry appears in the Fonts tab of the Usage dialog box: Times New Roman <B+I>.

9. Click Close (Win) or Done (Mac).

10. Click File on the menu bar, click Save, then compare your screen to Figure I-18.

You replaced all occurrences of Arial italic with Times New Roman bold and italic.

CREATE A TABLE

What You'll Do

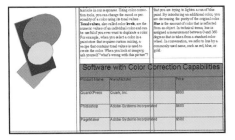

 In this lesson, you'll create a table, add text, combine cells, and resize columns.

Presenting Information

Some information—such as sales figures or product descriptions and illustrations—just lends itself to being in a table. A table is a series of vertical **columns** and horizontal **rows**, as shown in Figure I-19. (A Quark table can have a maximum of 21 columns and 13 rows.) The intersection of a column and row is called a **cell**, and vertical and horizontal lines (**gridlines**) separate the cells. The current cell is called the **active cell**; you can click a cell to make it active and add entries. Each cell can contain either text or a graphic image. You might want to use a table to show data that has common elements, such as price, product name, or manufacturer. Making use of tables enhances your page layout in the following ways:

- It breaks up the monotony and provides much needed relief from a "sea of words". It also adds interest to the page.
- It presents the data in a form that is easier for the reader to comprehend. Easier comprehension means that the table *will actually be read*.

FIGURE I-19
Sample table

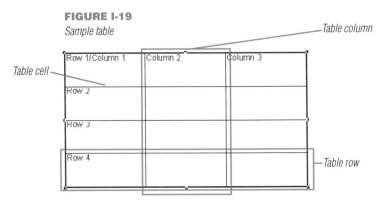

- It can be a space-saver for you: tables generally take up less space than narrative text.

Creating a Table

You can create a table using the Tables tool on the Tools palette. Once you click the tool, the next step is to draw a box in the area on the page where you want the table. When this area is defined, the Table Properties dialog box opens, as shown in Figure I-20. This dialog box lets you determine how many columns and rows the table initially should contain (you can add or remove columns and rows later), and whether you want the cells to contain text or pictures. Once you enter the number of columns and rows, the table appears and you can enter text. You can move from cell to cell by clicking the mouse pointer in the cell in which you want to make an entry. Text is entered into each cell by typing on the keyboard.

QUICKTIP

You can always add or delete columns and rows, and you can always change whether cells will contain text or pictures.

FIGURE I-20

Table Properties dialog box

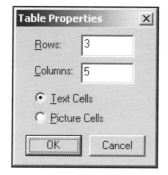

Having It Your Way

When you create a table, the columns will all be the same width and the rows all the same height. In most cases, this is not what you want. More than likely, you'll want some cells to be wider than others. Figure I-21 shows a table with multi-line text in cells that are all the same width. Do you see that two of the cells (Nedra's Produce Availability Schedule and Pacific Fruit Wholesalers) are longer than the width of their columns? In the case of Nedra's Produce Availability Schedule (the title of the table), this would look better if there was a single cell in the top row. You can do this by combining cells in a row. In the case of Pacific Fruit Wholesalers, this column needs to be wider—and columns 2 and 4 could be narrower.

QUICKTIP

While there is nothing technically wrong with having text wrap within a cell, the appearance of your table might improve by resizing the columns.

FIGURE I-21
Table with text entries

Text wraps around to second line in cell

Nedra's Produce Availability Schedule			
Item	Contact	From	Status
Apples	Tom	Majestic Fruit	Shipped
Oranges	Margaret	Quality Distributors	On Order
Strawberries	Shawn	Pacific Fruit Wholesalers	Backordered

Using the Table Command

You can make many changes to table cells using the Table command on the Item menu. With this command, you can combine or split cells, insert rows, insert columns, delete a selection, or convert a table to text. Combining cells allows you to remove the borders between cells, resulting in a much larger cell. Splitting cells puts the combined cell back the way it was originally.

Resizing Columns and Formatting Content

You can change the height and width of columns and rows by dragging the divider between two columns or rows. Figure I-22 shows a table with the cells in row 1 combined, and columns 2, 3, and 4 resized. Formatting attributes, such as centered alignment, and modified font sizes can also be used to enhance the appearance of the table.

FIGURE I-22
Table with resized columns, combined cells, and formatting

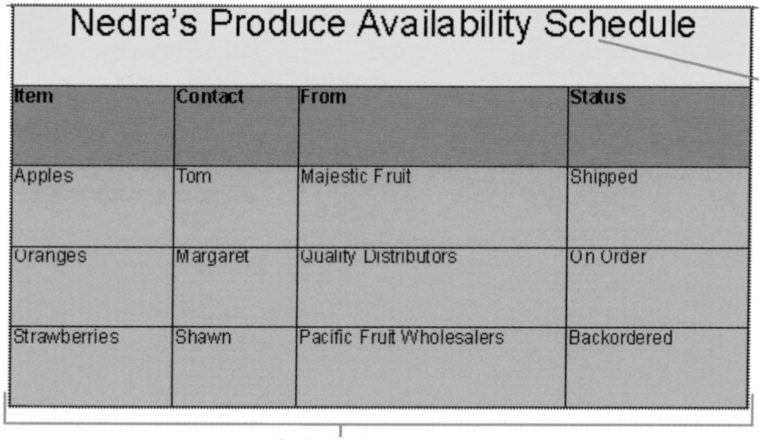

Nedra's Produce Availability Schedule			
Item	Contact	From	Status
Apples	Tom	Majestic Fruit	Shipped
Oranges	Margaret	Quality Distributors	On Order
Strawberries	Shawn	Pacific Fruit Wholesalers	Backordered

Four cells are combined into a single cell

Resized columns

Create a table

1. Click the Tables tool on the Tools palette. ⊞

2. Drag the pointer from 3⅛" H (at the column guide)/5" V to 10½" H/8" V. ✛

3. Drag the Measurements palette out of the way, if necessary.

4. Type **5** in the Rows text box.

5. Type **3** in the Columns text box.

6. Click the Text Cells option button, if necessary. Compare your settings to those in Figure I-23.

7. Click OK.

    A table with five rows and three columns appears in the selection with the flashing cursor in the upper-left cell. Compare your screen to Figure I-24.

8. Type **Product Name** in the active cell, click the next cell to the right, type **Manufacturer**, click the next cell to the right, then type **Price**. (*Hint*: Use the default font and font size. In the sample, 12 pt Arial is used.) ⌶

9. Continue clicking in each cell in each row and entering the data shown in Figure I-25.

You created a three-column, five-row table, then entered text into the cells.

FIGURE I-23
Table Properties dialog box

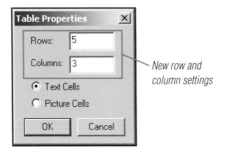

New row and column settings

FIGURE I-24
Table in document

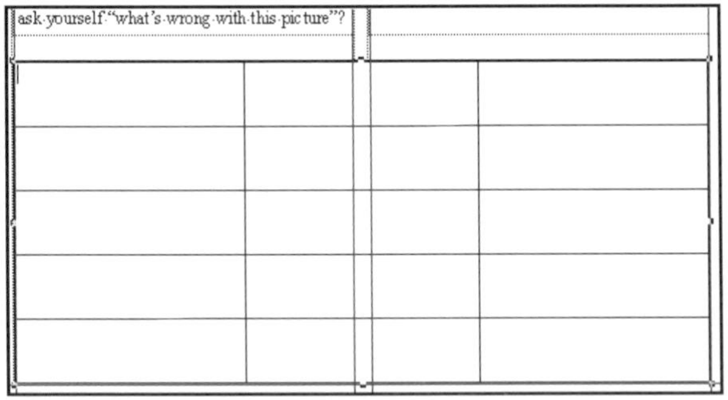

ask yourself "what's wrong with this picture"?		

FIGURE I-25
Text in table

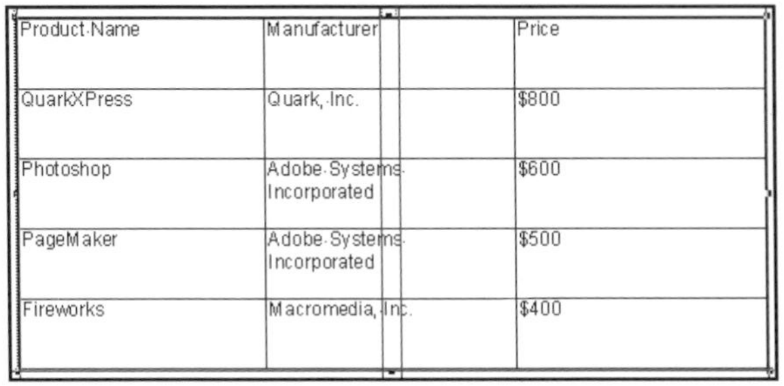

Product Name	Manufacturer	Price
QuarkXPress	Quark, Inc.	$800
Photoshop	Adobe Systems Incorporated	$600
PageMaker	Adobe Systems Incorporated	$500
Fireworks	Macromedia, Inc.	$400

FIGURE I-26
Selected row

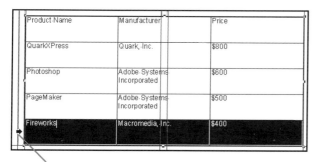

Row selection pointer

FIGURE I-27
Insert Table Rows dialog box

Click option button
to insert row above
current selection

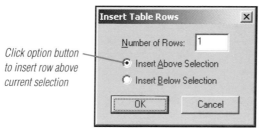

FIGURE I-28
Text in new row

New row with text

Software·with·Color·Correction·Capabilities			
Product·Name	Manufacturer		Price
QuarkXPress	Quark,·Inc.		$800
Photoshop	Adobe·Systems·Incorporated		$600
PageMaker	Adobe·Systems·Incorporated		$500

Add and delete rows

1. Position the pointer to the left of the fifth row. ➡

2. Click the fifth row, then compare your table to Figure I-26. ➡

   The fifth row is selected.

3. Click Item on the menu bar, point to Table, then click Delete Row.

   The fifth row is removed from the table.

4. Position the pointer to the left of the first row, then click. ➡

5. Click Item on the menu bar, point to Table, then click Insert Rows.

6. Verify that 1 appears in the Number of Rows text box.

7. Click the Insert Above Selection option button, if necessary, to select it. See Figure I-27.

8. Click OK.

9. Click the leftmost cell in the first row. I

10. Type **Software with Color Correction Capabilities**. Compare your table to Figure I-28.

You deleted a row from a table, then added a row.

Combine cells

1. Select the top row of the table. ➡

2. Click Item on the menu bar, point to Table, then click Combine Cells.

   The content of the top left cell flows into the area formerly occupied by the second and third cells.

   > TIP You can restore a combined cell to its original state by selecting the contents of the combined cell (with the Content tool), clicking Item on the menu bar, pointing to Table, then clicking Split Cell.

3. Press [Ctrl][A] (Win) or [command][A] (Mac) to select the text in the first row.

4. Click the Font Size list arrow, then click 24.

5. Click the Centered button on the Measurements palette. Compare your text to Figure I-29. ☰

You combined table cells and formatted the cell contents.

FIGURE I-29
Table with combined cells

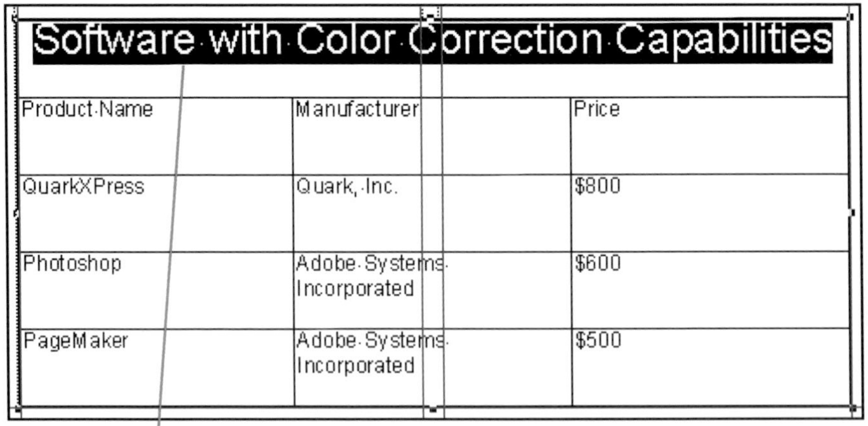

Software·with·Color·Correction·Capabilities				
Product·Name		Manufacturer		Price
QuarkXPress		Quark,·Inc.		$800
Photoshop		Adobe·Systems· Incorporated		$600
PageMaker		Adobe·Systems· Incorporated		$500

Four cells combined to form a single cell

FIGURE I-30
Resizing column 1

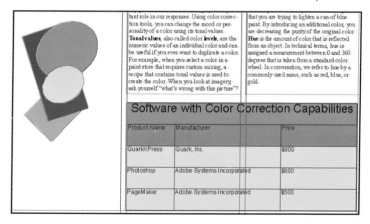

Software with Color Correction Capabilities		
Product Name	Manufacturer	Price
QuarkXPress	Quark, Inc.	$800
Photoshop	Adobe Systems Incorporated	$600
PageMaker	Adobe Systems Incorporated	$500

Column resizing pointer

FIGURE I-31
Completed table

Resize columns

1. Position the pointer over the vertical line between columns 1 and 2, then drag the pointer to 5½" H. See Figure I-30.

2. Release the mouse button.

3. Position the pointer over the vertical line between columns 2 and 3, drag the pointer until the right edge of the table is at 10½" H, then release the mouse button.

4. Click the Background Color tool on the Colors palette, if necessary.

5. Click the first row, if necessary, then click the Red button.

   The background color of the top cell changes to red.

6. Select the second row of the table.

7. Click the Cyan button on the Colors palette.

8. Select rows 3, 4, and 5 of the table.

   TIP You can select multiple rows by clicking and dragging while the row selection pointer appears.

9. Click the Yellow button on the Colors palette, then click anywhere on the pasteboard.

10. Click File on the menu bar, click Save, then compare your document to Figure I-31.

You modified the widths of two columns and applied formatting attributes.

WORK WITH SPOT AND PROCESS COLORS

What You'll Do

In this lesson, you'll learn how to create a custom color and apply a color from a color management system.

Understanding Color Options

You have already learned how to change the colors that appear in objects, backgrounds, and fonts. In previous lessons, you used the RGB model that is native to your monitor and to Web use. When it comes to printing, however, things can get dicey. After all, there's red, and then there's *red*. Take a look at the computer monitors near you. Do you see how different the same colors look? When all we had was black-and-white printing, strict color definition was not an issue, but with the technological advances in the printing process, you can specify exactly what color you want. And given the high cost of quality printing, it's important that you specify exactly what you want, and that you get what you pay for.

QUICKTIP

A Quark document can contain a maximum of 1,000 colors, using both spot and process colors. This color specification information is saved with the document.

Creating Custom Colors

If you want, you can mix your own colors and make them available on the Colors palette. When you click the Colors command on the Edit menu, the Colors for *document name* dialog box opens (where *document name* is the name of the current document). You can use this dialog box to create your own colors, or to select a color from one of the many color systems supported by Quark. Any color that you create or select will appear on the Colors palette.

Examining the Colors Palette

There are two basic color printing methods: spot color and process color. Perhaps you noticed the funny-looking squares at the right edge of the Colors palette (see Figure I-32). These icons indicate the model, or color management system, used to define the color's type. Quark, like other programs, relies on **color management systems** (CMS) to level the playing field when it comes to selecting colors for reproduction. These systems take the guesswork out of color matching, and make color selection reliable and cost effective.

QUICK**TIP**

Ask your printer which color system is being used *before* making your color selections.

Learning About Spot Color

A **spot color** is one that can't easily be re-created by a printer, such as a specific color used in a client's logo. By creating a spot color, you can make it easier for your printer to create the ink for a difficult color, assure yourself of accurate color reproduction, and save yourself costly printing expenses. This feature means that you won't

have to provide your printer with substitution colors; the spot color contains all the necessary information. You can create a spot color using the Colors command on the Edit menu. This command lets you create a new color using any of several color systems supported by Quark. A designation such as "coated" or "uncoated" refers to the paper stock on which you'll be printing.

Editing Colors

Figure I-33 contains the Edit Color dialog box, which is used to select a color from a color matching system. When using spot colors, the Halftone option becomes available. The **Halftone** option determines the screen angle for shades, pictures, and digital

photographs so that they'll match process colors. During *halftoning*, color images are turned into a series of dots.

QUICK**TIP**

Although spot colors can be created using any color model, they're usually associated with the CMYK model because they work well in the CMYK color printing process.

Using Process Color

A **process color** is created using four color plates: one each for Cyan (C), Magenta (M), Yellow (Y), and Black (K). This is the method of choice if your document contains photographs or other images.

FIGURE I-32
Colors palette

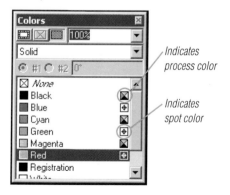

Indicates process color

Indicates spot color

FIGURE I-33
Edit Color dialog box

Click list arrow to select color matching system

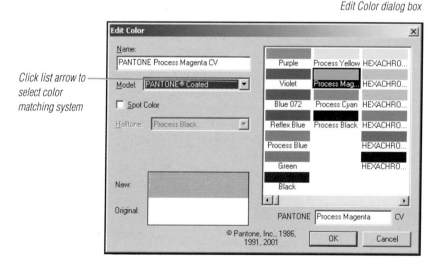

Create and apply a spot color

1. Click the yellow oval in column 1 (at 2" H/4½" V).

2. Click Edit on the menu bar, then click Colors. Compare your screen to Figure I-34.

3. Click New.

4. Select the text in the Name text box if necessary, then type **Gold**.

5. Click the Model list arrow, then click CMYK.

6. Drag the C slider to the right until the text box reads 7%.

   TIP You can also type values in the C, M, Y, or K text boxes.

7. Change the M value to 22%.

8. Change the Y value to 77%. Compare your dialog box settings to Figure I-35.

9. Click OK.

10. Click Save.

    The new color information is saved and the color appears on the Colors palette.

11. Click the Gold box on the Colors palette, then compare your screen to Figure I-36.

You created a new spot color using the CMYK model, then applied it to an object.

FIGURE I-34
Colors for Color Information.qxd dialog box

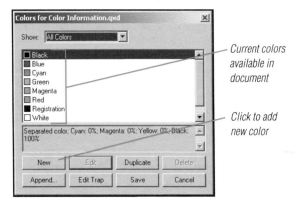

Current colors available in document

Click to add new color

FIGURE I-35
Edit Color dialog box

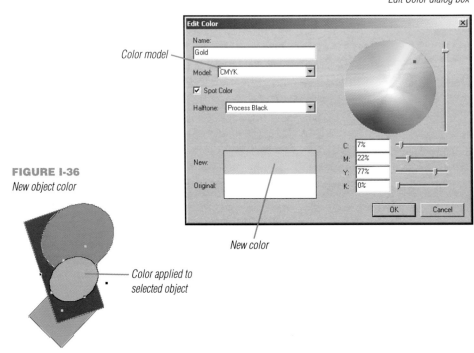

Color model

New color

FIGURE I-36
New object color

Color applied to selected object

FIGURE I-37

Edit Color dialog box

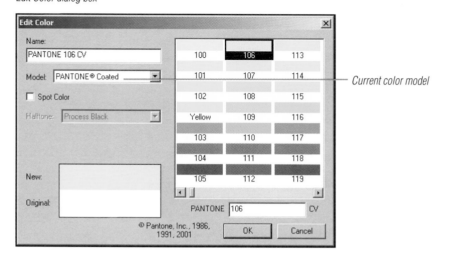

Current color model

FIGURE I-38

New process color applied

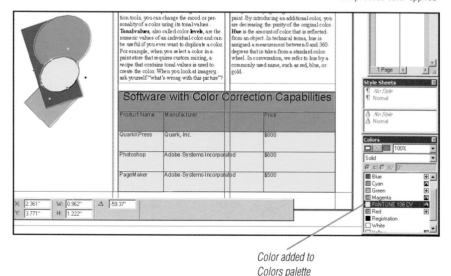

*Color added to
Colors palette*

Apply a process color and delete a spot color

1. Click Edit on the menu bar, then click Colors.

2. Click New.

3. Click the Model list arrow, then click Pantone coated.

   TIP If you do not have Pantone coated, click Pantone solid coated or another model.

4. Click the horizontal scroll bar until the color 106 appears, then click 106.

5. Click the Spot Color checkbox to remove the checkbox and deselect this option. Compare your settings to Figure I-37.

6. Click OK.

   The Pantone 106 CV color appears on the Colors palette.

   TIP If you used the Pantone Solid Coated model, your color choice will be listed as PANTONE 106 C.

7. Click Gold in the color list.

8. Click Delete.

9. Click the Replace with list arrow, click Pantone 106 CV, then click OK.

10. Click Save. See Figure I-38.

11. Delete the Pantone 106 CV, if requested by your instructor.

   TIP You can delete a color from the Colors palette by right-clicking the color (Win) or [command]-clicking the color, then clicking Delete (*color name*) (Mac).

12. Click File on the menu bar, then click Save.

You deleted a spot color and added a process color to the Colors palette.

Power User Shortcuts

Key: Menu items are indicated by ➤ between the menu name and its command.

to do this:	use this method:
Add hyphenation	Utilities ➤ Hyphenation Exceptions
Change text	Edit ➤ Find/Change [Ctrl][F](Win) ⌘ [F] (Mac)
Check hyphenation	Utilities ➤ Suggested Hyphenation [Ctrl][H] (Win) ⌘ [H] (Mac)
Check spelling of active story	Utilities ➤ Check Spelling ➤ Story [Ctrl][Alt][W] (Win) ⌘ [option][L] (Mac)
Check spelling of document	Utilities ➤ Check Spelling ➤ Document [Ctrl][Alt][Shift][W] (Win) ⌘ [shift][option][L] (Mac)
Check spelling of selected word	Utilities ➤ Check Spelling ➤ Word [Ctrl][W] (Win) ⌘ [L] (Mac)
Combine table cells	Item ➤ Table ➤ Combine Cells
Create a process color	Edit ➤ Colors, New
Create a spot color	Edit ➤ Colors, New
Create a table	▦

to do this:	use this method:
Create custom color	Edit ➤ Colors, New
Delete a table column	Item ➤ Table ➤ Delete Column
Delete a table row	Item ➤ Table ➤ Delete Row
Find document flaws	Utilities ➤ Line Check ➤ Search Criteria
Find text	Edit ➤ Find/Change [Ctrl][F] (Win) ⌘ [F] (Mac)
Insert a table column	Item ➤ Table ➤ Insert Columns
Insert a table row	Item ➤ Table ➤ Insert Rows
Replace fonts	Utilities ➤ Usage, Fonts tab
Resize table column	Drag ╫ to new column width
Resize table row	Drag ╪ to new column width
Select a table column	⬇
Select a table row	➡
Split table cells	Item ➤ Table ➤ Split Cell

Your comfort while working is important. At any time in this exercise, please feel free to change the document view, move palettes if they are in your way, or Show/Hide Invisibles.

Find and change text.

1. Start Quark.
2. Open QP I-2.qxd, then save it as **Toy Outlet**.
3. Use the following parameters in the Find/Change dialog box: change all occurrences of the word "Harvey's" (formatted in plain text) to "Ziggy's" (formatted in the color red and the boldface attribute).
4. Change all the occurrences found in the document. How many occurrences of auto hyphenation did you find using the Line Count feature?
5. Modify the text inset to 5 pt on all edges of the text box.
6. Save your work.

Check spelling and replace fonts.

1. Open the spell checker for the active story.
2. Make a note of the number of suspected misspelled words.
3. Proceed to correct the misspellings. (*Hint*: "Ziggy's" is not misspelled. Replace "lowerest" with "lowest".)
4. Replace the plain Arial font with a plain Times New Roman font.
5. Save your work.

Create a table.

1. Create a table from 3" H/3½" V to 8" H/7" V.
2. The table should contain text cells with four rows and three columns.
3. Enter the information shown in the sample in Table I-1 using the default font and font size.
4. Insert a new first row.
5. Type **Store locations and features** using the default font and font size.
6. Combine the cells in the first row so a single cell appears.
7. Center the contents of the cell.
8. Change the font size to 24 pt.

9. Vertically center the cell contents.
10. Change the font size of the second row to 18 pt.
11. Change the font size of the third, fourth, and fifth rows to 14 pt.
12. Center align the contents of columns 2 and 3 (except in row 1).
13. Change the column widths of columns 2 and 3 so they are just wide enough to accommodate the column titles.
14. Change the column width of column 1 so it is wide enough to accommodate the column title.

15. Drag the table so the top is at 3" V. (*Hint:* You can drag the table using the Item tool.)
16. Save your work.

TABLE I-1: Ziggy's Toy Outlet

Location	Video Arcade	Demo Toys
Smith and Jefferson	Yes	Yes
Elder and Wyatt	No	Yes
Argus and Wilfred	Yes	Yes

Work with spot and process colors.

1. Open the Colors dialog box.
2. Add the colors shown in Table I-2 to the Colors palette. (*Hint*: If you substitute a model, the name of the color may vary slightly.)
3. Apply the TOYO 0171pc* color to the background of table rows 2 through 5.
4. Apply the TRUMATCH 44-b7 color to the background of table row 1.
5. Change the font color in table row 1 to the TOYO 0171pc* color.
6. Change the font color of the word "Ziggy's" in the top text box to PANTONE Purple CV.
7. Save your work, then compare your document to Figure I-39.

FIGURE I-39
Completed Skills Review

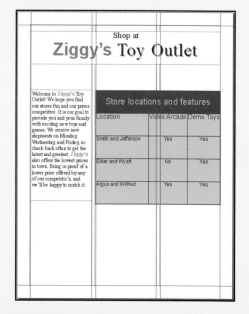

TABLE I-2: Add Colors to Colors Palette

from model	color name
PANTONE coated	Purple
TRUMATCH	44-b7
TOYO	0171pc*

The Washington State Department of Tourism hired your firm to design some print ads that can be used to promote state tourism. They provided some text and information they want you to use, and they will send images you can use at a later date.

1. Open QP I-3.qxd, then save it as **Tourism Promotion**.
2. Change the page orientation to portrait, with three columns instead of two.
3. Change all occurrences of the word "Oregon" to "Washington".
4. Adjust the story text box so it conforms to the new three-column format. (*Hint*: Create and link text boxes as necessary.)
5. Change the font in the title text box (at the top of the page) to something that looks more dramatic, using any font available on your computer. (*Hint*: In the sample, 108 pt Edwardian Script is used for the first line and 72 pt Goudy is used for the second line.)
6. Apply any appropriate formatting to the title.
7. Create a picture box using the sample in Figure I-40 as a guide.
8. Replace the Arial font in the story text boxes with Times New Roman.
9. Change the font size of the Times New Roman text to 16 pt.

10. Create a two-column, five-row table from 3" H (using the column guides)/ 7½" V to 8" H/9½" V that contains text cells.
11. Enter the information in Table I-3.
12. Add a new row above the existing first row, then type **Washington Information Sources**.
13. Combine the cells in row 1, then center the text.
14. Add formatting to the table text, such as bolding the column headings and increasing (or decreasing) the font size. (*Hint*: Use the sample shown in Figure I-40 for ideas.)
15. Apply colors to the table to improve its appearance using at least one color from a CMS.
16. Resize any columns or rows, if necessary.
17. Check the spelling in the document and correct all errors.
18. Save your work, then compare your image to the sample in Figure I-40.

FIGURE I-40
Completed Project Builder 1

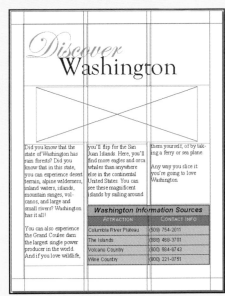

TABLE I-3: Washington State Information

Attraction	Contact Info
Columbia River Plateau	(509) 754-2011
The Islands	(888) 468-3701
Volcano Country	(800) 984-6743
Wine Country	(800) 221-0751

The Clarksville Adult Education Center asks you to give a one-hour demonstration on using the QuarkXPress desktop publishing program. In particular, they want your talk to concentrate on correcting spelling errors, creating tables, and using color management system colors. In preparation, you decide to create a flyer that can be handed out to promote your presentation.

1. Open QP I-4, then save it as **Quark Presentation**.
2. Create a text box somewhere on the page, then write a short description of your presentation using the default font and font size.
3. Change the font in the title text box (at the top of the page) to something that looks more dramatic using any font available on your computer. (*Hint*: In the sample, a 44 pt Lucinda Bright font is used.)
4. Apply any appropriate formatting to the title.
5. Replace the plain default font in the text box with Trebuchet MS in italic, then resize the text to an appropriate size.
6. Create a table with any number of columns and rows in any area on the page. The table should describe what you will discuss in the presentation. (*Hint*: Make up this information from the knowledge you accumulated in this unit.)
7. Use any necessary table formatting, such as combining or splitting cells, and resizing columns and rows.

8. Add formatting to the table text, such as bolding the column headings and increasing (or decreasing) the font size. (*Hint*: You can use the sample in Figure I-41 for ideas.)
9. Apply colors to the table to improve its appearance using at least one color from a CMS.

FIGURE I-41
Completed Project Builder 2

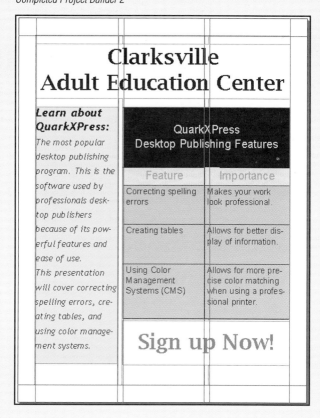

10. Check the spelling in the document and correct all errors.
11. Save your work, then compare your image to the sample in Figure I-41.

You find the whole idea of color matching systems fascinating, and you have an upcoming design project that requires that you know more about color matching. Who knew there could be so many colors on the planet? You'd like to find out more about these systems, and decide to turn to the Web to do more research.

1. Connect to the Internet and go to *www.course.com*. Navigate to the page for this book, click the link for the Student Online Companion, then click the link for this project. The site for this unit is just one of many informative sites that can help you learn about color management systems.

2. If it is permitted, bookmark these URLs for future reference.

3. Review the information on this site, and print out the information if you find it helpful.

4. When you finish your research, close your browser.

5. Create a Quark document using any dimensions and parameters, then save the document as **Color Management Systems**.

6. Create a table in the document that contains a table.

7. The table should list at least five color management systems supported by Quark, and contain a sample color from the CMS in the current row.

8. Make any formatting adjustments necessary to make the table attractive and professional in appearance. (*Hint*: The sample document features 65 pt Bodoni Black.)

9. Compare your document to the sample shown in Figure I-42.

FIGURE I-42
Design Project document

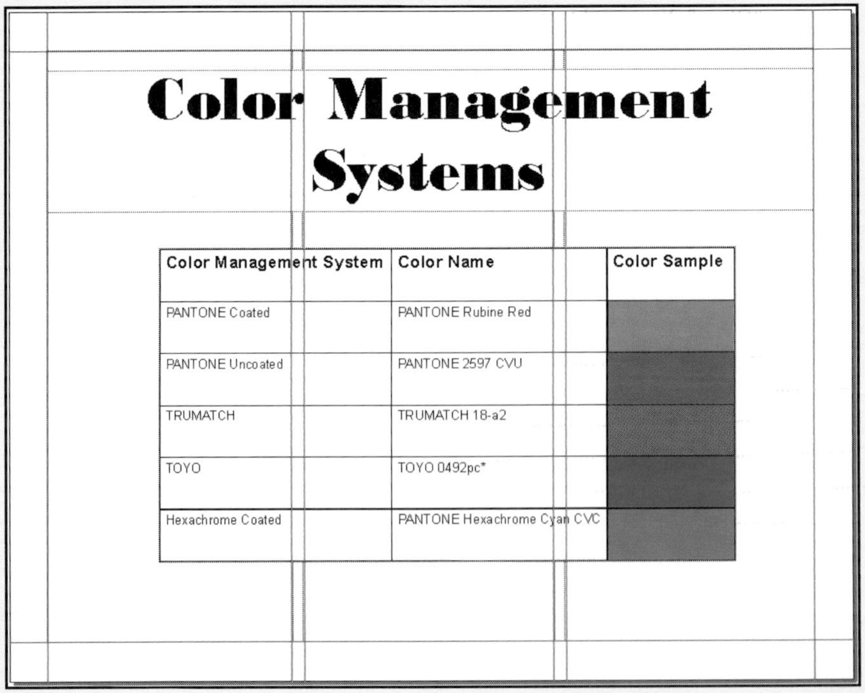

Color Management Systems

Color Management System	Color Name	Color Sample
PANTONE Coated	PANTONE Rubine Red	
PANTONE Uncoated	PANTONE 2597 CVU	
TRUMATCH	TRUMATCH 18-a2	
TOYO	TOYO 0492pc"	
Hexachrome Coated	PANTONE Hexachrome Cyan CVC	

Depending on the size of your group, you can assign elements of the project to individual group members, or work collectively to create the finished product.

Your cousin is a Silicon Valley industrialist. She asks you to be the creative force in designing a publicity sheet for an exciting, soon to be released microchip with the code name "Glory". You need to create a "look" for this new company.

1. One or more group members can outline a design scheme, including the size and orientation of the page.
2. Open a new document, then save it as **Glory**.
3. Create a text box and add some short, snappy promotional text.
4. Create some fancy heading text. (*Hint*: You might want to use a Bézier line to create a dramatic effect. In the sample, a 36 pt Bradley Hand ITC font is used.)
5. One or more group members can create a table that describes what makes this chip so exciting, as well as some descriptive text.
6. Create a text box and title. (*Hint*: In the sample, a 72 pt Poor Richard font is used.)
7. Make color selections and add colors from available color management systems.

8. Modify the insets for any text, including the table.
9. Resize any table column or row widths, as necessary.

10. Check the spelling in the document.
11. Save your work, then compare your document to the sample shown in Figure I-43.

FIGURE I-43
Completed Group Project

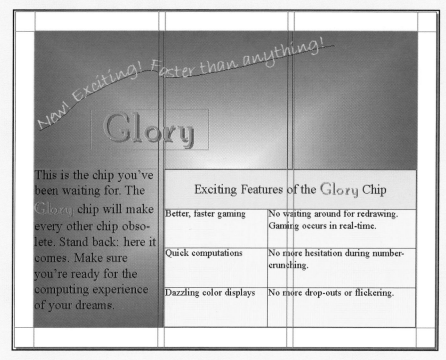

UNIT J

WORKING WITH BOOK TOOLS

1. Create a book.

2. Modify and organize a book.

3. Create a table of contents.

4. Work with indexes and libraries.

UNIT T
WORKING WITH BOOK TOOLS

Introduction

So, you're working on a bear of a project. It involves multiple documents that will ultimately be strung together to form one seamless-looking book. How do you take all these smaller documents and turn them into a larger one, and still maintain that consistent, professional look? Quark contains special tools specifically designed for the management of large projects.

Managing a Large Project

It makes perfect sense that when working on a large project, such as a book, you'd divide it up into manageable, bite-sized parts such as chapters. That way, instead of working towards the colossal (and overwhelming) goal of 200 or more pages, you have 10 to 20 chapters of approximately 20 pages each. This is much easier for your brains and psyche to deal with. Quark uses a similar approach for a large project in that it provides tools that let you manage all the pieces of the puzzle. For example, you can join all the chapters in a book using the Book palette. This feature takes advantage of automatic pagination by making the first page of the second chapter the number following the last page of the first chapter. You can also use the Book palette to change the order of the chapters. Can you imagine all the work you'd have to do if you had to *manually* change the page numbers after reordering the chapters?

Organizing Your Data

All of the Quark tools for large projects have one common objective: they make it possible to manage overwhelming amounts of data. For example, you can use the styles in your documents to create a table of contents. You can also create complex indexes using the Index palette. The Quark Library feature lets you create your own library file, which can be used to store frequently used objects such as text, tables, and graphic images.

QUICKTIP

For all you grammar buffs, *indexes* and *indices* are both considered acceptable plural forms of the word *index*.

Using Features to Create Additional Documents

You can use Quark features to create documents from existing files. For example, you can generate a table of contents and an index using information already in your files. You can generate a table of contents and verify the logical order of topics using styles that have been applied to text within a document. The generated list resembles an outline of topics, and shows as much or as little detail as you choose. You can generate an index of topics using the Index feature. The index, generally found at the end of a large publication, includes page references, and offers readers an alternative method of locating topics.

Tools You'll Use

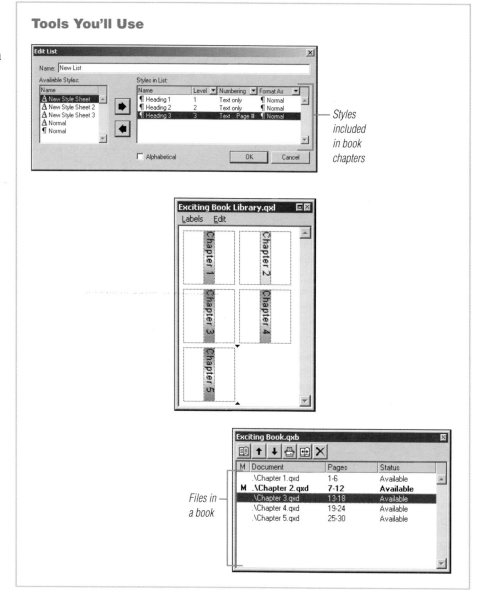

Styles included in book chapters

Files in a book

CREATE A BOOK

What You'll Do

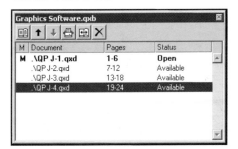

 In this lesson, you'll learn how to create a collection of document files using the Book palette.

Understanding a Complex Project

If you've never managed a large, cumbersome desktop publishing project, well, you're in for a treat. Don't run for cover: Quark manages to take a scary chore and turn it into a delightful little exercise. In Quark, a **book** is an organizational tool that lets you combine and rearrange multiple files to create a uniform document made up of separate components. When a book is created, it displays an icon and file extension that differ from those of a document. (Later, you'll learn how to create a library, which also has a different file extension.) Figure J-1 shows document, book, and library files and their extensions.

FIGURE J-1

Quark file extensions

Name	Size
Exciting Book.qxb	2 KB
Exciting Book Library.qxl	60 KB
Chapter 1.qxd	66 KB
Chapter 5.qxd	65 KB
Chapter 4.qxd	65 KB
Chapter 3.qxd	65 KB
Chapter 2.qxd	65 KB

Icon for Book — Extension for Book

Icon for Library — Extension for Library

Creating a book does *not* result in one enormous file. You still have individual document files, but the Book palette acts as a road map for the book by ensuring that pagination flows from one file to another, and creating an atmosphere of cohesion and uniformity.

Using the Book Palette

You can combine and organize documents to form a book using the Book palette. This palette is analogous to a *command center* because it organizes the entire project. You can use it to:

- Determine which documents are included in the book by adding and deleting files. Each book can have a maximum of 1,000 chapters, and you can add up to 25 chapters at a time.
- Rearrange the order in which documents occur, which affects pagination.

- Synchronize chapters to ensure that consistent styles are used throughout the book. Synchronizing the chapters is an essential step in ensuring that all styles and list information are available to all the files within the book. Without this process, you would find information—such as that used to create a table of contents—missing from the completed project. In order to synchronize the chapters, at least two chapters must be selected.
- Print the book.

The Book palette is unlike other palettes you've used in that you cannot open it using the View menu.

Working in the Book Palette

Let's take a look at the Book palette. The only way you can open this palette is by using the File menu. A new book is created by clicking File on the menu bar, pointing to New, then clicking Book. When you've done this, a palette will open on your work area.

There are no keyboard shortcuts for the Book palette, but you can maximize, minimize, or resize it. You can reopen an existing book using the Open command on the File menu.

Examining Book Palette Components

You can add documents to a book in any order you choose, but the first document you add is considered the master chapter. The master chapter is used to define the colors, styles, and other settings that will be used throughout the book. A Book palette containing four documents is shown in Figure J-2.

FIGURE J-2
Book palette

Click to move document up in the list

Click to add a document to the book

Indicates the master chapter

Click to move document down in the list

Click to synchronize the selection

Click to delete the selection

Indicates document status

Range of pages in each file

Click to print the selection

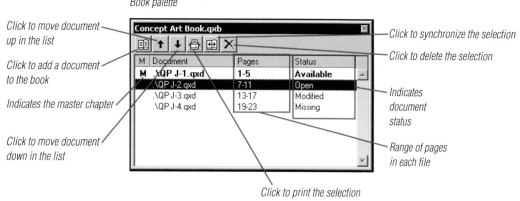

Understanding the Master Chapter

Did you notice that the master chapter is Chapter 1? It doesn't matter which document you choose to make the master, but remember that the file added first will be used to define all the settings for the other documents. Table J-1 describes the information found within the Book palette.

QUICKTIP

You can open any file on the Book palette by double-clicking its entry. If a file is missing, you can locate it by double-clicking its entry, then using the Locate dialog box.

Using Additional Book Settings

The master chapter in a book is used to define all the settings used in the project. These settings include Styles and Colors, as well as H&Js, Lists, and Dashes & Stripes. H&Js are rules that are used for hyphenation and justification, and are edited by clicking Edit on the menu bar,

TABLE J-1: Book Palette Information

column	description
Document	Lists each file name and path.
Pages	Tells you the range of pages in each document (assuming you used the automatic page numbering feature).
Status	Tells you about the file for each entry in the book.
	• Available means the file path has been verified but is not currently open.
	• Open means that the file path has been verified and is currently open.
	• Modified means that the individual file has been modified since it was last viewed using the Book palette.
	• Missing means that the file path could not be verified.

then clicking H&Js. **Lists** (covered later in this unit) make use of Style Sheets, and are used to generate a table of contents and check for logical progression of ideas.

Dashes & Stripes are collections of line patterns that you can choose to use within a document or book. You can edit the line types used within a document by clicking Edit on the menu bar, then clicking Dashes & Stripes.

Using a template to work smart

If all your documents are identical, it may make no difference which document you use as the master chapter. You can create documents with identical settings by creating a template. A **template** is a file with the extension .qxt (Win) that can be created from an existing document by clicking File on the menu bar, then clicking Save as. When the Save as dialog box opens, name the file, click the Type list arrow, click Template in the Save as dialog box, then click OK. A template can contain text, but what's more important when working with a large project is that it can contain text and picture boxes, styles, and other elements essential to maintaining a consistent look and feel among documents. When you start a new document based on this template, the document opens with all the information intact, but the file is unnamed. This preserves the template so it's always in its original form. And guess what? All the documents you create based on this template will have identical settings, such as margins and styles. The synchronization process further ensures that all the contributing documents have the same elements.

Create a book

1. Before you begin, create a new folder named **Copied Project Files** which you can use to store copied project files for this unit.

   Copying the project files ensures that the original files will be preserved so you can repeat this unit, if necessary. You can create the folder in any location, though you may wish to create in the same location where you store your other project files so that it's easy to locate. The book file you'll create must be able to locate these files in the course of your work.

   TIP If you do not know how to create a folder, or you need help choosing a folder location, consult your technical support person.

2. Copy project files QP J-1.qxd, QP J-2.qxd, QP J-3.qxd, and QP J-4.qxd into the new folder.

3. Start Quark, click File on the menu bar, point to New, then click Book.

   The New Book dialog box opens.

4. Navigate to the Copied Project Files folder if necessary, type **Graphics Software** in the File name text box (Win) or Book Name text box (Mac), then click Create. Compare your Book palette to Figure J-3.

   TIP You can open an existing book file by clicking File on the menu bar, then clicking Open. (Book files appear along with regular Quark files and templates, although their extensions and icons differ.) You can also open an existing book file by clicking Start on the taskbar, pointing to Documents, then clicking the book name (Win).

You created a book.

FIGURE J-3
New Book palette

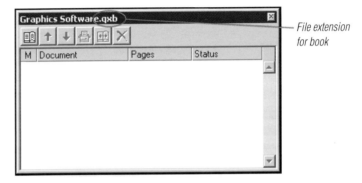

File extension
for book

Book palette with master chapter

Add Chapter tool

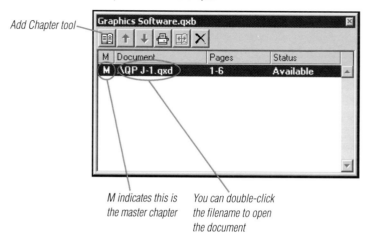

M indicates this is the master chapter

You can double-click the filename to open the document

FIGURE J-5
Book palette with four chapters

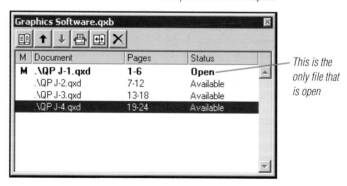

This is the only file that is open

Add chapters to a book

1. Click the Add Chapter tool on the Book palette.

   The Add New Chapter dialog box opens.

2. Open the Copied Project Files folder in the Add New Chapter dialog box if necessary, then double-click QP J-1.qxd.

   The file QP J-1.qxd (showing its status as 'Available') appears on the Book palette. See Figure J-4.

3. Double-click QP J-1.qxd on the Book palette.

   The file opens and you can see that the status of the master chapter changes to Open.

   > TIP It is not *essential* to have any book chapters open in order to create a book.

4. Click the Add Chapter tool on the Book palette.

5. Double-click QP J-2.qxd.

6. Repeat Steps 4 and 5 to add QP J-3 and QP J-4 so your Book palette looks like Figure J-5.

You added chapters to a book file, then you opened one of the chapters.

Synchronize book components

1. Click the entry for QP J-2.qxd on the Book palette.

2. Press and hold [Shift], then click the entry for QP J-4.qxd on the Book palette. Compare your palette to Figure J-6.

   TIP   In order to use the Synchronize feature, you must have *at least* one chapter other than the master chapter selected.

3. Click the Synchronize tool on the Book palette.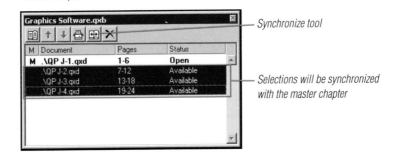

   The Synchronize Selected Chapters dialog box opens.

4. Click Include All at the bottom of the Available section.

   All of the available Style Sheets are included in the Include list, as shown in Figure J-7.

5. Click Synch All.

   TIP   Without synchronization, there would be no consistency among the chapters.

(continued)

FIGURE J-6
Selected chapters

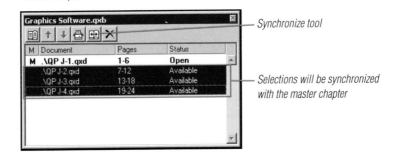

Synchronize tool

Selections will be synchronized with the master chapter

FIGURE J-7
Synchronize Selected Chapters dialog box

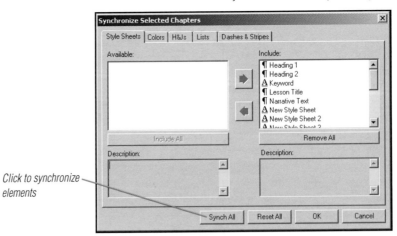

Click to synchronize elements

Click OK to close the Synchronize Selected Chapters dialog box.

7. Click OK to close the warning box shown in Figure J-8, if necessary.

The settings in the three selected chapters have been synchronized with the master chapter.

> TIP There are no visual signs indicating that synchronization is taking place.

You synchronized the three additional chapters with the master chapter.

FIGURE J-8
Synchronization warning box

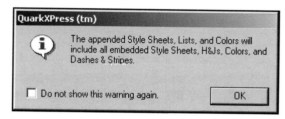

LESSON 2

MODIFY AND ORGANIZE A BOOK

What You'll Do

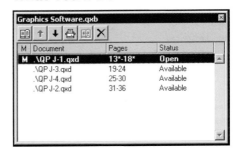

In this lesson, you'll learn how to reorder book chapters, and change the starting page in a section.

Creating a Logical Sequence

The order in which you add chapters to a book determines the order in which they appear on the Book palette. Assuming you used the automatic page numbering feature, the chapter order will also take care of correctly numbering your pages. But what do you do if you either add chapters in the wrong order, or decide later that a change of chapter order is warranted? Move the chapters around, of course.

Reordering Chapters

The order of chapters can be changed by selecting the chapter(s) you want to move, then clicking the Move Chapter Up or Move Chapter Down tools on the Book palette. It's not necessary to have these chapters open in order to move them, but their status does need to be either Open or Available. Figure J-9 shows a Book palette

with the chapters in their original order. Figure J-10 shows the same Book palette with the chapters reordered.

QUICKTIP

You can reorder one chapter at a time, and each chapter can belong to only one book at a time. If you want a chapter to belong to multiple books, you must make copies of the file.

Paginating Like a Pro

Earlier it may have seemed like overkill when you entered the codes that automatically paginated each page, but it's about to pay off *big time*. Because a large project may be done in a piecemeal fashion, you may not have every chapter when you expect it. If this is the case, you can change the starting page of any chapter, and all the pages within that chapter will reflect the change. In addition, all chapters following the file with the changed starting page number will also be modified.

Changing the Starting Page Number

You can change the starting page number of a book by clicking Page on the menu bar, then clicking Section. Using the Section dialog box, you can indicate the format of numbers (for example, 1, 2, 3, 4, or a, b, c, d) as well as any prefix you want to precede a number/letter. If you'll recall, you can create a section anywhere within a document, and all subsequent pages will be renumbered. The first page in a document that is renumbered has an asterisk by its icon on the Document Layout palette, as shown in Figure J-11.

FIGURE J-9
Original order of chapters

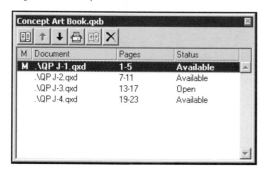

FIGURE J-11
Document Layout palette with renumbered pages

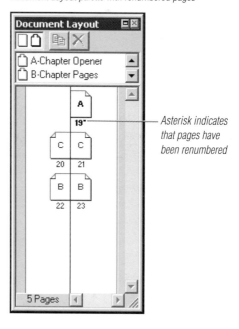

Asterisk indicates that pages have been renumbered

FIGURE J-10
Reordered chapters

Master chapter is the second chapter in the book

Pagination changes automatically with order of chapters

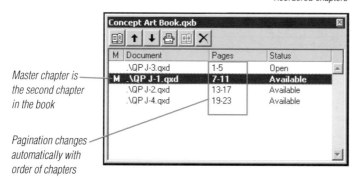

Modify the chapter order

1. Click outside the selection (Mac), then click QP J-2.qxd on the Book palette.

2. Click the Move Chapter Down tool. ↓

   The position of the selected file changes in the Book palette list. See Figure J-12.

3. Click QP J-4.qxd on the Book palette.

4. Click the Move Chapter Up tool. ↑

   The selected file is now the third chapter on the list on the Book palette, as shown in Figure J-13.

You used the Move Chapter Up and Move Chapter Down tools to reorder the chapters on the Book palette.

FIGURE J-12
Second chapter moved in the list

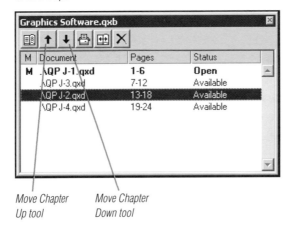

Move Chapter
Up tool

Move Chapter
Down tool

FIGURE J-13
Reordered chapters

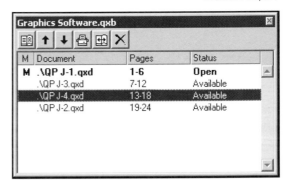

Printing a book

You can print one or more chapters in a book by clicking the chapters you want to print on the Book palette, then clicking the Print Chapters tool on the Book palette. You can only print a chapter if its status is Open or Available, and you can print multiple chapters by holding [Shift] while selecting the chapters you want to print, then clicking the Print Chapters tool on the Book palette.

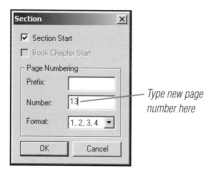

Type new page
number here

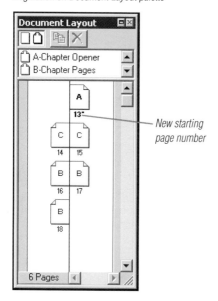

New starting
page number

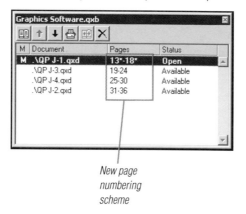

New page
numbering
scheme

Change the starting page number

1. Click QP J-1.qxd on the Book palette.

2. Click Page on the menu bar, then click Section.

3. Click the Section Start checkbox if it does not contain a checkmark, then double-click the Number text box.

4. Type **13**. Compare your settings to Figure J-14.

5. Click OK. Compare your Book palette to Figure J-15 and your Document Layout palette to Figure J-16.

6. Click File on the menu bar, then click Save.

   TIP There is no Save tool on the Book palette toolbar because saving changes to a book is an automatic process. The Save command that *is* available (if you have a file open) only affects the open document. The filename shown in the title bar indicates to which document the menu commands apply.

You changed the starting page in the book, which changed the pagination in all the chapters.

CREATE A TABLE OF CONTENTS

What You'll Do

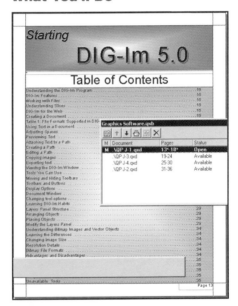

In this lesson, you'll create a list using styles in documents.

Streaming a Large Project Using Style Sheets

Maybe you thought that creating and using style sheets was just a way of giving your documents a consistent look. While this is one benefit of style sheets, you're about to see how they really earn their keep.

Creating List Criteria

Style sheets prove their usefulness when it comes time to generate a list. Style sheets are used to differentiate 'levels,' such as those you would normally find in an outline or table of contents. (This, in fact, is the same method many word processing programs use to generate lists.) Using a series of dialog boxes, you can make the following determinations:

- Which style sheets will be used to generate the list
- Which level will be assigned to each style sheet
- How each level will appear (with or without pagination)
- How each level will be formatted

Examining List Criteria

Figure J-17 shows the Edit List dialog box. Here you can see that four style sheets from the list of those that are available were added to the list. Levels were assigned to the style sheets, as well as numbering formats. When the list is generated (or built), each level in the list is automatically assigned the Normal paragraph style sheet (to give the list a more uniform appearance).

QUICKTIP

When creating the list parameters, it is only necessary to open the master chapter.

Choosing Levels

So how do you know how to assign levels? Well, assuming you have some knowledge of the text used to build the list, this shouldn't be too difficult. The only way you can know which style sheet should be a particular level is by logically determining how the list should read, or by having an agreed-upon system for which styles will be used in a particular manner. Once you know which levels are to be assigned to specific style sheets, you can select a style sheet, click the Level list arrow in the Edit List dialog box, then click the appropriate level.

QUICKTIP

To reiterate the obvious: the key to working effi-ciently—regardless of the size of your project—is planning. Knowing in advance that you'll want to generate a list should motivate you to take steps to avoid having to backtrack to create and apply styles.

Making Pagination Choices

Deciding which types of pagination should be included in a list is also part of the plan-ning process. During the planning process, it may have already been determined which levels will and won't display a page reference. Table J-2 shows the types of numbering formats that are available.

Building a List

Once you assign all the levels, formatting, and numbering choices, you can build the list in the document in which you want the list to appear using the Lists palette. Click the text box where the list will appear. You can apply formatting, such as styles, tabs, and indents, once the list is built.

QUICKTIP

When building the list, it is only necessary to open the Book palette on which you want the list generated.

FIGURE J-17
Edit List dialog box

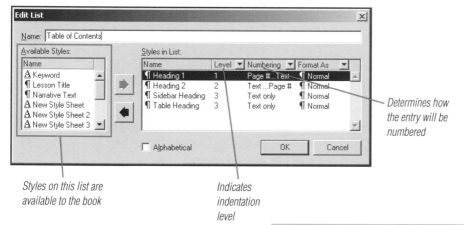

Styles on this list are available to the book

Indicates indentation level

Determines how the entry will be numbered

TABLE J-2: Numbering Formats

format	description
Text only	Displays the text in the level
Text ...Page #	Displays the text in the level followed by the page number
Page # ...Text	Displays the page number followed by the text in the level

Create list criteria

1. Click Edit on the menu bar, then click Lists.
   The Lists for QP J-1.qxd dialog box opens.

2. Click New.
   The Edit List dialog box opens.

3. Type **Graphics Software TOC** in the Name text box. Compare your dialog box to Figure J-18.

4. Click Heading 1 on the Available Styles list.

5. Press and hold [Ctrl] (Win) or [command] (Mac), click Heading 2, scroll down the list and click Sidebar Heading, click Table Heading (the paragraph style), then release [Ctrl] (Win) or [command] (Mac).

6. Click the Add Styles To List button. Compare your list to Figure J-19. ➡

   TIP You can display the *completed list* in alphabetical order by clicking the Alphabetical check-box.

You created a list using four styles within the master chapter.

FIGURE J-18
List name entered in Edit List dialog box

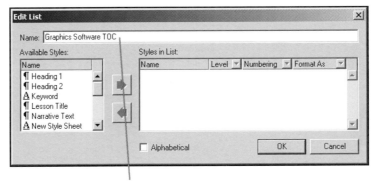

Type list name here

FIGURE J-19
Entries in Edit List dialog box

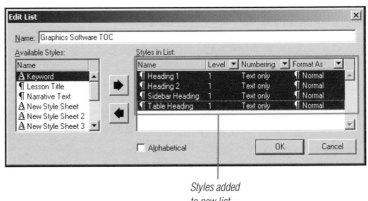

Styles added
to new list

FIGURE J-20

Levels and Numbering changes in Edit List dialog box

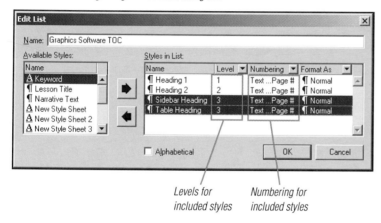

Levels for   Numbering for
included styles   included styles

1. Click the Numbering list arrow, then click Text ...Page #.

2. Click outside the selection (Mac), then click Heading 2 in the Styles in List box.

3. Click the Level list arrow, then click 2.

4. Click Sidebar Heading in the Styles in List box, press and hold [Shift], click Table Heading, then release [Shift].

   The Sidebar Heading and Table Heading styles are both selected.

5. Click the Level list arrow, then click 3.

   Level 3 will be applied to the selected styles. Compare your screen to Figure J-20.

You modified the levels and numbering scheme for the styles on a list.

View a list

1. Click OK, then compare your dialog box to Figure J-21.

2. Click Save to close the Lists for QP J-1.qxd dialog box.

3. Click View on the menu bar, then click Show Lists. Compare your Lists palette to Figure J-22.

4. Click File on the menu bar, then click Save.

You viewed a list for a chapter that is based on styles.

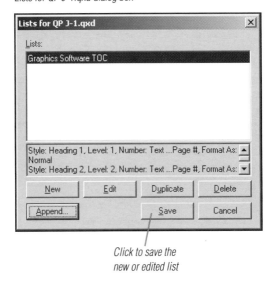

Click to save the
new or edited list

Preview of list
generated using
the styles

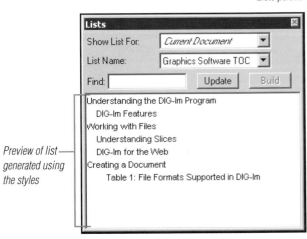

FIGURE J-23

Append Lists to Default Document dialog box

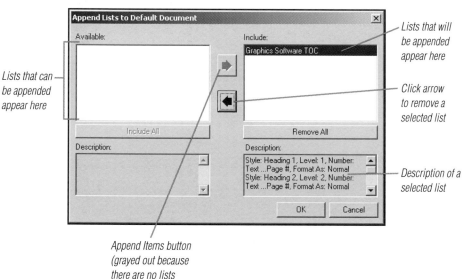

Lists that can be appended appear here

Lists that will be appended appear here

Click arrow to remove a selected list

Description of a selected list

Append Items button (grayed out because there are no lists available to be appended)

1. Click the Close button on the Lists palette.

2. Close QP J-1.qxd (leaving the Books palette open).

3. Click outside the selection on the Books palette, click Edit on the menu bar, then click Lists.

   The Default Lists dialog box opens.

4. Click Append, locate and click QP J-1.qxd, then click Open.

5. Click Graphics Software TOC in the Available list, then click the Append Items button. ➡

6. Compare your dialog box to Figure J-23, click OK, then click OK to close the warning box, if necessary.

7. If necessary, click the Repeat For All Conflicts checkbox to add a checkmark, then click Use Existing.

8. Click Save.

   The Default Lists dialog box closes.

You closed all the book chapters, then appended a list to a book.

Append and build a list

1. Select all four documents in the Book palette, then click the Synchronize tool.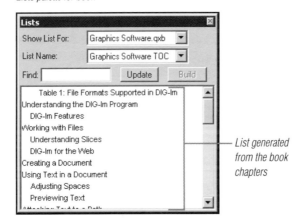
2. Click Synch All, then click OK.

   The appended list is synchronized in all the chapters. You might see QP J-1.qxd open during this process.
3. Click View on the menu bar, then click Show Lists. Compare your Lists palette to Figure J-24.

   The list contains entries from all the chapters in the book.
4. Double-click QP J-1.qxd on the Book palette.
5. Click the Content tool, if necessary, then click the lower text box (at 2" H/4" V).
6. Click Build on the List palette. Compare your table to Figure J-25.

   The contents of the List palette appears in the open document.

   TIP   Pagination is affected by the following variables: printer selection, font, and font size. Your page numbers may vary.

You synchronized the chapters in a book, then generated a list in a chapter.

FIGURE J-24
Lists palette for book

List generated from the book chapters

FIGURE J-25
Generated list

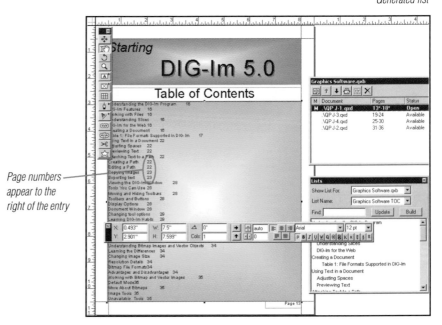

Page numbers appear to the right of the entry

Tab settings in Paragraph Attributes dialog box

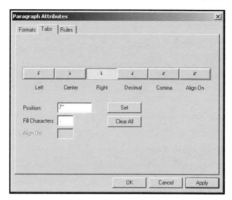

Format a list

1. Click the Close button on the Lists palette.

2. Click View on the menu bar, then click Fit in Window.

3. Press [Ctrl][A] (Win) or [command][A] (Mac) to select all the text in the list.

4. Click Style on the menu bar, then click Tabs.

   The Tabs tab in the Paragraph Attributes dialog box opens.

5. Click the Right Tab button.

6. Type **7"** in the Position text box.

7. Type **.** in the Fill Characters text box. Compare your tab settings to Figure J-26.

8. Click OK.

9. Click anywhere on the work area to deselect the text.

10. Click File on the menu bar, click Save, then compare your document to Figure J-27.

You used tabs to format the generated list.

FIGURE J-27
Formatted list

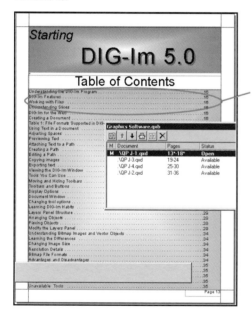

Tabs and dot leaders make the list more readable

Evaluating the process

Are you surprised at how complicated it is to generate a table of contents? Well, rest assured that this process would be a lot more difficult if you had to manually generate the same list. Just imagine if you had to open each document and manually type each heading and page notation. Then imagine that the order of the pages changes and you must—once again—make sure that all the pages are correctly cited in the list. I'll bet this doesn't seem quite so tedious now, does it? Also, consider what a difficult task this is. You are asking Quark to examine the contents of many individual files to compile an all-inclusive list: a very difficult task.

WORK WITH INDEXES AND LIBRARIES

What You'll Do

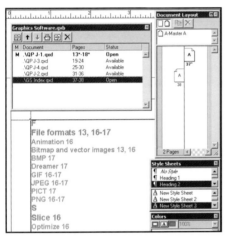

In this lesson, you'll create an index for a document and a library file.

Understanding the Importance of Indexes

It's nice to have a complete table of contents within a book, but to some, the real test of a user-friendly book is a complete index. If you've ever searched for a topic that you knew was in a book, but were unable to find it, then you understand the importance of this feature.

Using Indexing Tools

Like many other book features, indexing has its own palette. And, like the Lists feature, the Index palette is used to create the list criteria. Once the criteria are defined, you can generate an index. Table J-3 describes the tools on the Index palette.

TABLE J-3: Index Palette Tools

tool	name	description
▤+	Add	Adds a selected entry or reference to the list
▣+	Add All	Adds all occurrences of the selection to the list
⇥	Find Next Entry	Jumps to the next occurrence of the selection
✎	Edit	Lets you edit an entry or reference
✕	Delete	Lets you delete an entry or reference

Exploring the Index Palette

The Index palette, shown in Figure J-28, can be opened by clicking View on the menu bar, then clicking Show Index. There are three areas on the Index palette:

- Entry area: This area lets you specify each individual item that will be listed in the index, and determines how it will be sorted.
- Reference area: This area lets you specify the style sheet that will be applied and the scope (the range an entry spans), and creates cross-references.

- Entries list: This area displays each entry (indented by level), and the number of times it occurs in a document.

Items within a document are **marked**—that is, they are surrounded by brackets indicating that they will be placed in the index. Each entry can be defined as having a level. Once all the entries are marked and added to the Entries list, the index can be generated, or **built**, usually in a separate document.

Indexing a Book

Creating an index for an entire book can be tricky. It's important that you complete several steps in the following order:

- Create a document that will contain the index, otherwise the index will be added to the end of your current document.
- Add the index document to the book, preferably as the last chapter.
- Synchronize all the styles and lists in all the chapters.
- Build the index *for the entire book*.

FIGURE J-28
Index palette

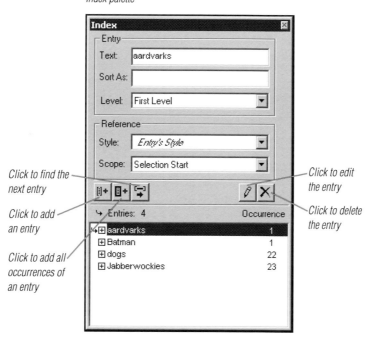

Click to find the next entry

Click to add an entry

Click to add all occurrences of an entry

Click to edit the entry

Click to delete the entry

QUICKTIP

When you build an index, it is always added to the end of the current document. By default, enough pages are added to accommodate the entries.

Using Libraries

A **library** is a storage and retrieval system you can create and use with any documents. You can use a library to store just about anything: text or objects. You can create a library (which has the extension .qxl) by clicking File on the menu bar, pointing to New, then clicking Library. Entries in a library can be named by double-clicking the library entry, typing a name in the Library Entry dialog box, then clicking OK.

QUICKTIP

Like the Book palette, the Library palette can only be opened using the Open command on the File menu.

Using the XTensions Manager

You may notice that another computer with QuarkXPress may have different features than the computer you're using. This can happen because many of the features in Quark are actually XTensions. **XTensions** are mini-programs (having the extension .xnt) that can be added to or deleted from QuarkXPress, *without* causing harm to the rest of the program. Some Quark XTensions are Jabberwocky, Index, Step and Repeat, and Guide Manager. You can check to see which XTensions are installed by clicking Utilities on the menu bar, then clicking XTensions Manager. The XTensions Manager dialog box, shown in Figure J-29, opens. This dialog box lists all the XTensions currently in your installation of Quark, and you can disable a selected XTension by clicking the Enable list arrow, then clicking No. If you are unsure what a particular XTension does, you can click the About button.

FIGURE J-29
XTensions Manager dialog box

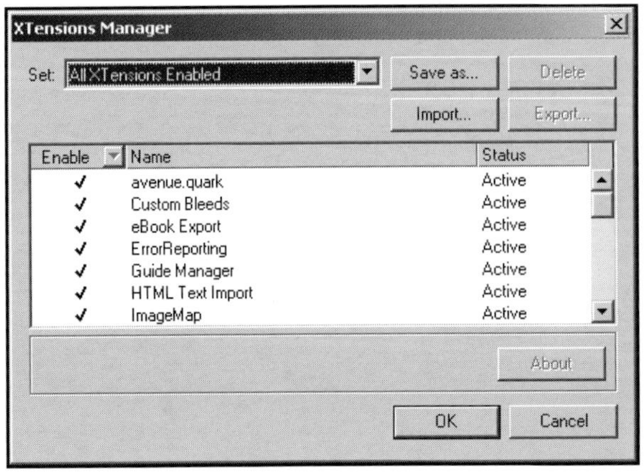

A description of the selected XTension appears at the bottom of the About dialog box as shown in Figure J-30.

QUICKTIP

Many programs use additional programs to augment functionality. In Microsoft Excel, for example, these mini-programs are called Add-ins.

Getting XTensions

If you are missing any QuarkXPress XTensions, the best place to check is on the Quark Web site (*www.quark.com*). This site changes often, so it's a good idea to visit it often. Here you'll find downloads and XTensions for QuarkXPress 5.0. When you find an XTension that you want for the platform you are using, click its link. (*Hint*: If a

dialog box opens asking you for a password, it means that site is busy and you should try again later.) Click the link to download the file, decompress it, if necessary, then drag the XTension file to the XTensions folder on your hard drive. (*Note*: If you are working in an institutional or networked environment, it's best to consult systems personnel *before* making any modifications.)

FIGURE J-30
About Jabberwocky dialog box

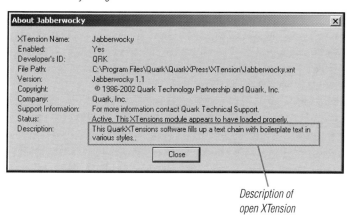

*Description of
open XTension*

Mark a document for indexing

1. Click View on the menu bar, then click Show Index.

2. Double-click the page 16 icon on the Document Layout palette.

   Page 16 of the active document appears.

3. Click the Content tool on the Tools palette, if necessary.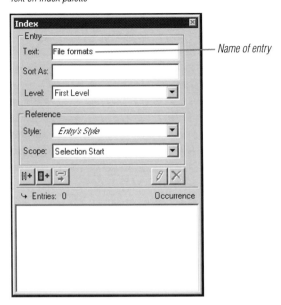

4. Select the text "file formats" (in column 1 at approximately 1" H/6¾" V).

   The selected text appears in the Text text box on the Index palette.

5. Select the "f" in file on the Index palette, then type **F**. Compare your Index palette to Figure J-31.

   The entry will appear in the index as "File formats" rather than "file formats" so that index entries are capitalized consistently.

6. Verify that Selection Start appears in the Scope list arrow. Additional Scope options are described in Table J-4.

You marked an item for inclusion in an index.

Name of entry

TABLE J-4: Scope Options

option	description
Selection Start	Searches from the currently selected text, which is surrounded by an open bracket
Selection Text	Searches between the open and closed brackets
To Style	Searches based on the style indicated in the Reference area
Specified # of ¶s	Searches through the number of paragraphs you specify
To End Of	Searches through the end of the story or document
Suppress Page #	Does not display the page number
X-Ref (Win) Cross-Reference (Mac)	Creates a cross-reference for the selection

Create index entries

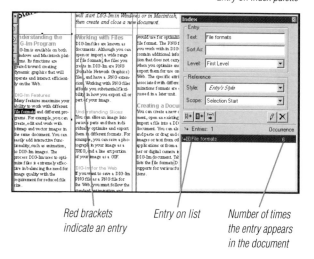

1. Click the Add All tool on the Index palette. The entry appears in the Entries list. 🗗⁺

   An entry appears in the Entries list, as shown in Figure J-32.

2. Double-click "PNG" in column 2 (at approximately 4½" H/5" V).

3. Click the Level list arrow, then click Second Level.

4. Click the Add All tool on the Index palette. 🗗⁺

   The Second Level entry appears on the Index palette with 10 occurrences. Compare your Index palette to Figure J-33.

You created two entries, then modified the level of one entry.

Red brackets indicate an entry

Entry on list

Number of times the entry appears in the document

FIGURE J-33

Second Level entry in Index palette

Edit tool

Edited entry is indented

Editing an index entry

At some point, you'll need to change the level of an index entry. You can do this by clicking the Edit tool in the Index palette. The Edit tool is a toggle switch: you click it once to turn it on, make your changes, then click it once to turn it off. Once the Edit tool is on, you can click the Level list arrow and change the entry's level.

Add entries and create an index document

1. Use the Add All tool on the Index palette to add the entries and their levels shown in Table J-5.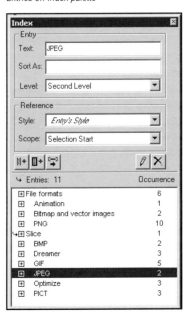

   The entries appear on the Index palette, as shown in Figure J-34.

   > TIP You can expand the length of the Index palette by dragging the bottom edge of the palette window.

2. Create a new document using portrait orientation facing pages, one column an automatic text box, and default margin settings, then save it as **GS Index** in the Copied Project Files folder.

You made additional index entries and created an index chapter.

FIGURE J-34
Entries on Index palette

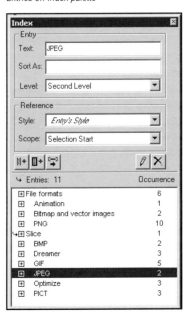

TABLE J-5: Additional Index Entries

text entry	location of text	level
Bitmap and vector images	p. 16, column 1 @ 1" H/7 ¼" V	2
Animation	p. 16, column 1 @ 2" H/8" V	2
Slice	p. 16, column 2 @ 3 ½" H/6 ¾" V	1
Optimize	p. 16, column 2 @ 3 ¾" H/7 ¼" V	2
Dreamer	p. 17, table column 3 @ 4 ½" H/6 ¼" V	2
GIF	p. 17, table column 1 @ 1 ½" H/6 ½" V	2
BMP	p. 17, table column 1 @ 1 ½" H/7" V	2
PICT	p. 17, table column 5 @ 6 ¾" H/7 ½" V	2
JPEG	p. 17, table column 2 @ 2 ½" H/8 ¼" V	2

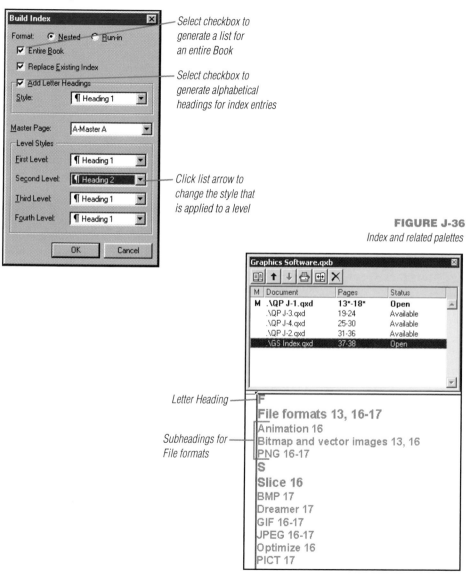

Select checkbox to
generate a list for
an entire Book

Select checkbox to
generate alphabetical
headings for index entries

Click list arrow to
change the style that
is applied to a level

FIGURE J-36
Index and related palettes

Letter Heading

Subheadings for
File formats

Synchronize chapters and build an index

1. Click the Add Chapter tool on the Book palette, then double-click GS Index.qxd. 📖

2. Move GS Index so it is the last chapter in the book if necessary. ↓

3. Click the Synchronize tool on the Book palette. ⊞

   TIP Without synchronization, you would not be able to index the entire book into a single file in a single step.

4. Click the Synch All button in the Style Sheets tab of the Synchronize Selected Chapters dialog box, then click OK to close the warning box.

   The style sheets and lists for all the book chapters have been synchronized.

5. Click Utilities on the menu bar, then click Build Index.

   The Build Index dialog box opens.

6. Make any necessary settings changes to the Build Index dialog box using Figure J-35 as a guide, click OK, then click OK to close the warning box (Mac) if necessary.

   The index is generated in GS Index. Compare your screen to Figure J-36.

You synchronized book chapters, then built an index.

Create a library

1. Click File on the menu bar, point to New, then click Library.

2. Save the new file as **GS Library** in the Copied Project Files folder.

   The GS Library.qxl palette appears.

   > TIP In the New Library dialog box, you click Create after naming the file. In the Save as dialog box, you click Save after naming the file.

3. Click the Item tool on the Tools palette.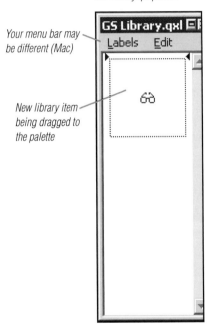

4. Display QP J-1.qxd if necessary, then double-click the page 17 icon on the Document Layout palette if page 17 does not appear in QP J-1.

5. Click the table at 4" H/7" V.

6. Drag the selection onto the Library palette.

   Did you notice that the pointer turned into miniature glasses, shown in Figure J-37, as you dragged the table?

   (continued)

FIGURE J-37
GS Library.qxl palette

Your menu bar may be different (Mac)

New library item being dragged to the palette

When you finished dragging the table, the table appeared on the Library palette. See Figure J-38.

> TIP   You can place a library entry into a file by dragging a library icon into any document.

7. Double-click the table icon on the Library palette.

8. Type **Standard table**, then click OK.

9. Click File on the menu bar, click Exit (Win) or Quit (Mac), then click Yes to save each modified document.

You created a library file, then added and named an entry.

GS Library.qxl palette with table entry

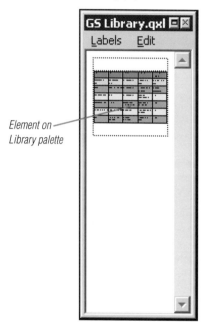

Element on Library palette

Power User Shortcuts

to do this:	use this method:
Add a document to a book	📖
Add all entries to list	📄+
Add an entry to list	📄+
Add document styles to list	➡
Build an index	Utilities ➤ Build Index
Change starting page number	Page ➤ Section
Create a Book palette	File ➤ New ➤ Book
Create a library	File ➤ New ➤ Library [Ctrl][Alt][N] (Win) ⌘ [option][N] (Mac)
Create a template	File ➤ Save as [Ctrl][Alt][S] (Win) ⌘ [Alt][S] (Mac)
Create list criteria	Edit ➤ Lists
Delete the entry	✖ (Win)
Display Index palette	View ➤ Show Index
Display Lists palette	View ➤ Show Lists

to do this:	use this method:
Edit the entry	✎
Find the next entry	➡
Generate a list	Build
Move a document down	⬇
Move a document up	⬆
Name a library entry	Double-click entry on Library palette
Open a document in a book	Double-click chapter name on Book palette
Open a library	File ➤ Open [Ctrl][O] (Win) ⌘ [O] (Mac)
Open an existing Book palette	File ➤ Open [Ctrl][O] (Win) ⌘ [O] (Mac)
Print book chapters	🖶
Synchronize chapters	🔃
View installed XTensions	Utilities ➤ XTensions Manager

Before beginning this Skills Review, please make a copy of QP J-5, QP J-6, QP J-7, QP J-8, and QP J-9, and place them in the Copied Project Files folder you created earlier in this unit.

Your comfort while working is important. At any time in this exercise, please feel free to change the document view, move palettes if they are in your way, or Show/Hide Invisibles.

Create a book.

1. Start Quark.
2. Create a new book file, then save it as **Tornado** in the Copied Project Files folder.
3. Add the following files to the book from the Copied Project Files folder: QP J-5.qxd, QP J-6.qxd, and QP J-7.qxd.
4. Open the file QP J-5 from the Book palette.
5. Select all chapters in the book, then synchronize all the styles.

Modify and organize a book.

1. Change the order of the chapters to the following: QP J-5, QP J-7, QP J-6.
2. Change the starting page of the master chapter to 53.
3. Save your work in the open document.

Create a table of contents.

1. Create a new list for the open chapter called **Tornado TOC**.
2. Include the following style sheets: Heading 1, Heading 2, and Sidebar Heading.
3. Heading 1 should be at Level 1 and should use the Text ...Page# page numbering.
4. Heading 2 should be at Level 2 and should use the Text ...Page # page numbering.
5. Sidebar Heading should be at Level 3 and should use the Text ...Page# page numbering.
6. Save the Tornado TOC list.
7. Show the Lists palette.
8. Save and close the open book chapter, then close the Lists palette.

9. Edit the lists for the book by appending the Tornado TOC in QP J-5.
10. Save the appended list in the book, synchronize all the list information in all the chapters, then open the Lists palette.
11. Open QP J-5 using the Book palette, then click the text box at 4" H/4" V with the Content tool. (*Hint*: You may have to close and then reopen the Lists palette to display the list.)
12. Build the TOC in the text box.
13. Select all the text in the generated list.
14. Change the selected text to 18 pt Arial.
15. Create a right-aligned tab at 7 ¼" with a dash (-) as a fill character.
16. Deselect the text, then close the Lists palette.
17. Save your work.

Work with indexes and libraries.

1. Show the Index palette.
2. Open each of the remaining chapters.
3. Add all the occurrences of the words (each with initial capital letters in the Text text box) listed in Table J-6. (*Hint*: You can use the Find/Change command to locate entries.)
4. Save the changes made to each open chapter.
5. Create a new document using portrait orientation, one column, and default margin settings. Make sure the Facing Pages and Automatic Text box checkboxes are selected, then save the document as **Tornado Index**.

6. Add the new document to the Book palette, then move it to the end of the list if necessary.
7. Synchronize all the style sheets and lists by appending the items.
8. Build the index using the entire book, adding Letter Headings, and using Heading 1 as the Style for the First Level, and Heading 2 as the Style for the Second Level.
9. Create a library called **Tornado Library**.
10. Place the following items in the library: the sidebar element on page 55 in QP J-5, and the TIP element on page 63 in QP J-6.

11. Save the changes made to each open chapter.
12. Display the list on page 53 of QP J-5.
13. Save your work, then compare your list, Book palette, and Library palette to Figure J-39.

FIGURE J-39
Completed Skills Review

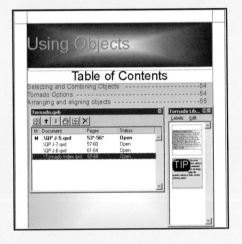

TABLE J-6: Index Entries

document	text entry to add	level
QP J-5	Vector shapes	1
	Group and Combine commands	2
	Combine options	2
	Layers panel	1
	Boomerang	2
QP J-7	Fill panel	1
	Pattern	2
QP J-6	Effects panel	1
	Xtras	2

One of your classmates missed the lecture in which building a table of contents was covered. You promised to explain this process to him, and you created a simple, single project file that you can use to demonstrate how to build a list using style sheets.

1. Open QP J-8.qxd, then save it as **TOC Demo**.
2. Open the Edit Lists dialog box, then create a new list called **Table of Contents**.
3. Add the following available styles to the list: Heading 1, Heading 2, and Heading 3.
4. Each style should be formatted with the Normal style, and should use the Text ...Page # numbering.
5. Heading 1 should be at Level 1, Heading 2 should be at Level 2, and Heading 3 should be at Level 3.
6. Save the Table of Contents list.
7. Display the Lists palette.
8. Click the lower text box on page 1 at 4" H/4" V.
9. Build the list in the active text box.
10. Change the font size of the list to 18 pt and add the italic attribute.
11. Create a right-aligned tab at 6 ¾" that uses a period (.) as a fill character.
12. Change the left margin of the Level 1 headings to 1". (*Hint*: Drag the upper-left triangle in the displayed Tabs ruler to the 1" mark.)

13. Change the left margin of the Level 2 headings to 1 ½", and change the left margin of the Level 3 headings to 2".

14. Close the Lists palette and deselect the text.
15. Save your work, then compare your image to the sample in Figure J-40.

FIGURE J-40
Completed Project Builder 1

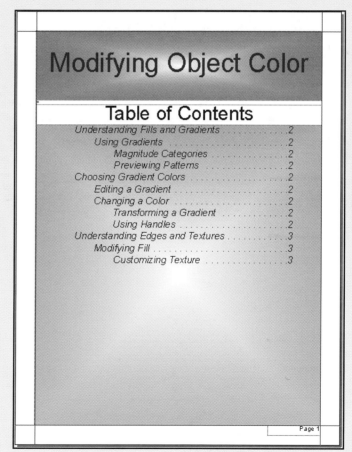

Once again you are proving yourself to be invaluable to your instructor. She is scheduled to speak at an international symposium this week, and asks you to deliver the lecture on building an index to another class. She prepared the project file, as well as the lesson plan. All you have to do is review the lesson and deliver the lecture, then answer questions.

1. Open QP J-9.qxd from the Copied Project Files folder, then save it as **Index Lesson**.
2. Change the starting page number to 17.
3. Change all instances of "Effect panel" to "Effects Panel". (*Hint*: You should have 12 instances changed.)
4. Show the Index palette, then mark the document using the Index palette shown in Figure J-41 for the entries and their levels.
5. Build the index with letter headings using the Heading 1 style for the Letter Headings and the Normal style for the First Level and Second Level entries.
6. Cut the index entries on page 22 of the document, then paste them into the text box at 4" H/ 4" V on page 21.
7. Delete the newly added page 22.
8. Save your work, then compare your index and Index palette to the sample in Figure J-41.

FIGURE J-41
Completed Project Builder 2

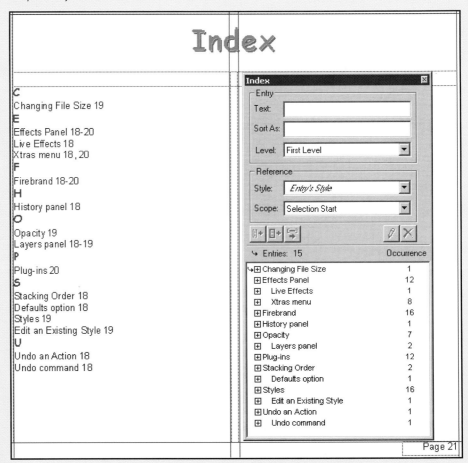

It strikes you as somewhat magical that Quark can generate a table of contents or an index using information found in one or more documents. You're curious as to whether or not this process is available in other programs, and if it's done in a similar fashion. You decide to use the Internet to conduct some research on these procedures.

1. Connect to the Internet and go to *www.course.com*. Navigate to the page for this book, click the link for the Student Online Companion, then click the link for this unit. The site for this unit is just one of many informative sites that can help you learn about color management systems.

2. If it is permitted, bookmark these URLs for future reference.

3. Review the information on this site, and print it out if you find it helpful.

4. When you finish your research, close your browser.

5. Create a document using either a word processor or a presentation graphics program that contains your observations, then save the document as **List Generation**.

6. Add your observations to the List Generation document. (*Hint*: You can take screen shots of individual Web pages by pressing the [Print Screen] key when

viewing a page in your browser. Insert the screen shots into your active document by pressing [Ctrl][V] (Win).)

7. Compare your document to the sample shown in Figure J-42.

FIGURE J-42
Design Project sample

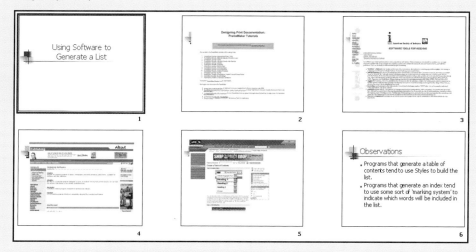

Before beginning this Group Project, please make a copy of any existing documents that will be used in this project, and place them in the Copied Project Files folder you created earlier in the unit for storing copies of project files.

You are in charge of the final project in your computer class and want to combine the skills you have learned in Quark to make your other project more spectacular. (Since several of your teammates are taking both classes, it was an easy sell.) Since you and your teammates are all working separately on documents, you decide to combine all your documents into a book that contains a table of contents and an index.

1. One or more group members can outline a design scheme, including the size and orientation of the page.
2. One or more group members can create at least three short, simple documents. (*Hint*: You can use any documents available on your computer, if necessary. If you create new documents, you can use any naming scheme you choose.)
3. One or more group members can add two or more elements to the library, which can be used throughout this exercise.
4. Create and apply style sheets.
5. Open a new book, then save it as **Final Project**.
6. One or more group members can build a table of contents, and assign levels and pagination styles.

7. Format the table of contents according to the heading levels.
8. Create a document that will contain the index (saved as **Final Project Index**).
9. Mark each of the documents for index entries.
10. Synchronize the documents and build the index.
11. Create a library called **Final Project Library**.
12. Save your work, then compare your document to the sample shown in Figure J-43.

FIGURE J-43

Completed Group Project

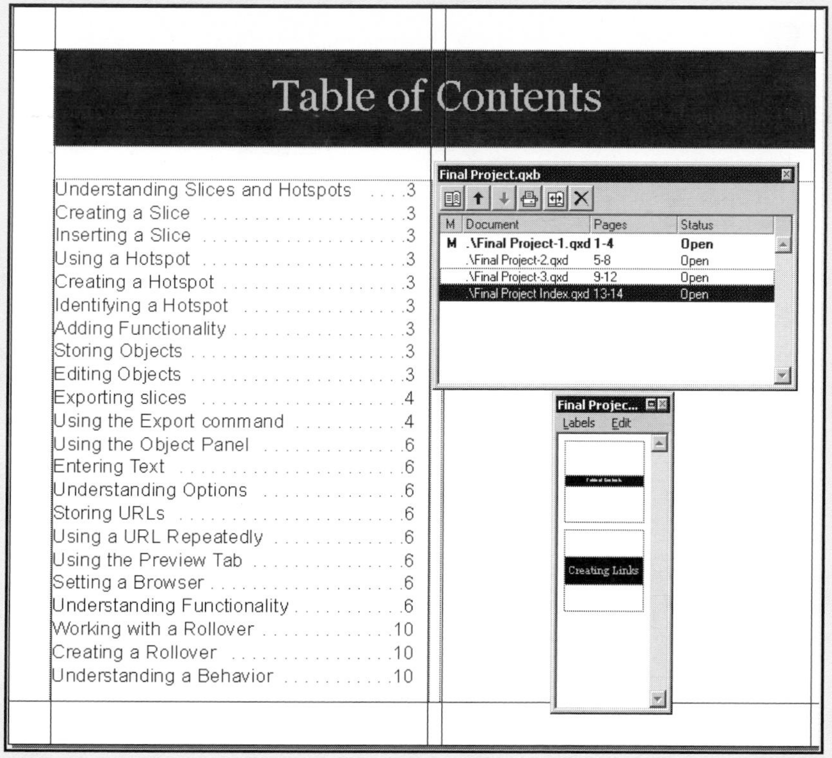

Table of Contents

Final Project.qxb

M	Document	Pages	Status
M	**.\Final Project-1.qxd**	**1-4**	**Open**
	.\Final Project-2.qxd	5-8	Open
	.\Final Project-3.qxd	9-12	Open
	.\Final Project Index.qxd	13-14	Open

Final Projec...

Labels   Edit

Table of Contents

Creating Links

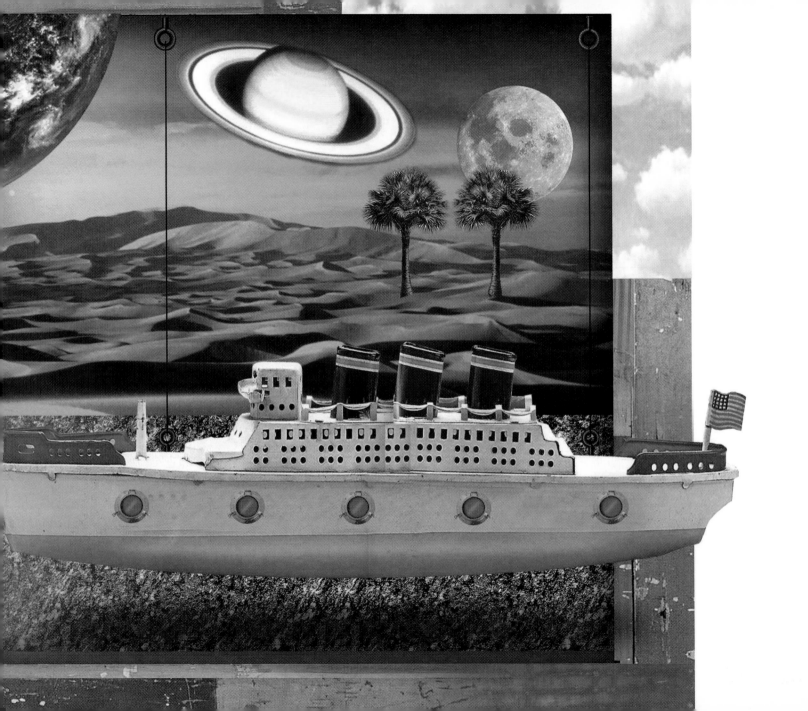

CREATING CONTENT FOR WEB USE

1. Create and modify a Web document.

2. Enhance a Web page.

3. Collect and display Web information.

4. Export content with XML.

UNIT K
CREATING CONTENT FOR WEB USE

Introduction

By now, you're familiar with Quark's strengths as a page layout program. You can also use it to create surprisingly sophisticated Web pages for publishing to the World Wide Web. Quark contains a special Web palette to facilitate this process. All you need are your Quark skills and your keen eye for design.

Presenting Information

Unlike a novel, Web page information is meant to be scanned rather than pored over word for word. Information that you want to convey to your readers should be easy to read quickly, and colors should be complementary. If you are designing a Web page for a business, bear in mind that most businesses have competitors, and if a Web site is irritating or obtuse, a customer can—and will—go elsewhere. On the Web, our attention spans are often shorter than usual. People rarely put up with annoying Web sites.

QUICKTIP

Avoid jarring colors and blinking doo-dads. Such effects may seem cute at first, but they grow tiresome quickly.

Using Old and New Tools

Web pages are different from paper pages in that you needn't be concerned about page count as you would in a lengthy document. You create many Web page elements using the same tools you use to create paper pages, such as the Rectangle Text Box tool to insert text, and the Rectangle Picture Box tool to insert graphic images. In addition, the Web palette contains tools just for working with Web pages. This palette appears whenever you create or open a Web document.

QUICKTIP

You should be concerned with page height and width as not everyone uses the same resolution, and you don't want readers to have to scroll too much either right-left or up-down.

Creating Special Web Elements

Tools on this palette are used to create Web-specific elements, such as form boxes and the elements found within them. In addition to being able to add graphic images—all important in the highly visual world of the Web, you can also create effects that become active based on the position of the mouse pointer.

Designing For All Systems

When designing your page layout, remember that not everyone has a cool 21-inch monitor on his or her desk. Some folks are still using 15-inch monitors with 640 × 480 resolution. Make sure you test your pages at a lower resolution, either on a smaller monitor, or by adjusting your monitor's settings, if necessary. The goal is to have your pages look terrific everywhere.

QUICKTIP

A special tool at the bottom of the Quark window lets you view your work in your Web browser so you'll always be able to see your progress, and know how your document will appear to others.

Tools You'll Use

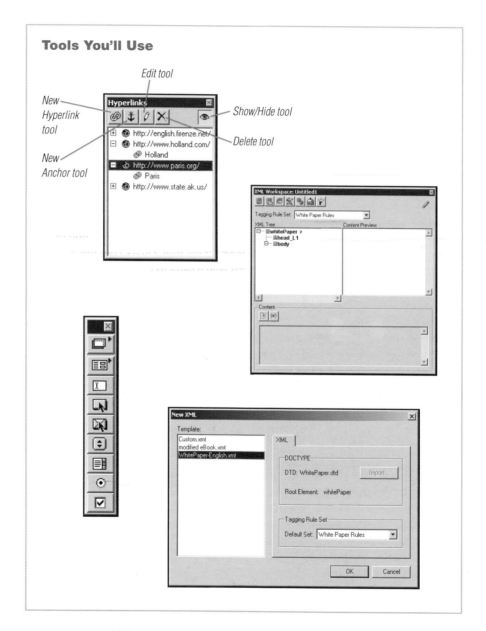

Edit tool

New Hyperlink tool

New Anchor tool

Show/Hide tool

Delete tool

CREATE AND MODIFY A WEB DOCUMENT

What You'll Do

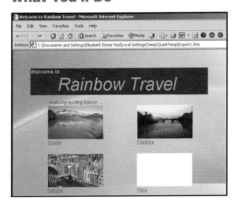

In this lesson, you'll learn how to create and modify a Web document by adding a background and text hyperlinks.

Creating a Web Page

Creating a Web page is nearly identical to creating a document. To do so, you click File on the menu bar, point to New, then click Web Document. See Figure K-1.

QUICKTIP

You can open an existing Web page in the same way you would open any other Quark file: click File on the menu bar, then click Open.

Understanding a Web Page

Before the page opens, the New Web Document dialog box opens, as shown in Figure K-2. Here you can determine the Page Width, and whether you want to use a graphic image as a background. You can also specify colors for Text, Background, and Links. A new Web page is shown in Figure K-3. There are several differences between a regular document and a Web document:

- A Web document contains no margins, but displays a dark blue line that indicates the right-page border.

- The ruler in a Web document appears in pixels.
- An HTML Preview tool appears on the status bar to let you see how your page will look on the Web.
- Different color options (on the Colors palette) are available. These Web colors make up a standardized collection that is universally displayed by most browsers. Using these specialized colors means that the purple color you apply to text will look similar on another computer.

FIGURE K-1
File menu options

Be forewarned that using non-'Web colors' can make for potentially bad—as in unusual and unpredictable—results. Make sure that if you *do* use colors other than those designed for the Web, you test your results on several other computers to ensure that the colors meet your expectations.

■ The names of exported pages appear on the Document Layout palette instead of on master pages.

When you finish modifying your settings, click OK and the Web document opens.

You can always modify color and dimension settings by clicking Page on the menu bar, then clicking Page Properties.

Adding a Background Image
Suppose you forget to add that perfect image to the background of your page? You can add the image by clicking Page on the menu bar, then clicking Page Properties. The Page Properties dialog box is similar to the New Web Document dialog box, except that it also lets you assign a title to the page.

The Web page title is what appears in the title bar when viewing the page in your browser.

FIGURE K-2
New Web Document dialog box

Use list arrows to determine hyperlink columns

Click checkbox to assign an image to the background

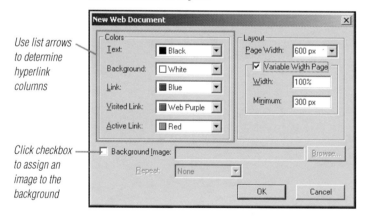

FIGURE K-3
New Web page

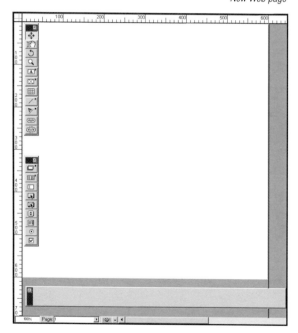

Inserting Text Hyperlinks

One of the most important features of a Web page is the use of hyperlinks. If you've spent any time browsing Web sites, you probably take for granted the fact that you can click a special text selection or picture, and your browser automatically jumps to a different Web page. Hyperlinks are what make this process so seamless. A hyperlink is a Web address (URL) that is assigned to text or an image, so that when a user clicks the text or image, the browser displays the contents of the linked address. There are two kinds of hyperlinks: absolute and relative. An absolute hyperlink links to a specific URL site, such as *www.quark.com*. A relative hyperlink links to a page *within your own site*, and should be specified using the prefix ../, (which tells your browser to look for the page within the folder containing the current page).

QUICKTIP

So why would you care if a hyperlink is relative or absolute? Only because you need to be aware of this distinction when creating links to your own site, or to the sites of others.

Assigning a Hyperlink

Assigning a hyperlink is a simple process. First you select the text or picture to which you want to assign the link. Next, you use the New Hyperlink tool on the Hyperlink palette, or click Style on the menu bar, point to Hyperlink, then click New. Tools available on the Hyperlinks palette are shown in Table K-1.

QUICKTIP

Selected text to which a hyperlink has been assigned appears underlined, in the color defined (the default is Blue).

TABLE K-1: Hyperlinks Palette Tools

tool	name	description
🔗	New Hyperlink	Applies a URL to the selection.
⚓	New Anchor	Applies a marker to a specific selection within a document, versus the top of a page.
✎	Edit	Lets you modify an existing selected hyperlink or anchor.
✕	Delete	Lets you delete an existing selected hyperlink or anchor.
👁	Show/Hide	Lets you show/hide selected text or picture anchors.

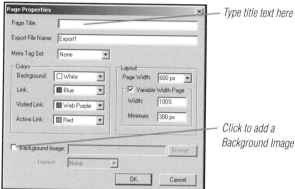

Type title text here

Click to add a
Background Image

Your list
may differ

Your file location
may differ

Click to locate
the Image Files

Add a page title and background image

1. Start Quark, open QP K-1.qwd, then save it as **Rainbow Travel**.

   The Web document opens, as well as the Web Tool palette. Some features (which will be covered in more detail later in this unit) have already been added to this page.

   > TIP   Mac users must boot using the OS 9.x operating system.

2. Click Page on the menu bar, then click Page Properties.

   The Page Properties dialog box opens, and the cursor is in the Page Title text box.

3. Click the Variable Width Page checkbox if necessary. Compare your settings to Figure K-4.

4. Type **Welcome to Rainbow Travel**.

   When viewed in a browser, the text in the Page Title text box will appear in the title bar.

5. Click the Background Image checkbox.

6. Click the Browse button (Win) or Select button (Mac), then locate and click Rainbow.jpg. Compare your dialog box to Figure K-5.

7. Click Open.

8. Click the Repeat list arrow, then click Tile.

   The Repeat list arrow lets you determine whether and how the background image will repeat on the page. In this case, the image is tiled, as necessary, to fill the page.

9. Click OK, then click OK to close the warning box if necessary. Compare your screen to Figure K-6.

You added a title to the page, and inserted a graphic image for the background.

Create text hyperlinks

1. Select the Content tool on the Tools palette, if necessary.

2. Click the Paris text box (at approximately 350 H/380 V) to select it, then double-click "Paris".

   Did you notice that these measurements are different than what you've seen on regular document pages? The default units of measurement on Web pages are pixels, not inches.

3. Click Style on the menu bar, point to Hyperlink, then click New.

   The New Hyperlink dialog box opens.

4. Click the URL list arrow, then click http://.

5. Deselect the selected text, if necessary; click to the right of the text, then type **www.paris.org**. Compare your dialog box with Figure K-7.

6. Click OK.

   The text "Paris" is selected, but the color of the text changed, and it is underlined.

7. Double-click the text "Alaska" to select it.

8. Click Style on the menu bar, point to Hyperlink, then click http://www.state.ak.us.

You added a new hyperlink to selected text, then applied an existing hyperlink to selected text.

FIGURE K-7
New Hyperlink dialog box

Web address
in text box

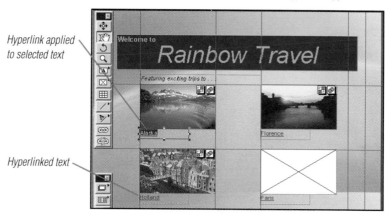

Hyperlink applied to selected text

Hyperlinked text

View a Web page

1. Click File on the menu bar, then click Save. Compare your page to Figure K-8.

2. Click the HTML Preview tool on the status bar. Compare your screen to Figure K-9.

3. Click the Close button on the browser.

You viewed a page in a Web browser.

FIGURE K-9

Page in browser

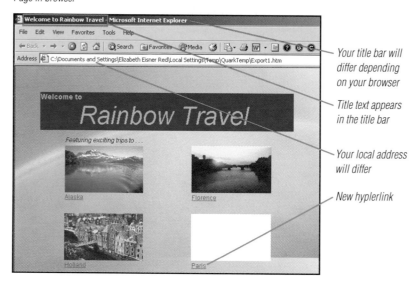

Your title bar will differ depending on your browser

Title text appears in the title bar

Your local address will differ

New hyplerlink

ENHANCE A WEB PAGE

What You'll Do

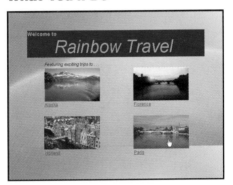

In this lesson, you'll learn how to create a rollover effect, and apply a hyperlink to an image.

Using Special Effects

You can add a special effect to an image that causes a different image to appear in place of the initial image within a picture box. This effect, called a **rollover**, is initiated when the user moves (or "rolls") the mouse pointer over the image. Once a picture box contains one image, you can add an additional image as a rollover. You can also add a hyperlink to the image, so that no matter which image the user clicks, the browser will jump to the assigned hyperlink. When you add either a rollover image or a hyperlink, an additional icon appears in the upper-right corner of the initial image within the Quark window, as a reference for you. These icons don't appear in Preview mode because Preview mode shows only what the user will see. Figure K-10 shows an image in Quark with the additional icons.

QUICKTIP

When you hold the mouse pointer over the Rollover icon (while still in Quark), a ScreenTip will tell you the name of the rollover file. When you hold the mouse pointer over the Hyperlink icon, a ScreenTip will display the hyperlinked URL.

Including an e-mail hyperlink

One of the most important hyperlinks you can (and should) include on a Web page is one that lets your readers communicate with you. This type of hyperlink is called the mailto: link. When clicked, the mailto: link opens a new message in the default e-mail application with the linked address. You can attach an e-mail hyperlink to selected text or a picture box by clicking Style on the menu bar, pointing to Hyperlink, then clicking New. Click URL list arrow, click mailto:, type the address where you want these messages delivered, then click OK.

Creating a Rollover

You can create a rollover for a selected picture box by clicking Item on the menu bar, pointing to Rollover, then clicking Create Rollover. This command opens the Rollover dialog box. You can modify an existing rollover in a picture box by clicking Item on the menu bar, pointing to Rollover, then clicking Edit Rollover to change the rollover image location, or Remove Rollover to completely delete the rollover effect. The Rollover dialog box lets you assign the default image and the rollover image, and also lets you assign a hyperlink.

QUICKTIP

The initial image, or default image, can also be assigned using the Rollover dialog box.

Rolling Over an Image

There's no secret to making a rollover happen, but it always impresses people. Once the default and rollover images are assigned, all users must do to see the rollover effect is move the mouse pointer over the original image. Figure K-11 shows the default image in HTML Preview (the browser). Figure K-12 shows the image when the mouse pointer is held over it. Pretty neat, huh?

Adding a Hyperlink to an Image

You can further enhance an image by adding a hyperlink. You can add a hyperlink in the Rollover dialog box, or by clicking Style on the menu bar, pointing to Hyperlink, then clicking New.

FIGURE K-10
Image with Rollover and Hyperlink icons

Icon indicates
a hyperlink

Icon indicates
a rollover

FIGURE K-11
Image in browser

FIGURE K-12
Rollover image

Pointer causes
rollover image
to appear

Lesson 2 Enhance a Web Page

Insert an image in a picture box

1. Click the picture box (at approximately 400 H/300 V) above "Paris".

2. Click File on the menu bar, then click Get Picture.

   The Get Picture dialog box opens.

3. Locate and click Paris.jpg, then click Open.

4. Click Style on the menu bar, then click Fit Picture To Box.

   The image is fit to the dimensions of the picture box, as shown in Figure K-13.

You inserted an image in an existing picture box, then fit the image to the box.

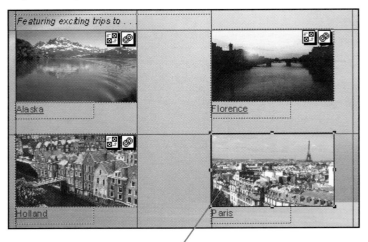

Newly inserted image

FIGURE K-14

Completed Rollover dialog box

Your file locations will differ

FIGURE K-15

Rollover and hyperlink applied to image

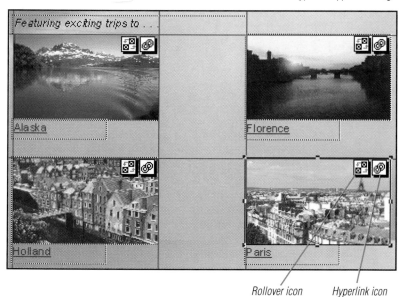

Rollover icon   *Hyperlink icon*

Create a rollover

1. Click Item on the menu bar, point to Rollover, then click Create Rollover.

   The Rollover dialog box opens.

2. Click the Rollover Image Browse (Win) or Select (Mac) button, then locate and click Seine.jpg.

3. Click Open.

4. Click the Hyperlink list arrow, then click http://.

5. Deselect the selected text, if necessary; click to the right of the text, then type **www.paris.org**. Compare your dialog box with Figure K-14.

6. Click OK. Compare your page to Figure K-15.

   Did you notice that two icons appear in the upper-right corner of the Paris image?

You created a rollover effect and added a hyperlink to the rollover.

Test a rollover and a hyperlink

1. Click File on the menu bar, then click Save.

2. Click the HTML Preview tool on the status bar. Compare your screen to Figure K-16.

3. Position your pointer over the Paris image to see the rollover effect.

4. Click the Close button on the browser.

   > TIP   You can also click your Web browser's Refresh button to view the changes, as an alternative to closing and reopening the browser.

You applied a hyperlink to an image.

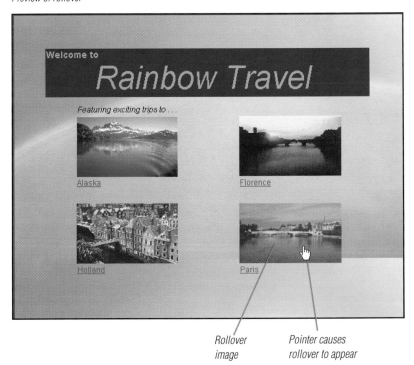

Rollover image

Pointer causes rollover to appear

FIGURE K-17

Mailto: hyperlink added to text

Hyperlinked text

1. Click the Rectangle Text Box tool on the Tools palette. $\boxed{A}$
2. Drag the pointer from 100 H/680 V to 200 H/700 V. ╋

   Did you notice that the length of the page "grew" to accommodate the new text box?
3. Type **Click to contact us** using the default font and size. ⊺
4. Select the text you just typed.
5. Click Style on the menu bar, point to Hyperlink, then click New.
6. Click the URL list arrow, then click mailto:.
7. Press [RightArrow], type **www.r-travel.com**, then click OK. (*This is a fictitious URL, for practice purposes in this unit only.*)
8. Click the Background Color tool on the Colors palette, then click None.
9. Deselect the text box, click File on the menu bar, then click Save. Compare your screen to Figure K-17.

You added a mailto: hyperlink to a Web document.

Planning for customer service

One of the most problematic areas of business planning is customer service. Even with earnest research efforts, the demand for a product or service is truly determined only in the marketplace. Underestimating demand for a product or service can lead to outstripped supply. Overestimating can lead to idle capacity, underutilized workers, and eventually, perhaps, layoffs and/or bankruptcy. When developing a Web site, consider the developmental and maintenance costs carefully. Unless visitors perceive value in a return visit, either to purchase additional product or read updated content, the number of visits to a site will drop off. Changing content requires an investment of time and energy on the part of developers and management. You must plan for direct contact with visitors to your site, too. While e-mail responses can be standardized and automated to respond to customer needs, someone must make sure that the responses are timely, and accurately answer the customers' questions. If you don't satisfy your customers' needs, someone else will.

COLLECT AND DISPLAY WEB INFORMATION

What You'll Do

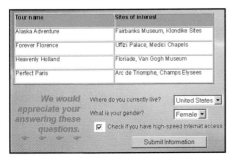

 In this lesson, you'll create form elements and a table on a Web page.

Using Form Elements To Collect Data

Web pages are useful not only for displaying information, but also for collecting it. You can use a form to gather marketing information about visitors to your Web page, allow visitors to order materials or products, let them register for special deals or events, and for many other purposes. Forms and their elements play an important part on Web pages for the following reasons:

- They are visually appealing
- They make it easy to identify options for the Web visitor, and clarify the type of information sought by the Web host.

- They provide consistency in data collection. For example, if you didn't supply a pop-up menu, a simple request for a reader's gender might result in a dozen different responses. Most data has many uses, and many companies "mine" the data they collect. For example, they might use consumer responses to determine if a product is worth maintaining or is cost-effective.
- They're fun to fill out, and make readers feel like they're contributing to your business.

QUICKTIP

Whenever possible, keep it simple. It should be easy for your Web visitors to *get* information, and it should be equally easy for them to *give* information. If it's not easy, they won't play.

Understanding Form Tools

Form tools are found on the Web Tool palette, and are shown in Figure K-18. These tools are described in Table K-2. Each form element performs a specific task. The Image Map tools, for example, allow you to define a hot area. A hot area is an area within an image that is clickable. The Form Box tool defines the area in which the form elements are stored. A selected form element can be modified by clicking Item on the menu bar, then clicking Modify. Within a Web page, a Radio button and a checkbox have similar applications.

FIGURE K-18
Web Tool palette

QUICKTIP

Remember that the Web Tool palette appears only when a Web document is open.

Getting to the Point

If there is information you want your reader to know, tell them as quickly as possible. Don't make them hunt for the facts. Tables are an effective method of displaying otherwise dull collections of words. You can create tables on a Web page using the same Tables tool (on the Tools palette) you use on a regular page.

TABLE K-2: Form Elements

tool	name	description
	Rectangle Image Map tool	Defines a rectangular hot area in an image.
	Oval Image Map tool	Defines an oval hot area in an image.
	Bézier Image Map tool	Defines a freeform hot area in an image.
	Form Box tool	Defines the area in which the form elements are stored.
	File Selection tool	Creates a Browse button that lets a user locate a file.
	Text Field tool	Creates a text field.
	Button tool	Creates a rectangular button that contains a text label.
	Image Button tool	Creates a button that contains an image.
	Pop-up Menu tool	Creates a multi-selection list that pops up when its list arrow is clicked. The list size is determined by the number of choices, and may contain a default selection.
	List Box tool	Creates a multi-selection list that displays choices. The list size is predetermined, may contain scroll bars, if necessary, and may contain a default selection.
	Radio Button tool	Creates a circular button that can be selected.
	Check Box tool	Creates a box that can be selected.

FIGURE K-19

Edit Menu dialog box

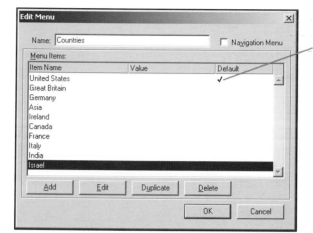

Checkmark indicates default value

FIGURE K-20

Modify dialog box

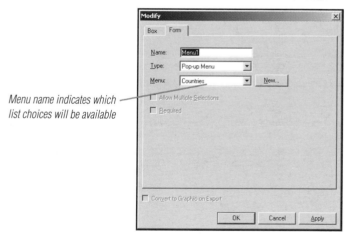

Menu name indicates which list choices will be available

FIGURE K-21

Pop-up menu in browser

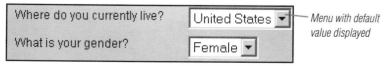

Menu with default value displayed

Add a pop-up menu

1. Click the Pop-up Menu tool on the Web palette. ⊟

2. Drag the pointer from 440 H/570 V to 470 H/590 V. ┼

   A blank pop-up menu opens. Don't worry if it's not exactly where you want it; you can nudge it into place later.

3. Click Item on the menu bar, then click Modify.

4. Click the Form tab if necessary, then click New (to the right of the Menu text box).

   The Edit Menu dialog box opens.

5. Type **Countries** in the Name text box, then click Add.

   The Menu Item dialog box opens.

6. Type **United States**, click the Use as Default checkbox, then click OK.

7. Click Add in the Edit Menu dialog box, then continue to add entries using Figure K-19 as a guide; *do not click the Use as Default checkbox for any of these new entries.*

8. Click OK to close the Edit Menu dialog box, click OK in the warning box if necessary, compare your settings to Figure K-20, then click OK to close the Modify dialog box.

9. Click the Item tool on the Tools palette, then press [DownArrow] until the bottom of the pop-up menu is aligned with the text box to its left. ⊕

10. Save the document, then click the HTML Preview tool on the status bar. ⊡

11. Compare your screen to Figure K-21, then click the Close button on the browser.

You created a pop-up menu on a form.

Add a checkbox and buttons

1. Click the Check Box tool on the Web palette. ☑

2. Drag the pointer from 270 H/620 V to 300 H/640 V. ┼

   TIP Don't worry if you cannot drag the shape past 360 H; the tool will expand when you add text.

3. Click Item on the menu bar, then click Modify.

4. Click the Initially Checked checkbox, then compare your dialog box to Figure K-22.

5. Click OK.

6. Click the Button tool on the Web palette. ⬚

7. Drag the pointer from 350 H/650 V to 375 H/670 V. ┼

8. Verify that the Content tool is selected, then type **Submit Information**. See Figure K-23.

9. Click File on the menu bar, then click Save.

10. Click the HTML Preview tool on the status bar. ⚙ ▼ Compare your screen to Figure K-24.

11. Click the Close button on the browser.

You added a checkbox and button to the form.

FIGURE K-22
Modify dialog box

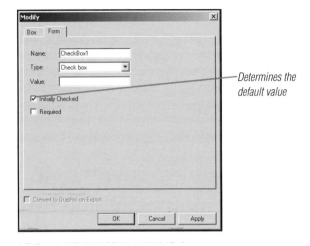

Determines the
default value

FIGURE K-23
Completed button and checkbox

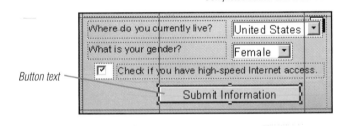

Button text

FIGURE K-24
Form elements in browser

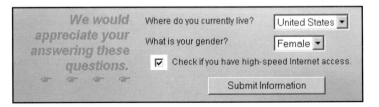

FIGURE K-25
Table Properties dialog box

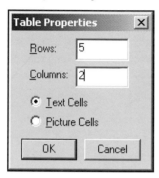

FIGURE K-26
Table information

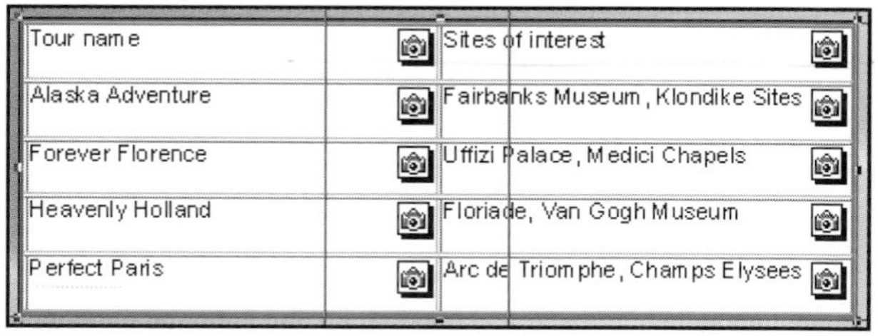

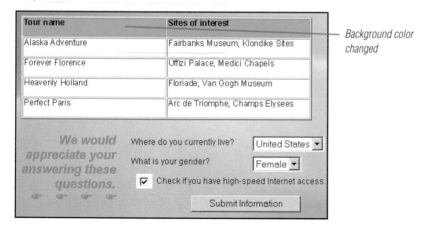

FIGURE K-27
Completed table

Background color changed

Add and format a table

1. Click the Tables tool on the Tools palette.
2. Drag the pointer from 100 H/400 V to 530 H/550 V.

   The Table Properties dialog box opens.
3. Type **5** in the Rows text box, then type **2** in the Columns text box. See Figure K-25.
4. Click OK.
5. Click the Content tool, if necessary, then type the information shown in Figure K-26.
6. Make the text in the first row bold.
7. Position the pointer to the left of the first row in the table, then click.
8. Click the Background Color button if necessary, then click Web Aqua on the Colors palette.
9. Deselect the table, click File on the menu bar, then click Save.
10. Click the HTML Preview tool on the status bar. Compare your screen to Figure K-27.
11. Click the Close button in the browser.
12. Proceed to the Skills Review (Mac) or to the next lesson (Win).

You added a table to the form, then formatted its contents.

EXPORT CONTENT WITH XML

What You'll Do

Understanding Animation

Animation means motion, although the movement may not always seem to flow evenly from one action to the next. The solution is to ease the transition between motion frames-the more frames in an animation, the smoother it plays.

Tweening adds frames in between selected frames so that the movement appears more fluid and less jerky. In Wingman, you can add as many tweening frames as you need to create just the effect you want.

Using Animation Symbols
When you animate a selection, Wingman automatically converts the selected object to a symbol, a graphic that represents an object, text, or combination group. Copies of symbols are known as instances-when you edit the original symbol, all instances of the symbol update as well. You need at least two instances of a symbol in order to create animation-one for the start of the animation, the other for the end. You can create animation that is more complex by adding more instances.

Importing and Creating an Image
You can import or create any image you want to animate and convert it to a symbol. Wingman adds the new symbol to the Library panel and the original object used to create the symbol becomes an instance of that symbol in the document window. Wingman stores symbols on the Library panel, where you can edit and reuse them in other documents.

Understanding Frame Delay
You can fine-tune your animation by adjusting the display time for each frame, known as frame delay. Frame delays are measured in hundredths of a second-even a small change can dramatically affect your animation. If the frame delay is too short, the image will appear indistinct, if it's too long, the image will appear jerky or erratic. The frame delay displays in the right column of the Frames panel.

 In this lesson, you'll learn to create and modify an XML document using avenue.quark and a text editor.

Understanding XML

What is XML and why should you care? Well, XML (which stands for eXtensible Markup Language) is a powerful language that is similar to HTML (HyperText Markup Language) in that it is used to create Web documents. The difference is that XML is designed to enhance and strengthen HTML: it is not a replacement. Using XML, you can take existing Quark documents and quickly make them Web-ready.

> **QUICKTIP**
>
> XML has many uses. Converting Quark documents for Web use is just a sample of its strength.

Making Use of Your Documents

Suppose your company wants you to take the existing employee handbook and post it on the corporate Web site. There are several ways you can make these documents Web-ready. One way—the least appealing—is to have someone (preferably not you) go through the laborious process of applying HTML tags to the document text. That doesn't sound like fun! Another way is to use a program included in QuarkXPress called avenue.quark that inserts tags (codes that surround important text) in the document so it becomes a useful Web document that can be browsed, searched, and so on. By inserting XML tags and special Web-designed style sheets, you can easily convert a regular document into one that can be used on the Web.

Understanding Cascading Style Sheets

You've already seen how style sheets can make your life easier when it comes to making documents look consistent, or when trying to generate a table of contents. Well, style sheets can be used in Web documents, too. Many Web browsers support Cascading Style Sheets, which means that you can vary the appearance of a document by changing a single reference in the XML codes. A Cascading Style Sheet (CSS) is a document that contains objects and formatting instructions that can be applied using styles.

Preparing a Document for XML

Every XML document needs a DTD, or Document Type Definition. The DTD describes and defines the XML elements (such as company name). How do you get the tags into the Quark document? Just follow these steps:

- Make sure that your Quark document is open and has styles utilized by a CSS.
- Open a new Quark XML document (by clicking File on the menu bar, pointing to New, then clicking XML). Select a set of tagging rules, such as White Paper Rules. Figure K-28 shows a tagging rule selection in the New XML dialog box.

- Drag coded text boxes from the Quark document into the XML Workspace. The XML tags are automatically applied to the corresponding styles in the document. Figure K-29 shows tags in the XML Workspace dialog box that were derived from a document. This dialog box is actually a workspace where you can create XML tags.
- Save the XML tags in a document with the filename .xml.
- Modify the XML document using a text editor so your browser knows which CSS should be applied, then view the document in your browser. A text editor is used to add an instruction that tells your browser which CSS should be used.

FIGURE K-28
New XML dialog box

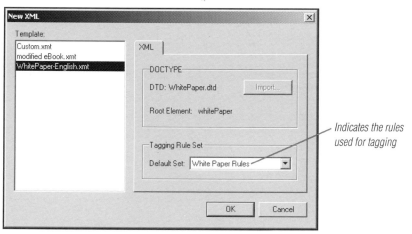

Indicates the rules used for tagging

FIGURE K-29
XML Workspace

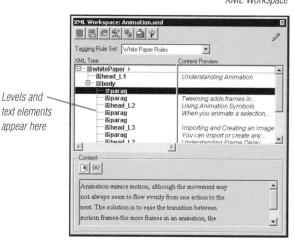

Levels and text elements appear here

Tag a document

NOTE: The steps in this lesson are for Windows users only.

1. Copy the following files (added to your hard drive during the Quark installation process) to the folder location where your project files are stored: wp.css, wp2.css, diagram1.gif, sidestripe_72.gif. The files are located in \Program Files\Quark\ QuarkXPress\ Tutorials\avenue.quark Tutorial.

   This protects the original files in your Program Files folder from any inadvertent modification.

2. Open QP K-2.qxd.

3. Click File on the menu bar, point to New, then click XML.

   The New XML dialog box opens.

4. Make sure the WhitePaper-English option is selected, then click OK to accept the default Template and Tagging Rule Set.

   The XML dialog box opens.

5. Press and hold [Ctrl], click and drag the text box containing the title text at 2" H/1" V to head_L1 in the XML Workspace dialog box, then release [Ctrl].

   A message box opens, as shown in Figure K-30, informing you that tagging is complete.

6. Click OK.

   "Understanding Animation" appears in the Content Preview of the XML Workspace dialog box.

You tagged a document using the XML Workspace.

FIGURE K-30
Message box indicates tagging is complete

FIGURE K-31

Tags in XML Workspace

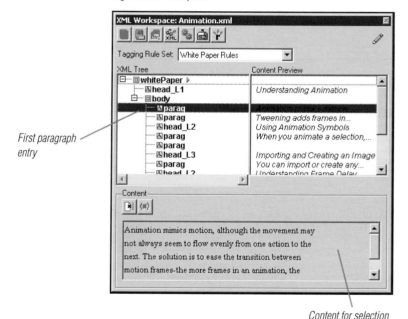

First paragraph entry

Content for selection appears here

Insert a CSS code in a text file

NOTE: The steps in this lesson are for Windows users only.

1. Open a text editor, such as WordPad.

   It is recommended that you *not use* Microsoft Word since this program might automatically modify several crucial characters. Using Microsoft Notepad also may cause poor results.

2. Open Animation.xml. Compare your screen to Figure K-32.

3. Position the pointer at the end of the first line, then press [Enter].

4. Type **<?xml-stylesheet type="text/css" href="wp.css"?>**. See Figure K-33.

   > TIP Make sure you type this instruction exactly as it appears or you may have different results.

5. Save the document in the text editor in a text-only format, replacing the original file when prompted.

6. Open your Web browser, then open Animation.xml. Compare your screen to Figure K-34.

You modified an XML document using a text editor, inserted a code that determines which CSS will be used, then viewed the document in your browser.

FIGURE K-32

XML document in text editor

Your text editor
may look different

FIGURE K-33

Cascading Style Sheet code in XML document

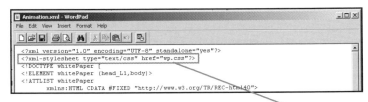

Code determines which
CSS will be used

FIGURE K-34

XML text with initial CSS

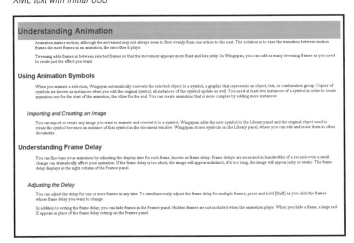

Creating Content for Web Use   Unit K

FIGURE K-35

Edited CSS code in text editor

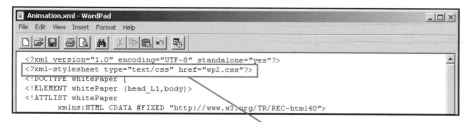

```
Animation.xml - WordPad                                    _ □ ×
File  Edit  View  Insert  Format  Help

  □ ☞ ◾ ◾ ◾ ◾ ◾ ◾ ◾ ◾ ◾

  <?xml version="1.0" encoding="UTF-8" standalone="yes"?>
  <?xml-stylesheet type="text/css" href="wp2.css"?>
  <!DOCTYPE whitePaper [
  <!ELEMENT whitePaper (head_L1,body)>
  <!ATTLIST whitePaper
           xmlns:HTML CDATA #FIXED "http://www.w3.org/TR/REC-html40">
```

Modification changes the CSS that is applied to this document

FIGURE K-36

XML text with alternate CSS

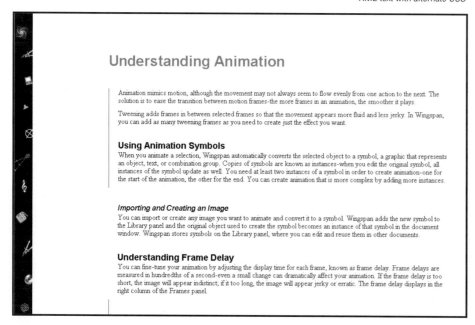

Understanding Animation

Animation mimics motion, although the movement may not always seem to flow evenly from one action to the next. The solution is to ease the transition between motion frames-the more frames in an animation, the smoother it plays.

Tweening adds frames in between selected frames so that the movement appears more fluid and less jerky. In Wingspan, you can add as many tweening frames as you need to create just the effect you want.

Using Animation Symbols

When you animate a selection, Wingspan automatically converts the selected object to a symbol, a graphic that represents an object, text, or combination group. Copies of symbols are known as instances-when you edit the original symbol, all instances of the symbol update as well. You need at least two instances of a symbol in order to create animation-one for the start of the animation, the other for the end. You can create animation that is more complex by adding more instances.

Importing and Creating an Image

You can import or create any image you want to animate and convert it to a symbol. Wingspan adds the new symbol to the Library panel and the original object used to create the symbol becomes an instance of that symbol in the document window. Wingspan stores symbols on the Library panel, where you can edit and reuse them in other documents.

Understanding Frame Delay

You can fine-tune your animation by adjusting the display time for each frame, known as frame delay. Frame delays are measured in hundredths of a second-even a small change can dramatically affect your animation. If the frame delay is too short, the image will appear indistinct; if it too long, the image will appear jerky or erratic. The frame delay displays in the right column of the Frames panel.

Modify a CSS code in a text file

NOTE: The steps in this lesson are for Windows users only.

1. Open the text editor window.

   > **TIP** You can leave the Quark, text editor, and Web browser windows open as you switch back and forth between programs.

2. Position the pointer to the right of "p" in the CSS text you typed earlier.

3. Type **2**. Compare your screen to Figure K-35.

4. Save the document in the text editor in a text-only format.

5. Open the browser window, then refresh the document image. Compare your screen to Figure K-36.

6. Close the browser window.

7. Close the text editor.

You modified the CSS code in the XML document, then viewed the document in your browser.

Power User Shortcuts

to do this:	use this method:
Add a background image	Page ➤ Page Properties [Ctrl][Alt][Shift][A] (Win) ⌘ [alt][shift][A] (Mac)
Add a hyperlink to a rollover image	Style ➤ Hyperlink ➤ New
Add a hyperlink to text	Style ➤ Hyperlink ➤ New
Add a page title	Page ➤ Page Properties [Ctrl][Alt][Shift][A] (Win) ⌘ [alt][shift][A] (Mac)
Add an anchor	
Create a Bézier image map	
Create a Browse button	
Create a button containing an image	
Create a check box	
Create a form box	
Create a list box	
Create a pop-up menu	

to do this:	use this method:
Create a Radio button	
Create a rectangular button	
Create a rectangular image map	
Create a rollover	Item ➤ Rollover ➤ Create Rollover
Create a text field	
Create an oval image map	
Create an XML document	File ➤ New ➤ XML
Delete a hyperlink	
Edit a hyperlink	
Modify a form element	Item ➤ Modify [Ctrl][M] (Win) ⌘ [M] (Mac)
Modify XML code	Use text editor
Preview a Web page in browser	
Preview XML code	
Show/Hide a hyperlink	

Your comfort while working is important. At any time in this exercise, please feel free to change the document view, move palettes if they are in your way, or Show/Hide Invisibles.

To complete the Skills Review, Mac users should boot using the OS 9.x operating system, and should skip the "Collect and display Web information" Skills Review.

Create and modify a Web document.

1. Start Quark.
2. Open QP K-3.qwd, then save it as **Relaxation Spa.**
3. Change the page title to "Relaxation Spa Getaway Specials".
4. Change the hyperlink color to Web Maroon.
5. Change the visited hyperlink color to Web Navy.
6. Use Water.jpg as the page background with tiled repetition.
7. Select the text "our latest travel getaway".
8. Create a hyperlink to this Web site: *www.beaches.com.*
9. Save your work.

Enhance a Web page.

1. Select the empty picture box in the document.
2. Get the picture Map.jpg.
3. Fit the picture to the box.
4. Add a solid, 6 pt Web Maroon border to the picture frame.

5. Add Castle.jpg as a rollover image.
6. Add the Web site *www.beaches.com* as the hyperlink to the rollover image.
7. Create a mailto: hyperlink to "Ask us" using (*fictional address*) *beachmaven@relaxationspa.com.*

FIGURE K-37
Skills Review in progress

8. Save your work.
9. View your page in your browser. See Figure K-37.

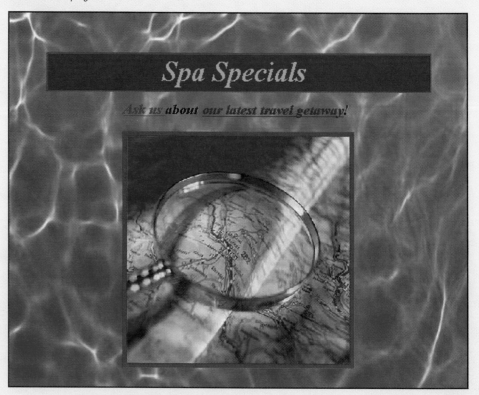

Collect and display Web information.

1. Create a rectangular text box from 50 H/480 V to 250 H/520 V using a bold, center-aligned 14 pt Times New Roman font.
2. Type **Please take a moment to answer our informal survey**.
3. Change the text box background so the background image is visible.
4. Create a form box from 300 H/480 V to 550 H/575 V.
5. Create a rectangular text box from 310 H/490 V to 410 H/550 V.
6. Type **Choose one dream getaway location**, using a right-aligned 14 pt Times New Roman font.
7. Change the text box background so the background image is visible.
8. Create a list box from 420 H/490 V to approximately 450 H/540V.
9. Create a new menu called Getaways, then add the following items to the list: Australia, Bali, Belize, Bermuda, Brazil (the default selection), Caribbean, Costa Rica, and France. (This list is not required and should not allow multiple selections.)
10. Create a button from 420 H/550V to approximately 445 H/570 V.
11. Type **Send Choice** on the button face.
12. Save your work.
13. Preview the page in your Web browser. Compare your screen to Figure K-38.

FIGURE K-38
Skills Review in progress

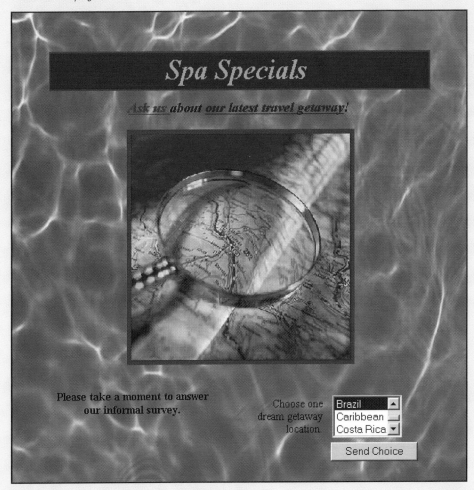

Export content with XML.

NOTE: The steps below are for Windows users only.

1. Open QP K-4.qxd.
2. Open a new XML document using the WhitePaper-English template and the White Paper Rules set.
3. Drag the text box at 5" H/5" V to body in the XML Workspace. (*Hint*: Make sure you close the message box.)
4. Drag the text box at 5" H/1" V to head_L1 in the XML Workspace.
5. View the XML code.
6. Save the XML tags as a standalone document called **Image Meister**.
7. Close the XML Workspace.
8. Open Image Meister.xml in your text editor.
9. Type the following line after the existing first line: **<?xml-stylesheet type="text/css" href="wp2.css"?>**.
10. Save the modified file using a text-only format.
11. View the document in your browser.
12. Modify Image Meister.xml in your text editor by changing wp2.css (in line 2) to "wp.css".
13. Save the modified file using a text-only format.
14. View the document in your browser, then compare your document to Figure K-39.

FIGURE K-39
Completed Skills Review

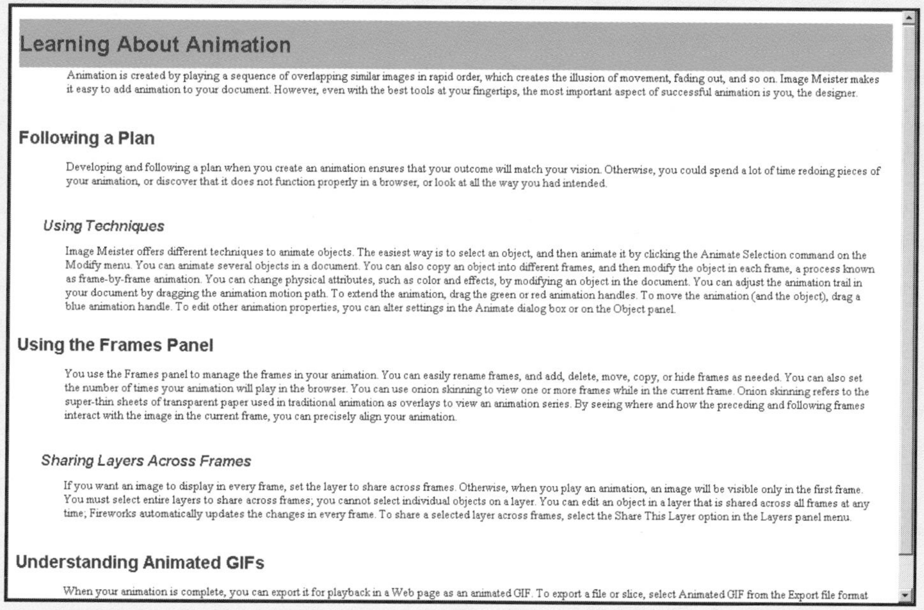

Learning About Animation

Animation is created by playing a sequence of overlapping similar images in rapid order, which creates the illusion of movement, fading out, and so on. Image Meister makes it easy to add animation to your document. However, even with the best tools at your fingertips, the most important aspect of successful animation is you, the designer.

Following a Plan

Developing and following a plan when you create an animation ensures that your outcome will match your vision. Otherwise, you could spend a lot of time redoing pieces of your animation, or discover that it does not function properly in a browser, or look at all the way you had intended.

Using Techniques

Image Meister offers different techniques to animate objects. The easiest way is to select an object, and then animate it by clicking the Animate Selection command on the Modify menu. You can animate several objects in a document. You can also copy an object into different frames, and then modify the object in each frame, a process known as frame-by-frame animation. You can change physical attributes, such as color and effects, by modifying an object in the document. You can adjust the animation trail in your document by dragging the animation motion path. To extend the animation, drag the green or red animation handles. To move the animation (and the object), drag a blue animation handle. To edit other animation properties, you can alter settings in the Animate dialog box or on the Object panel.

Using the Frames Panel

You use the Frames panel to manage the frames in your animation. You can easily rename frames, and add, delete, move, copy, or hide frames as needed. You can also set the number of times your animation will play in the browser. You can use onion skinning to view one or more frames while in the current frame. Onion skinning refers to the super-thin sheets of transparent paper used in traditional animation as overlays to view an animation series. By seeing where and how the preceding and following frames interact with the image in the current frame, you can precisely align your animation.

Sharing Layers Across Frames

If you want an image to display in every frame, set the layer to share across frames. Otherwise, when you play an animation, an image will be visible only in the first frame. You must select entire layers to share across frames; you cannot select individual objects on a layer. You can edit an object in a layer that is shared across all frames at any time; Fireworks automatically updates the changes in every frame. To share a selected layer across frames, select the Share This Layer option in the Layers panel menu.

Understanding Animated GIFs

When your animation is complete, you can export it for playback in a Web page as an animated GIF. To export a file or slice, select Animated GIF from the Export file format

The local chapter of dairymen advised your art gallery, Innovation, that July is National Ice Cream month. They asked you to help them promote ice cream by holding a special exhibit of artwork featuring the confection. You decide to advertise the exhibit on the gallery's Web site.

NOTE: Mac users should first boot using the OS 9.x operating system.

1. Open QP K-5.qwd, then save it as **Ice Cream Exhibit**.
2. Add the following page title "Ice Cream Exhibit" to the page.
3. Add the file Art Background.jpg to the background using the tile repeating format.
4. Add the VanillaCone.jpg file to the picture box, then fit the picture to the box. (*Hint*: You can reposition the picture box if you wish.)
5. Format the second text box from the top by changing the Background color, Text color, and Text alignment. (*Hint*: In the sample, the Background is changed to Web Purple, and the text is centered and italicized.)
6. If you choose, you can add a colorful border to the top text box.
7. Add the ChocolateCone.jpg image as a rollover.
8. Hyperlink the image to http://www.ice-cream.org/.
9. Create a text box that says "*Click here for more information*".
10. Create a mailto: hyperlink using this text box and your own e-mail address.
11. Format the hyperlink text using any formatting you choose. The sample shows 18-point Arial font and center alignment.
12. Save your work.
13. View the document in your browser, then compare your image to the sample in Figure K-40.

FIGURE K-40
Completed Project Builder 1

You work for Bobcat Books, a small independent publisher of technical manuals. Your boss doesn't understand the implications of XML to her market, and is afraid that it will be too difficult for the company to move hard-copy texts into the eBooks market. You decide to demonstrate how easy it is to convert a sample Quark document into an XML page.

NOTE: The steps below are for Windows users only.

1. Open QP K-6.qxd.
2. Open a new XML document using White Paper Rules.
3. Drag the document title to head_L1 in the XML Tree.
4. Drag the three-column text box to body in the XML Tree.
5. Save the tags as **XML Chapter** (a standalone document).
6. Close the XML Workspace.
7. Open XML Chapter.xml in a text editor.
8. Add the following to the document **<?xml-stylesheet type="text/css" href="wp2.css"?>** as the second line.
9. Save the document using a text-only format.
10. View the document in your browser, then compare your document to Figure K-41.

FIGURE K-41
Completed Project Builder 2

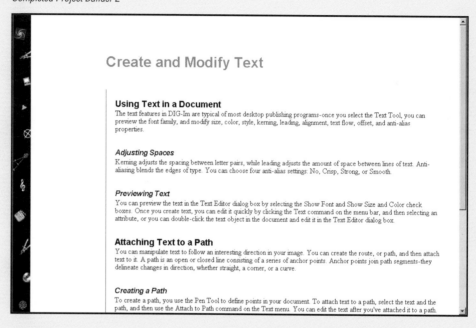

Create and Modify Text

Using Text in a Document
The text features in DIG-Im are typical of most desktop publishing programs-once you select the Text Tool, you can preview the font family, and modify size, color, style, kerning, leading, alignment, text flow, offset, and anti-alias properties.

Adjusting Spaces
Kerning adjusts the spacing between letter pairs, while leading adjusts the amount of space between lines of text. Anti-aliasing blends the edges of type. You can choose four anti-alias settings: No, Crisp, Strong, or Smooth.

Previewing Text
You can preview the text in the Text Editor dialog box by selecting the Show Font and Show Size and Color check boxes. Once you create text, you can edit it quickly by clicking the Text command on the menu bar, and then selecting an attribute, or you can double-click the text object in the document and edit it in the Text Editor dialog box.

Attaching Text to a Path
You can manipulate text to follow an interesting direction in your image. You can create the route, or path, and then attach text to it. A path is an open or closed line consisting of a series of anchor points. Anchor points join path segments-they delineate changes in direction, whether straight, a corner, or a curve.

Creating a Path
To create a path, you use the Pen Tool to define points in your document. To attach text to a path, select the text and the path, and then use the Attach to Path command on the Text menu. You can edit the text after you've attached it to a path.

DESIGN PROJECT

You know how to convert a regular Quark document into an XML document, but you're not really sure you understand the concept of the Cascading Style Sheets. To get a better understanding, you decide to turn to the trusty Internet.

1. Connect to the Internet and go to *www.course.com*. Navigate to the page for this book, click the link for the Student Online Companion, then click the link for this project. This site is just one of many

informative sites that can help you learn about color management systems.

2. If it is permitted, bookmark these URLs for future reference.
3. Review the information on this site, and print it out if you find it helpful.
4. When you finish your research, close your browser.
5. Create a document using either a word processor or a presentation graphics program in which you can record pertinent facts about Cascading Style Sheets, then save the document as **CSS Information**.

6. Add your observations to the CSS Information document. (*Hint*: You can take a screen shot of individual Web pages by pressing the [Print Screen] key when viewing a page in your browser. Insert the screen shot into your active document by pressing [Ctrl][V] (Win).
7. Compare your document to the sample shown in Figure K-42.

FIGURE K-42
Design Project sample document

Creating Content for Web Use   Unit K

NOTE: This project is for Windows users only.

Depending on the size of your group, you can assign elements of the project to individual group members, or work collectively to create the finished project. Your uncle has been a photographer for many years and has always sold his images by word-of-mouth. You're able to convince him that it's time to enter the modern age and sell his images on a Web site. The good news is that you convinced him. The bad news is that he puts you and your team in charge of developing an initial page for his approval.

1. One or more group members can decide on a general layout for the sample page.
2. Open a new Web document and save it as **Photography**.
3. One or more group members can locate images. (*Hint*: You can take images with a digital camera, scan existing images in your possession, or use images existing on your computer.)
4. One or more group members can place text and picture boxes on the page.
5. Create a striking text box that contains the artist's name.
6. Create at least one hyperlink or form element. (*Hint*: The hyperlinks in the sample are fictitious.)
7. Create at least one rollover.

8. Preview the finished document in a browser. Compare your document to the sample shown in Figure K-43.

FIGURE K-43
Completed Group Project

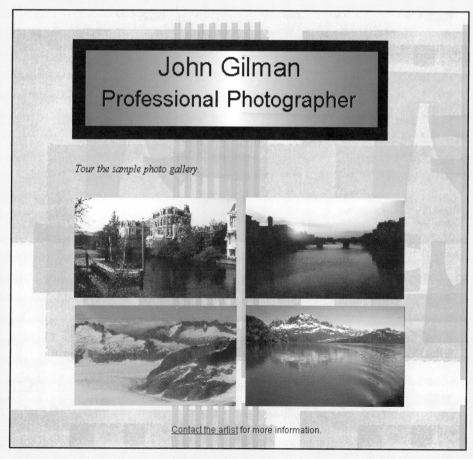

Unit K   Creating Content for Web Use

Unit	Lesson	Steps Title	Summary	Page
A	Start QuarkXPress 5.0	Start QuarkXPress (Windows)	You started QuarkXPress for Windows.	8
		Start QuarkXPress (Macintosh)	You started QuarkXPress for Macintosh.	9
	Learn how to open and save a document	Open a File	You used the Open command on the File menu to locate and open a file.	12
		Use the Save As command	You used the Save As command on the File menu to save the file with a new name.	13
	Examine the QuarkXPress Window	Select a tool	You selected the Rectangle Text Box tool on the Tools palette, used shortcut keys to select another tool in the Tools palette, then you reset the Tools palette to its default setting.	16
		Hide and show palettes	You used the View menu to show and hide palettes.	17
	Use Help to learn about QuarkXPress	Find information in Help Contents	You used the Contents tab in Help to view and print a topic.	19
		Find information in the Index	You used the Index tab in Help to view a topic.	20
		Keep Help information on top	You made the Help window visible on top of the Quark window.	20
		Get information using Find	You found information in Help by typing text using the Find tab.	21
	View and print a document	Use the Zoom tool	You used the Zoom tool to visually enlarge and reduce an area of the document.	24
		Examine print settings	You changed the print orientation and printed a document.	25
	Close a document and exit QuarkXPress	Close the document and exit Quark	You closed the active document, saved your changes, then exited QuarkXPress.	27
B	Set preferences	Set Auto Save options	You started QuarkXPress, opened a new document with a landscape orientation, then you modified the Auto Save preference.	41
		Set Drag and Drop option	You turned on the Drag and Drop Text option in the Preferences dialog box.	43
	Add text to a document	Create a text box and add text	You created a text box with the Rectangle Text box, entered text in the text box, then enlarged the text using the Measurements palette.	46
		Draw ruler guides	You created vertical and horizontal ruler guides.	47
	Modify and reposition a text box	Modify a text box	You modified the height and width of a text box using the rulers and the Measurements palette.	52

STEPS SUMMARY

Unit	Lesson	Steps Title	Summary	Page
		Reposition a text box	You moved the text box using the arrow keys, and dragged it to a new location. The Snap to Guides feature helped you align the text box quickly and precisely.	53
	Copy and move text	Cut and paste text, then Undo	You used the Cut and Paste commands on the Edit menu to cut and paste text, then used the Undo Paste command to eliminate the results of the Paste command.	56
		Use Revert to Saved, and drag-and-drop text	You used the Revert to Saved command to restore the last saved version of the file, then you used Drag and Drop to move text.	57
C	Format text to add emphasis	Get text	You started QuarkXPress, opened a document, then imported text from an existing document.	71
		Show invisibles	You displayed invisible symbols in the document.	72
		Apply attributes	You applied color and different attributes to selected text.	73
	Modify text flow and add drop caps	Manually link text boxes	You linked two text boxes, which eliminated the text overflow problem.	76
		Delete text and create a drop cap	You deleted a line of text, and created and formatted a drop cap in a paragraph.	77
	Modify paragraph characteristics	Change text alignment	You changed the text so it is center-aligned.	81
		Change tracking and kerning	You modified the alignment and kerning of the contents of a text box.	82
		Modify line spacing	You changed the leading within a text box, then modified the font size.	83
	Enhance the appearance of a text box	Modify a text box frame	You used the Modify dialog box to enhance the frame of the text box.	86
		Change background color	You used the Color palette to add color to the text box background, then you subdued the color by adjusting the Blend style.	87
D	Add and delete pages in a document	Add document pages	You added pages to an existing document using the Page menu and the Document Layout palette, and linked a story with overflow text.	100
		Delete document pages	You deleted pages using the Page menu and the Delete tool on the Document Layout palette.	101

Unit	Lesson	Steps Title	Summary	Page
	Add numbers to identify pages	Add page numbers	You created a text box, and added page numbering.	104
		Display page numbers	You displayed automatic page numbering.	105
	Change vertical alignment	Modify vertical alignment	You vertically aligned text.	108
		Modify text and background colors	You created reversed text.	109
	Rearrange pages in a document	Create facing pages and rearrange pages	You changed the pages so they are facing pages, then you moved a page by dragging page icons in the Document Layout palette.	112
		Work in Thumbnails view	You used the Thumbnails view to rearrange pages.	113
	Add continuation notices	Add a continued from notice	You created a continued from notice for a linked story.	116
		Add continued on notice	You created a continued on notice for a linked story.	117
		Set up tabs	You created a text box for tabbed text, then you created a right-aligned tab using the Paragraph Attributes dialog box.	118
		Create tabbed text	You typed tabbed text, then you applied attributes to the text and the text box.	119
E	Use a style sheet to work efficiently	Create a style sheet using the Edit menu	You created a paragraph style sheet containing character attributes, using the Style Sheets command on the Edit menu.	134
		Create a style sheet using the Style Sheets palette	You created a character style sheet using the Style Sheets palette.	135
		Modify a style sheet	You modified a style sheet using the Style Sheets palette.	136
		Apply a style sheet	You applied two character style sheets and one paragraph style sheet to a document.	137
	Use master pages to maintain consistency	Create a master page	You created a new master page and added formatting to it.	140
		Modify a master page	You modified the formatting in the A-Master A page.	141
		Apply a master page	You applied two different master pages to document pages.	142

Unit	Lesson	Steps Title	Summary	Page
		Rename a master page	You renamed a master page, then you changed the background color of text boxes to none so the color on the master page would be visible.	143
	Create headers and footers	Create a header/footer	You created a text box to use as a footer on a master page.	146
		Copy and format a header/footer	You copied and pasted a text box, then changed the text alignment of footers on facing pages.	147
	Lock master page elements and indent text	Lock objects on a master page	You locked multiple objects on a master page.	150
		Create a first line indent	You indented a first line indent in a paragraph.	151
F	Layer objects	Use the Item menu to reorder objects	You used the Item menu to reorder stacked objects.	167
		Create layers using the Layers palette	You used the Layers palette to create three new layers.	168
		Assign objects to layers	You assigned an object to each layer on the Layers palette.	169
		Rename a layer	You renamed a layer in the Layers palette.	170
		Reorder layers	You modified the stack order on the Layers palette.	171
	Modify the alignment of objects	Align objects	You vertically aligned a text box and an object.	174
		Group objects	You horizontally aligned two text boxes.	175
	Rotate an object	Rotate an object	You rotated an object using the Measurements palette and Rotation tool.	179
	Duplicate an object	Duplicate an object	You duplicated an object and placed it on the pasteboard.	183
G	Place a picture on a page	Create a picture box and insert an image	You created a picture box, then used the File menu to get an image.	197
		Reposition an image in a picture box	You used the Content tool to move the image within the picture box, resized the picture to the box, undid this change, and then resized the box to the picture.	198
		Move and resize a picture box	You moved a picture to a new location, resized the picture box proportionally, then fit the picture to the box.	199

Unit	Lesson	Steps Title	Summary	Page
	Change margins and add placeholder text	Change margins and columns	You modified the number of columns and the top, bottom, inside, and outside margins using the Master Guides dialog box.	203
		Add nonsense text	You modified the default Jabberwocky language, created a text box, and filled it with nonsense text.	204
		Modify a text box	You adjusted the text inset in a text box.	205
	Modify picture box properties	Adjust offset and scale an image	You scaled an image, then you offset it using the Modify dialog box.	208
		Frame and flip an image	You modified the color of the picture box and the frame, and horizontally flipped the image.	209
	Modify color contrast	Change the color model	You changed the color model to CYMK.	213
		Adjust contrast using the CMYK model	You modified Cyan, Yellow, Magenta, and Black using the CMYK model.	214
		Adjust contrast using the HSB model	You modified the Saturation and Brightness using the HSB model.	215
H	Use a line as a design tool	Create and modify a straight line	You created a line and modified its length using the Measurements palette.	228
		Duplicate a straight line	You duplicated a straight line, then moved each line between columns of text.	229
	Work with special line types	Create a Bézier line	You created a three-segment Bézier line on the upper portion of the page.	232
		Modify a line style	You modified the Width, Arrowhead, Color, and Line Style of a Bézier line.	233
	Create text on a path	Convert a Bézier line to a text path	You converted a Bézier line to a text-path, then added and modified text.	236
		Modify text path	You used handles on the text-path to reposition the curve, then applied attributes to the text.	237
	Control image runaround	Modify runaround settings	You modified the Runaround settings so text wraps to an image in a picture box.	240
		Create a mask and layer objects	You created a mask using a text box, then rearranged layers so an object would be hidden from view.	241

Unit	Lesson	Steps Title	Summary	Page
I	Find and change text	Set find and change parameters	You modified the parameters to find and change text.	256
		Find and change text	You replaced all occurrences of the word "image" with the word "picture" formatted in Arial italic text.	257
		Use Line Count	You used the Line Count feature to identify flaws.	258
		Fix an identified flaw	You fixed a widow line problem identified using the Line Count feature.	259
	Check spelling and replace fonts	Correct spelling errors	You used the Check Spelling feature to determine whether the document contained spelling errors, then you corrected the errors.	262
		Change document fonts	You replaced all occurrences of Arial Italic with Times New Roman bold and italic.	263
	Create a table	Create a table	You created a three-column, five-row table, then entered text into the cells.	268
		Add and delete rows	You deleted a row from a table, then added a row.	269
		Combine cells	You combined table cells and formatted the cell contents.	270
		Resize columns	You modified the widths of two columns and applied formatting attributes.	271
	Work with spot and process color	Create and apply a spot color	You created a new spot color using the CMYK model, then applied it to an object.	274
		Apply a process color and delete a spot color	You deleted a spot color and added a process color to the Colors palette.	275
J	Create a book	Create a book	You created a book.	292
		Add chapters to a book	You added chapters to a book file, then you opened one of the chapters.	293
		Synchronize book components	You synchronized the three additional chapters with the master chapter.	295
	Modify and organize a book	Modify the chapter order	You used the Move Chapter Up and Move Chapter Down tools to reorder the chapters on the Book palette.	298
		Change the starting page number	You changed the starting page in the Book, which changed the pagination in all the chapters.	299
	Use Style lists to create a table of contents	Create list criteria	You created a list using four styles within the master chapter.	302

Unit	Lesson	Steps Title	Summary	Page
		Organize list criteria	You modified the levels and numbering scheme for the styles in the list.	303
		View a list	You viewed a list for a chapter that is based on styles.	304
		Generate a book list	You closed all the book chapters, then appended a list to a book.	305
		Append and build a list	You synchronized the chapters in a book, then generated a list in a chapter.	306
		Format a list	You used tabs to format the generated list.	307
	Work with indexes and libraries	Mark a document for indexing	You marked an item for inclusion in an index.	312
		Create index entries	You created two entries, then modified the level of one entry.	313
		Add entries and create an index document	You made additional index entries and created an index chapter.	314
		Synchronize chapters and build an index	You synchronized book chapters, then built an index.	315
		Create a library	You created a library file, then added and named an entry.	317
K	Create and modify a Web document	Add a page title and background image	You added a title to the page, and inserted a graphic image for the background.	333
		Create text hyperlinks	You added a new hyperlink to selected text, then applied an existing hyperlink to selected text.	334
		View a Web page	You viewed a page in a Web browser.	335
	Enhance a Web page	Insert an image in a picture box	You inserted an image in an existing picture box, then fit the image to the box.	338
		Create a rollover	You created a rollover effect and added a hyperlink to the rollover.	339
		Test a rollover and a hyperlink	You applied a hyperlink to an image.	340
		Add a mailto: hyperlink	You added a mailto: hyperlink to a Web document.	341
	Collect and display Web information	Add a pop-up menu	You created a pop-up menu in a form.	345
		Add a checkbox and buttons	You added a checkbox and button to the form.	346

Unit	Lesson	Steps Title	Summary	Page
		Add and format a table	You added a table to the form, then formatted its contents.	347
	Export content with XML	Tag a document	You tagged a document using the XML Workspace.	350
		Save an XML document	You saved tags created from a Quark document as an XML document.	351
		Insert a CSS code in a text file	You modified an XML document using a text editor, inserted a code that determines which CSS will be used, then viewed the document in your browser.	352
		Modify a CSS code in a text file	You modified the CSS code in the XML document, then viewed the document in your browser.	353

Read the following information carefully!!

Find out from your instructor the location of the Project Files you need and the location where you will store your files.

- To complete many of the units in this book, you need to use Project Files. Your instructor will either provide you with a copy of the Project Files or ask you to make your own copy.

- If you need to make a copy of the Project Files, you will need to copy a set of files from a file server, stand-alone computer, or the Web to the drive and location where you will be storing your Project Files.

- Your instructor will tell you which computer, drive letter, and folders contain the files you need, and where you will store your files.

- You can also download the files by going to www.course.com. See the inside back cover of the book for instructions to download your files.

Copy and organize your Project Files.

- Use the Project Files List to organize your files to a zip drive, network folder, hard drive, or other storage device.

- Create a subfolder for each unit in the location where you are storing your files, and name it according to the unit title (e.g., Quark Unit A).

- For each unit you are assigned, copy the files listed in the **Project File Supplied** column into that unit's folder.

- Store the files you modify or create in each unit in the unit folder.

Find and keep track of your Project Files and completed files.

- Use the **Project File Supplied** column to make sure you have the files you need before starting the unit or exercise indicated in the **Unit** column.

- Use the **Student Saves File As** column to find out the filename you use when saving your changes to a provided Project File.

- Use the **Student Creates File** column to find out the filename you use when saving your new file for the exercise.

Files used in this book

UNIT	Project File Supplied	Student Saves File As	Student Creates File	Used in
A	QP A-1.qxd	Excelsior Newsletter.qxd		Lesson 2–6
	QP A-2.qxd	Faraway Travel.qxd		Skills Review
				Project Builder 1
			Sample Document.qxd	Project Builder 2
				Design Project
				Group Project
B			About Quark.qxd	Lesson 2–4
			Volunteering.qxd	Skills Review
	QP B-1.qxd	Eiffel Tower.qxd		Project Builder 1
			Leadership Topic.qxd	Project Builder 2
				Design Project
	QP B-2.qxd	Birthday Card.qxd		Group Project
C	QP C-1.qxd QP C-2.doc	Text Design Element.qxd		Lesson 1–4
	QP C-3.qxd QP C-4.doc	About Hydrangeas.qxd		Skills Review
	QP C-5.qxd QP C-6.doc	Zion National Park.qxd		Project Builder 1
	QP C-7.qxd	New Bike Card.qxd		Project Builder 2
				Design Project
			Quark Promotion.qxd	Group Project
D	QP D-1.qxd	Headliners.qxd		Lesson 1–4
	QP D-2.qxd	Super Bowl Facts.qxd		Skills Review
	QP D-3.qxd	Trip to London.qxd		Project Builder 1
	QP D-4.qxd	Name Game.qxd		Project Builder 2
				Design Project
			Software Review.qxd	Group Project
E	QP E-1.qxd	Eye Care.qxd		Lesson 1–4
	QP E-2.qxd	Vacation Therapy.qxd		Skills Review
	QP E-3.qxd	Safe at Home.qxd		Project Builder 1

UNIT	Project File Supplied	Student Saves File As	Student Creates File	Used in
	QP E-4.qxd	Mayoral Sign.qxd		Project Builder 2
			Master pages and style sheets.ppt*	Design Project
			Ergonomics.qxd	Group Project
F	QP F-1.qxd	ArtsREACH.qxd		Lesson 1–4
	QP F-2.qxd	Psychology Update.qxd		Skills Review
	QP F-3.qxd	Futuroscope.qxd		Project Builder 1
	QP F-4.qxd	Glacier Cruise.qxd		Project Builder 2
				Design Project
			Mugworts.qxd	Group Project
G	QP G-1.qxd QP G-2.tif	Sandy Beach.qxd		Lesson 1–4
	QP G-3.tif	Cold Front.qxd		Skills Review
	QP G-4.qxd QP G-5.TIF	Helicopter.qxd		Project Builder 1
	QP G-6.TIF	Karate.qxd		Project Builder 2
			Color Experiment.qxd	Design Project
			Art Review.qxd	Group Project
H	QP H-1.qxd	New Car.qxd		Lesson 1–4
	QP H-2.qxd	Pyramid.qxd		Skills Review
	QP H-3.qxd	London Guard.qxd		Project Builder 1
	QP H-4.qxd QP H-5.tif	Bridge.qxd		Project Builder 2
			Bezier Research.ppt*	Design Project
			Publishing Contest.qxd	Group Project
I	QP I-1.qxd	Color Information.qxd		Lesson 1–4
	QP I-2.qxd	Toy Outlet.qxd		Skills Review
	QP I-3.qxd	Tourism Promotion.qxd		Project Builder 1
	QP I-4.qxd	Quark Presentation.qxd		Project Builder 2
			Color Management Systems.qxd	Design Project
			Glory.qxd	Group Project

*Document type of saved file will vary.

UNIT	Project File Supplied	Student Saves File As	Student Creates File	Used in
J	QP J-1.qxd QP J-2.qxd QP J-3.qxd QP J-4.qxd	Graphics Software.qxb	GS Index.qxd GS Library.qxl	Lesson 1–4
	QP J-5.qxd QP J-6.qxd QP J-7.qxd	Tornado.qxb	Tornado Index.qxd Tornado Library.qxl	Skills Review
	QP J-8.qxd	TOC Demo.qxd		Project Builder 1
	QP J-9.qxd	Index Lesson.qxd		Project Builder 2
			List Generation.ppt*	Design Project
			Final Project.qxb Final Project Index.qxd Final Project Library.qxl	Group Project
K	QP K-1.qwd Rainbow.jpg Florence.jpg Alaska.jpg Canal.jpg Tower.jpg Holland.jpg Paris.jpg Seine.jpg Mountains.jpg QP K-2.qwd	Rainbow Travel.qwd	Animation.xml	Lesson 1–3
				Lesson 4
	QP K-3.qwd QP K-4.qxd	Relaxation Spa.qxb Image Meister.xml		Skills Review
	QP K-5.qwd ChocolateCone.jpg VanillaCone.jpg	Ice Cream Exhibit.qxd		Project Builder 1
	QP K-6.qxd	XML Chapter.xml		Project Builder 2
			CSS Information.ppt	Design Project
			Photography.qwd	Group Project

Document type of saved file will vary.

A

Absolute hyperlink
Code assigned to text or an image that links to a specific URL site when clicked.

Active cell
The current cell in a table.

Append style sheets
To copy style sheets from one document to another.

Attributes
Effects that change the appearance of one or more characters.

B

Bézier line
Composed of curved or straight segments whose properties are determined by the segments that join them.

Bitmap image
Image composed of many dots forming a pattern.

Bleed
A technique in which a graphic image exceeds page margins, giving the illusion (after the paper is cut to size) that the image was printed all the way to the edge of the page.

Book
An organizational tool that lets you combine and rearrange multiple files to create a uniform document made up of separate components.

Book palette
An onscreen palette that you can use to combine and organize Quark documents to form a book.

Build
To compile or create an index using entry items that have been marked in the text of one or more Quark documents.

C

Cascading Style Sheet (CSS)
A document that contains objects and formatting instructions that can be applied using styles.

Cell
The intersection of a column and row.

Character style sheet
Formatting instructions that can only be applied to specifically selected characters.

Clipboard
A temporary storage area that can contain a selection.

Clipping path
An image that has areas within it cropped to conform to elements within it.

Closed path
One continuous path without endpoints, such as a circle.

Color management systems (CMS)
Professional designed systems that make it easy to select colors for reproduction.

Color model
A reference key that specifies how pigments combine to produce resulting colors.

Compound path
A shape that has more than one open or closed path.

Content management
A key tool in the process of organizing and formatting all types of information so it can be easily accessed by end users.

Continuation notice
A text box that automatically locates linked text that precedes or follows the text in the active text box.

Copyfitting
The art of fitting text within a text box.

Cropping
The process of hiding specific areas in an image.

Cutting
Removing a selection from its current location.

D

Default path
The drive and folder location where a specific file, type of file, or set of files.

Document

A file created in Quark. Each document can contain up to 2000 pages.

Document window

The window beneath the program title bar and menu bar that includes the document image, rulers, and other objects.

Dot leaders

Characters that precede a decimal tab and help the reader interpret information in columns or separated by tabs.

Drag-and-drop

Allows you to select text, then move it in one motion, without using the Clipboard.

DTD (Document Type Definition)

Describes and defines XML elements.

Endpoints

A line segment with at least one segment, and anchor points at either end.

Facing pages

Sheets that are generally bound in book or magazine format, with one page facing left and one page facing right.

Font

A complete set of characters, letters, and symbols for a particular typeface.

Footer

Repetitive information that appears at the bottom of every page, or on every page to which a particular master page is applied.

Gridlines

Vertical and horizontal lines that separate the cells in a table.

Grouped object

Also called a grouping or a group, a collection of multiple objects that can be formatted or moved as a single object.

Gutter width

The space between each column on a page, or between a column and the inner edge of a page.

Halftone

An option that determines the screen angle for shades, pictures, and digital photographs.

Handles

Small boxes that appear around an object's perimeter when it is selected.

Header

Repetitive information that appears at the top of every page, or on every page to which a particular master page is applied.

Histogram

In Quark, a graph displaying the numeric values of colors.

Hot area

An area within an image that is clickable.

Hue

The amount of color that is reflected from an object.

Hyperlink

A code assigned to text or an image that jumps to a new page when clicked. There are two kinds of hyperlinks: absolute and relative.

Hyphenation

The separation of syllables using a dash.

Indent

A distance specified for text to wrap from the left and/or right margin.

Insertion point

The flashing cursor that displays when characters are typed. Typed characters always occur to the right of the insertion point.

Jabber

Gibberish or nonsense text, used to quickly populate a text box during the design phase of a publication.

Jabbering

Creating gibberish text using the Jabber feature.

Kerning

The vertical space that occurs between individual characters.

Landscape orientation

A document printed with the long edge of the paper along its top.

Layer objects

To position objects so that they appear to be laying on top of one another.

Layers palette

An onscreen palette that provides an intuitive way of reorganizing a stack of objects.

Leading

The horizontal space that occurs between each line of text.

Library

A Quark feature that lets you store and retrieve information that can be used in documents.

Line segment

A portion of a line created by clicking the starting point of a line tool, then by dragging the mouse to an ending point.

Links

Connections you create between text boxes so the reader's eye can travel easily from one column to the next on a page, and from page to page.

Locking

Feature used to protect the contents of a master page, making it safe from inadvertent alteration.

Lorem ipsum

Gibberish text, also known as Jabber, that is commonly used to fill text boxes during the design phase of a publication.

Margin guides

Onscreen lines (blue by default) that indicate the margins on the page.

Margins

Border areas at the top, bottom, left, and right edge of each column on a page, and of each page itself.

Marked

Text entries that are surrounded by brackets indicating that they will be included in the index when it is built.

Mask

A text or picture box that can be strategically positioned so that parts of an image are not displayed.

Master chapter

Defines the overall colors, styles, and other settings that will used throughout a book.

Master Guides

Overall settings for the columns and margins.

Master Page

Template for a type of page in a document that contains repetitive elements.

Matte

An opaque box behind an object that makes the object stand out.

Measurements palette

A context-sensitive onscreen palette that displays measurements and formatting settings for the selected text, chart, or picture and lets you modify these settings.

Media-independent publishing

Creating a document, and letting software make the necessary adjustments for the media you choose to publish to, such as a printer or the World Wide Web.

Menu bar

Contains menus from which you can choose Quark commands.

Native format

A file having the default file extension from the program in which you are currently working.

Normal

The name of the default character or paragraph style sheet in a Quark document.

Nudge

To slightly move a selected picture box or text box using the [Up Arrow], [Down Arrow], [Left Arrow], and [Right Arrow] keys.

Object

Any item that, when selected, is surrounded by handles, indicating that you can move, copy, delete, or modify it. (You can select an object by clicking it.)

Orientation

The direction of an image on the page.

Orphan

A stray word at the top of a page or column.

Pagination

The numbering of pages.

Palette

A small moveable window you can use to verify and modify settings. Palettes contain buttons that let you make changes in a document; they can be opened and closed using commands on the View menu.

Paragraph style sheet

Contains character attributes that are based on a specific character style sheet, and can be applied to an entire paragraph.

Pasteboard

The area surrounding the document that can be used to create or modify elements, or as a holding area for future use.

Pasting

Placing a selection from the Clipboard to a new location.

Path

An individual line having two distinct endpoints. (Also called an open path.)

Path component

Consists of one or more anchor points joined by line segments.

Picture box

An object that contains a picture, used to position the picture on the page.

Picture format

Electronic file format that determines qualities such as the number of colors that are used, and the program used in its creation.

Point of origin

The upper-left corner of an image.

Portrait orientation

A document printed with the short edge of the paper along its top.

Preferences

Settings you can adjust to make your working environment more pleasant, comfortable, and convenient.

Printable area

The total dimensions of the page that are accessible by the printer.

Program title bar

Displays the program name and the filename of the open document.

Relative hyperlink

Code assigned to text or an image that links to a page within the same document or Web site.

Repurposing

Adapting one type of content, such as a paper-based document, to another format such as a Web page.

Reversed text

Light characters appearing on a dark background. This effect makes text look as if it were cut out of the background.

Rollover

Effect in which one image switches to another image when the mouse points to the initial image.

Ruler guides

Onscreen lines (green by default) that you can drag from the horizontal and vertical rulers to make it easier to align objects.

Rulers

Onscreen measurement guides that help you precisely measure and position objects in the work area.

Runaround
A setting that controls how closely text wraps around an object.

Sans serif font
Characters in this type of font do not include tails, or strokes, at their top or bottom; commonly used in headlines and headings.

Saturation
The purity of a particular color.

Secondary paragraph
A paragraph that follows a heading.

Serif fonts
Characters in this type of font include tails, or strokes, at the top or bottom of some characters; commonly used in body text.

Signature
A count of pages grouped in a multiple of 8.

Single pages
Individual sheets that have top, bottom, left, and right margins.

Snap to
An effect that occurs as you drag an object towards a margin or ruler guide, causing it to align with the margin or guide. By default, this feature is turned on in Quark.

Splash screen
A window that displays information about the software program you are opening.

Spot color
A specific color not easily recreated by a printer.

Stack
A cluster of objects.

Starting point
The left-most endpoint on a text path.

Status bar
Located at the bottom of the program window (Win) or the document window (Mac) and displays current page and magnification information.

Story
The contents of a text box.

Style sheet
A document that stores formatting information you plan to use repeatedly. There are two types of style sheets: those that affect characters and those that affect paragraphs.

Symbol fonts
Used to display unique characters (such as $, ÷, or ™).

Tab
An alignment feature that makes it easy to line up characters beyond the limitations of a text box.

Table
A series of vertical columns and horizontal rows, used to organize information for easy scanning and reference.

Tags
Codes that surround important text; used in XML and other programming languages.

Template
File that contains standard formatting and text or graphics which you wish to use as the basis for other Quark documents; Quark template files have the file extension .qxt.

Text box
An object that contains text; used to position the text on a page.

Text inset
The area—measured in points—between the actual text box frame and the words within the box.

Text paths
Line segments that can display text.

Thumbnails view
View of the Quark window in which each page is represented by a miniature image that includes just enough detail to make each page recognizable.

Toggle key
A button or key that turns a feature on or off when clicked.

Tonal values

The numeric values of an individual color. Also called color levels.

Tracking

The process of adjusting the amount of space to the right of each selected character.

Ungroup

To restore a grouped object to its original components.

Vector image

An image composed of line and pattern information.

Vertical alignment

The positioning of text between the top and bottom of a text box.

White space

The design term for space on a page that is not covered with printed or graphic material.

Widow

A single line at the top of a page or column. Also called a widow line.

XML (eXtensible Markup Language)

A powerful language that is similar to HTML but is used to further customize information. In Quark, XML is used to make existing documents Web-ready.

XTensions

Mini-programs (having the extension .xnt) that can be added to or deleted from QuarkXPress without causing harm to the program.